Folk Dance as Ecumenical Communication

Folk Dance as Ecumenical Communication

A Theological Vision and Mission

A. Temjen Jamir

Christian World Imprints

First Published in 2020 by
Christian World Imprints
Christian Publishing & Books from India
C-3, Wazirpur Industrial Area
Delhi-110052
cwidelhi2017@gmail.com
www.ChristianWorldImprints.com
Phone: +91 11 41526079

ISBN: 978-93-5148-472-1 (HB)
ISBN: 978-93-5148-473-8 (PB)

Printed in India.

Contents

Foreword

During the recent decades, emergence of young minds among the indigenous scholars who are not only interested for academic adventurism but are committed to explore the dynamics that are principal foundations for our identity, ethnicity, history and also for community co-existence in the contemporary indigenous communities is notable. Such commitment motivates them to consciously gaze at their everyday-life culture. For them, the study of everyday interaction is as important as the processes governing the everyday life of their people and thus cannot afford to neglect it. As such, scholars interested to explore social dynamics of indigenous communities consciously go beyond earlier methodological roots that are modeled after the natural sciences, rather go beyond observable, quantifiable and measurable phenomena. Secondly, another new development in the indigenous scholarship is to consciously go beyond our long standing preference for investigation of issues with direct "important" social policy implications. In other words, in the contemporary indigenous studies, young minds are advocating that the study of everyday relations be considered a central area of social sciences in its own right. More so, social scientists cannot afford to neglect the study of everyday life, not necessarily to embrace community's everyday way of life but simultaneously be exploring the limits and potentialities of human being's relations with each other. This is, by any standard, an important endeavour in the present academic research.

Research and discussion on everyday life is never simply the accumulation of data. Whatever the form it takes, the data are always there, accessible to everyone not only within the researched community but by and large accessible to everyone. Thus, the most critical challenge for scholars involved in the exploration of everyday life is to develop explanation of how the data make sense in the first place, meaningful in the second place and usable in the third place. In the process of research one may locate the historical roots and political economy of a particular everyday life. Scholars may help the community see a familiar set of facts from new angles and so add new dimensions to our understanding and further attempt to employ such new dimensions to penetrate the obvious and thereby reveal underlying aspects of people's everyday life.

On the other hand, social scientist interested in phenomena such as religious devotion (commitment) should not just investigate what goes on in churches and Christian ministry. Any everyday day life and events, whether diverse or similar might also be understood as expressions of religious devotion. So also, the same intensity and reverence associated with religious rituals underlie the various phenomena as well. Obviously, content, context or social situations or even traditional religious content differs quite widely with the content and practice of the Church, nevertheless display common social and communication forms.

At the backdrop of this supposition, though very important, critical analysis of Folk Dance in Naga society is virtually non-existent even though most of the Naga scholars refer to their folk dance in their text often to support in their narration of history, identity and culture. Similarly, most of the scholars either fail to notice the folk dance or classify it as spectacle, therein eliding its signifying practices with aesthetic standards of judgement. More so, heavily influenced by Western theatrical and critical traditions, representations of Folk Dance in contemporary Naga society, somewhat ambivalently, with themes of harmony or chaos in the world of spectator's entertainment.

Dramaturgically speaking, enactment of some kind of folk dance in Naga narratives does a number of things to the text. As a focalizing agent, folk dance draws attention to the rhetoric of embodiment in all performance, something which is less apparent in simply dramatization of dialogue, especially within the conventions of realism. Even while bringing body into focus, folk dance also spatializes, which is to say that it foregrounds proxemics relations between character, spectator and features of the set.

In imperial historical account (indigenous) Naga folk dance has been encoded as the expression of savage or exotic 'otherness' within a discourse which represents Nagas as objects to be looked at, and their folk dance as piece of spectator's entertainment. Similar to what W. Robertson, for example, wrote in 1928, 'aboriginal dance…as the picturesque signifier of less-than human-behaviour'. Such descriptions though purportedly historical accounts clearly influenced scholars for so long and look at the folk dance as a primitive performance event designed for consumption by the imperial spectators, and in our case unfortunately even by the Western missionaries.

The premise of the present book explores the Naga Folk Dance's potential as transformative agent that invoke, rather necessitate ecumenical communication among various denominational groups in Nagaland. Dr. Temjen Jamir in his writing approach Naga Folk Dance not only as enacted performance of their past within the imperialistic notion or even patriarchal discourses but as a mode of empowerment and attempt to propose an active self-constituting process for ecumenical communication that expiate relationship, participation, development, revitalization of tribal spirituality, unity and harmony. He further argues that Naga

Folk Dance is always an "everyday" community centered activity and functions as a mode of empowerment for all of its participants in their "everyday way of life."

Author's main contribution in this research, which hopefully can be valued as crucial and undeniable strength in Tribal/Naga Cultural Studies is his attempt to read, explore and method of interpreting Naga Folk Dance *As Text*. Even so not that explicit in the content, the author calls for decolonizing our relationship with Naga Folk Dance (only) as primitive performance for entertainment and consumption by exclusive spectators. Reasonably, the author concludes that Naga Folk Dance can be a strategic use for both dialogical communication among different denominational groups as well as can be a common ecumenical sphere where people can come together for mutual participation, inclusive empowerment and a common space that generate common voice for Social Justice and Peace. To put in one simple sentence, the book is about "Countering the Dynamic of "Us-Them" Polarization through Naga Folk Dance."

Prof. Dr. L. Imsutoshi Jamir
Professor of Communication and Cultural Studies
Clark Theological College

Acknowledgement

I thank the almighty God for his abundant grace in keeping me safe and sound throughout my research work. I am indebted to Rev. Dr. John Joshva Raja for his invaluable suggestions, comments and guidance. I express my heartfelt thanks to Rev. Dr. Sebastian Periannan, Rector, St. Peter's Pontifical Seminary, Bangalore, for his valuable observations, suggestions, and constant guidance, encouragement and support. The observations and comments of Dr. Jolyon Mitchell, Senior Lecturer, The University of Edinburgh were very helpful and I am grateful to him.

I also thank all the people who have helped me during my field research and agreed to be interviewed. I also wish to express my gratitude to the Librarians, especially the United Theological College, Bangalore, the School of Divinity library, Moria House Library, and the Main library, the University of Edinburgh. I gratefully acknowledge my Sponsors, the World Association for Christian Communication (WACC), South Asia Theological Research Institute (SATHRI), and the Clark Theological College (CTC), for their financial support and help. I also thank all my friends and relatives for their support and encouragement. A special word of thanks goes to Professor Santiago and Rev. Arun Kumar Wesley who patiently read the drafts and made valuable suggestions for correction. Finally, I am sincerely grateful to my wife, L. Atula Lkr., and my two sons, Imkongnuksung and Medemkaba, for their unceasing support and encouragement throughout the journey of my studies and ministry. I dedicate this research work to them.

A. Temjen Jamir

List of Abbreviations

ABAM	Ao Baptist Arogo Mungdang
ABC	Assam Baptist Convention
AG	Assembly of God
APBC	Arunachal Pradesh Baptist Convention
CBCAM	Council of Baptist Churches in Assam and Manipur
CBCNEI	Council of Baptist Churches in North East India
CC	Christian Communication
CFS	Christian Folk Song
CNI	Church of North India
CPR	Church's Public Relations
CSI	Church of South India
CUM	Church Union Movement
EC	Ecumenical Communication
EDC	Exclusive Denominational Communication
ECS	Ecumenical Common Sphere
GBC	Garo Baptist Convention
JPIC	Justice, Peace and Integrity of Creation
KABC	Kabir Anglong Baptist Convention
MBC	Manipur Baptist Convention
MF	Moatsu Festival
NABM	North American Baptist Mission
NBCC	Nagaland Baptist Churches Council
NCCI	National Council of Churches in India

NCRC	Nagaland Christian Revival Church
NEI	North East India
NEICC	North East India Christian Council
NEIZCC	North East India Zonal Cultural Council
NF	Naga Festivals
NFD	Naga Folk Dance
NFS	Naga Folk Song
NT	New Testament
OR	Osservatore Romano, English Edition
OT	Old Testament
RC	Roman Catholic
UNESCO	United Nations Educational, Scientific and Cultural Organization
WACC	World Association for Christian Communication
WCC	World Council of Churches

Chapter 1

Introduction

1.1. Rationale for the Research Work

This study investigates how the celebration of Naga cultural festivals and folk dances can help bring the people together on a common platform for interaction and participation irrespective of their status, background and religious affiliations. Second, the research examines the presence of ecumenical communication in folk dance which can be acknowledged and incorporated in the church to promote contact, relationship and participation between churches in Nagaland. In this regard, it should be kept in mind that ecumenical communication is meant to encourage Christians of different denominations coming together to interact and develop relations and unity among themselves. The Church can be a place for promoting ecumenism and participation among the Christians of different denominations. In addition, Christian communication may not confine itself to one's local Church alone, but extend itself to other denominations and religions. For instance, there are different churches in Nagaland such as the Baptists, the Roman Catholics, the Pentecostals, the Nagaland Christian Revival Church, and the Assembly of God. They have been involved and engaged in evangelization and in social communication. It has been observed that there is a lack of ecumenical communication among the Christians of different denominations as they promote an exclusive denominational communication among themselves in the church. This shows that there appears to be a lack of ecumenical relationships amongst them.

The researcher believes that folk dance can be considered a powerful means of communication for bringing people together on a common platform for mutual participation and sharing with one another in the North East India, especially in Nagaland.[1] In this connection, the researcher observed that the churches in Nagaland are obsessed with the mass media for communicating the gospel, and for giving information to the people in the church. Though the mass media may serve as useful tools for promoting ecumenical communication, in reality, they have certain limitations, as they tend to provide most often a one-way traffic with minimal feedback. As such, there are less opportunities for people's active participation. Thus, it may not often cater to the needs of the people. In this context, folk media of communication will be more effective for communicating and exchanging ideas, information, and the Christian message to one another.

Naga Festivals and Folk Dances

In Nagaland, all the tribes celebrate their distinct seasonal festivals[2] with dances, songs and feasts, though the styles vary from one tribe to another. During the festival, both men and women including children participate and share with one another with a sense of unity, love, and equality. Thus, these festivals provide a space for communication and unity of all the villagers. In addition, it also enhances and expresses their communitarian values and the tribal identity as Nagas.

Folk dance is very much at the centre of the Naga community life. There are varieties of Naga dances such as the war dance, the agricultural dance, the spear dance, the harvest dance, the bamboo dance, and the marriage dance,[3] in which

---

1 Nagaland is a vibrant State found in the northeastern part of India. It is largely a mountainous State. The Naga Hills rise from the Brahmaputra valley in Assam to about 2000 feet and rise further to the southeast as high as 6000 feet. "Nagaland," www.http://en.wikipedia.org/wiki/nagaland, 7th May 2007. Browsed on 23-11-07. The present State of Nagaland covers an area of 6,366 sq. miles Asoso Yonuo, *The Rising Nagas: A Historical and Political Study.* (New Delhi: Vivek Publishing House, 1974), p. 2. with a 1,988,656 population (2001). P. C. Muanthanga, *Transforming Eastern India Region.* (Shillong: North East India Mission and Resources Centre (NEIMARC), p. (Inside Cover page). Nagaland has a largely monsoon climate with high humidity levels. The State of Nagaland was formally inaugurated on 1st December, 1963, as the 16th State of the Indian Union. Nagaland is bounded by Myanmar in the East, Assam in the West, Arunachal Pradesh in the North and Manipur in the South. There are twelve district headquarters in the State, namely, Dimapur, Kiphire, Kohima, Longleng, Mokokchung, Mon, Noklak, Peren, Phek, Tuensang, Wokha and Zunheboto. Kohima is the capital city of the State. Dimapur is the largest metropolitan city in the State.

2 Festivals of Nagaland are observed in the following months by different tribes: Angami Naga – Sekrenyie festival in February; Chakhesang – Tsukhenyie in March or April; Konyak & Phom – Aoling & Monyu in April; Ao – Moatsü in May & Tsüngrem Mong in August; Chang – Nakyulum in July; Sema – Tuluni & Anni in July; Yimchunger – Medemneo in August; Sangtam – Mongmong in September; Kachari – Bushu in January; Khaimniungan – Miu in May and Tsokum in October; Kuki – Mimkuut in January; Pochury – Yemshe in October; Lotha – Tokhu Emong in November; Rengma – Ngada in November; Zeliang – Nag-ngai in December. Alongla P. Aier, ed., *From Darkness to Light* (Kohima: Nagaland Baptist Church Council, 1997), pp. 11-12; Also see http://www.tourismnagaland.com/Festivals.html, 2007 Nagaland Tourism. Browsed on 19-01-08.

3 Asoso Yonuo, op. cit., p. 33.

men and women dance together as well as separately. These dances reflect the ancient rituals, some of which are solemn and grave, while others express joy and gaiety. Naga folk dances need not only be considered as an optional entertainment but also understood as a vehicle for promoting participation and relationship among people in the community. At this point, one can see an ecumenical presence in the Naga folk dance as a medium for building relationships, as it promotes participation, learning and unity among people in the community. Thus, if the churches recognize such a sphere of tribal identity[4] in the folk dance, it may become a point of contact leading towards a significant ecumenical unity among Christian denominations. The concept of ecumenism is not only a process of discussion for the unity of the Church but it also includes ecumenical activities towards achieving peace, justice, and unity of the whole creation. In this context, it must be stated that the sphere of tribal unity needs to go beyond the unity of the Church to widen it to the realm of ecumenical activities related to development, freedom, peace, justice and human dignity.

The analysis and the assessment of the existing problem of denominationalism and the absence of ecumenical communication amongst the people are crucial for this study. In this connection, the research methods employed in this investigation will be discussed to find out if such a space for communication is available outside the church in the celebration of Naga cultural festivals and folk dances among the people for the promotion of ecumenism in the church and society. In fact, the tribe and clan traditions and loyalties play an important part in the life of Nagas. Dancing, singing and music are natural gifts of the Naga tribes[5] which provide them space for communication, interaction and participation, promoting unity, relationship, cooperation and development among the people in the Church and society. Accordingly, it is surmised that it may in turn facilitate more interactive and ecumenical communication towards promoting ecumenical relations and cooperation among Christians of different denominations. In addition, it also may promote their communitarian values and identity in the society. Further, the Churches can speak with one voice towards fulfilling the agenda of Christian and ecumenical communication in terms of involving themselves in God's mission in the world in the ecumenical spirit to promote peace, justice, freedom and solidarity.

4 In this research, the term "Tribal Ecumenism" or "Tribal Identity" refers to the sphere of ecumenical presence in Naga folk dance that can be recognized and extended by the churches for the promotion of ecumenism between Christian denominations in Nagaland.

5 There are about sixteen major tribes in Nagaland. The following are the sixteen major tribes of Nagaland: Angami, Ao, Chakhesang, Chang, Kachari, Khiamnuingan, Konyak, Kuki, Lotha, Phom, Pochury, Rengma, Sangtam, Sumi, Yimchunger, and Zeme-Liangmai (Zeliang). These tribes speak their own tribal languages and dialects belonging to Sino-ibetan family of languages. They also communicate with each other in Nagamese which is most widely spoken market language. English, the official State language, is widely spoken in the official circles and is the medium for education in Nagaland.

The majority of the people are Christians in Nagaland where "Christians form 90 percent of the population."[6] Baptists, Roman Catholics, Revivalists, Pentecostals and Assambly of God are the Christian denominations found in the State. Among them, Baptists are the predominant group constituting more than 75 percent of the State's population. Catholics are found in significant numbers in parts of Wokha district as well as in the urban areas in Kohima and Dimapur. The Ao Naga area where the social anthropological study was conducted is located in Mokokchung district in the State.

1.2. Research Setting

The field research was personally conducted for data collection in a few selected places in Nagaland. In this connection, the social anthropological study of participant observation was conducted in Ao Naga area in three places; in Mokokchung town, Ungma, and Chuchuyimlang, during the celebration of Moatsü festival from the first of May to the third, 2006. In addition, in-depth interviews were arranged and held in Kohima, Dimapur and the above mentioned places in Nagaland during the Moatsu festival celebration, which is during the first week of May. In this research, the researcher also investigated the presence of ecumenical communication in Naga folk dance during the celebration of the Moatsu festival which can promote their communitarian values and identity, such as, interaction, equality, sharing, relationship, unity, peace and development in the community. The researcher also investigated the possibility of such a space for communication in the church for mutual participation, and interaction among the people in promoting relationship and unity in the Church and society.

The majority of the people of Nagaland are Christians. The census of 2001 recorded the State's Christian population at 1,978,502 as (90.02%) of the State's population.[7] However, they are divided among themselves as there are many Christian denominations in the State.[8] Amongst the churches, the Baptist Church enjoys the highest number of members. Christian denominations are engaged in ecumenical relationship within their own denominational group. It was also noticed that, outside their church relationship, Christians of different denominations living together in the neighbourhoods often communicate and socialize with each other, which is being the normal lifestyle of the people in the locality.

Nevertheless, officially, there exists less ecumenical communication among these Christian denominations. This shows the need for relationship overcoming denominational divisions among the churches. So far, churches have not attempted

6 "Nagaland," www.http://en.wikipedia.org/wiki/nagaland, 7th May 2007. Browsed on 23-11-07.

7 "Nagaland," www.http://en.wikipedia.org/wiki/nagaland , Browsed on 28-03-2020.

8 These are the Christian denominations in Nagaland - the Baptist Church, the Roman Catholic Church, the Ceylon Pentecostal Church, the Revivalist Church, the Assembly of God, the Seventh Day Adventist Church, and the Jehovah's Witnesses.

to establish an ecumenical common sphere,[9] instead, they have maintained a segregated denominational sphere among themselves. In this connection, each denomination tries to strengthen its members' faith in the church and often tends to highlight its doctrinal differences from that of other denominations. In addition, the church members are also discouraged from entering into any doctrinal discussion or associating with members of other denominations. Often, people ignore the similarities among themselves but highlight the differences whenever they meet. It indicates that the existing problem of non-ecumenical spirit and behaviour among the members are mainly connected with the leadership of the church. The churches do not even see the need and importance of coming together for official communication.[10] This shows that the church does not provide a common ecumenical sphere for communication within the church. In addition, in my observation, there is no wider ecumenical initiative in relation to peace, justice and development. Despite the denominational segregation and non-ecumenical spirit in the church, the people in Nagaland come and dance together during the celebration of their cultural festivals[11] and other cultural programmes to affirm their communitarian identity. At this point, the cultural space and celebration outside the church may provide a space for people to come together ecumenically and tribally as well. Such a space that provides for interaction and participation among the people can be seen as an ecumenical common sphere.

1.3. The Objectives and Importance of the Research

i. First, in this research work the researcher investigated how such cultural performances at Naga festivals could bring people together enabling them to establish contact, relationship and understanding outside the church regardless of their denominational affiliation.

---

9 The term 'ecumenical common sphere' refers to an ecumenical space, which may allow the Christians of different denominations to make contact with and relate to each other. 'At the national level in the North East India, since 1940s there have been church union negotiations among the Christian denominations, initiated by the North East India Church Council, though there has been so far no positive result.' Frederick S. Downs, Christianity in North East India: Historical Perspectives (Delhi: ISPCK, 1983), pp. 155-157.

10 Official communication can be seen as an ecumenical dialogue between the Christians of different denominations, centered within the sphere of the church under the high level church leadership and official representations.

11 There are many performing arts in Naga culture such as folk theatre, folk dance, folk songs, etc., which are associated with different festivals. Folk dances and music are the important features of these festivals. For example, during the celebration of Moatsü festival of Ao Naga in the month of May, regardless of their denominational differences, the Naga folk dance and other performances enable the community members to come to a common platform and dance together without a barrier.

ii. Second, the researcher examined how such a space for communication in Naga folk dance can be recognized as a *common ecumenical sphere*[12] to promote ecumenical relations between churches in Nagaland.

One problem in the Naga society is that of lack of communication between Christian denominations. The present problem of lack of communication and strained relationships among the Christians of different denominations in the North East India (NEI) in general and in Nagaland in particular is the problem of denominationalism. Although, at an earlier period, the work of a particular Christian mission helped to develop a sense of tribal solidarity in the North East India, it created its own problems.[13] For instance, in Nagaland, Tripura, South Mizoram, and Garo hills, Baptists are the dominant Protestant Christian community since the American Baptist Mission specifically concentrated their work in these regions. This situation did not help them in accepting the idea of ecclesiastical pluralism[14] such as Roman Catholics, Pentecostals, Assembly of God, and Jehovah's Witnesses, or relating themselves with other Christian denominations in the regions. In such a context, it is surmised that the intrusion of a particular denomination into another territory where a particular denomination was already predominant might have created barriers to ecumenism such as lack of communication, prejudices, and negative attitudes between churches.

In this connection, in Nagaland, the growth of Christian denominations such as Roman Catholics, Pentecostals, Assembly of God, and Nagaland Christian Revival Church along with Baptists in Nagaland grew out of an unfriendly climate through sheep stealing from the established Baptist Church and out of differences in the practice of doctrinal beliefs.[15] Thus at present, the increasing number of Christian denominations contributes towards more divisions among them. Does

12 The term 'common ecumenical sphere' refers to an ecumenical space, which is being created by the celebration of folk dance and festivals. So that it may allow the Christians of different denominations to make contact with and relate to each other.

13 Downs uses the terms tribal ecumenism, tribal integration and tribal solidarity synonymously. According to him, these identical terms are relevant because of the coming of Christianity to the North East India, in developing new relationships and strengthening their tribal identity with wider ecumenical consciousness in the context of traditionally hostile relationships among villages of the same tribe, between different tribes, and with those outside the tribal community. Downs, F. S. "Tribal Ecumenism in North East India: The Christian Role in Solidarity Movement" in Renthy Keitzar, Ed., A Trainer of Leaders: Essays in Honour of Jonathan H. Thumra Special issue of ETC Journal, Vol. 2, No. 2, 1989, p. 49; Merithung Tüngoe, Administrators Missionaries and a World Turned Upside Down. (New Delhi: ISPCK & ETC, 2000), pp. 85-86.

14 Frederick S. Downs, "Imported Substitution: Reflections of the Indigenization of Ecclesiastical Conflict in Northeast India," in Indian Missiological Review (Special Issue on the Centenary of the Church of Northeast India 1890-1990). Vol. 12, No. 2 & 4. Sept. – Dec. 1990, p. 79.

15 A. Bendangyabang Ao, History of Christianity in Nagaland: Social Change 1872-1972 (Bangalore: Shalom Ministry Publications, 2004), pp. 261-263.

this show that they have negative attitudes and prejudices towards each other? Is this why they tend to distance themselves from each other, instead of coming together to have ecumenical fellowship and interaction? At this point, the Church should be the place for ecumenism but there is no space for ecumenical contact and unity among Christians of different denominations. Nevertheless, in such a context, Naga folk dance as a common cultural construct could bring all the community members together and provide a space for mutual participation and interaction with one another, to move towards an ecumenical fellowship among churches.

In this context, this research could encourage the churches to develop an ecumenical relationship and participation by coming together on a common platform in celebration with one another.

a) Ecumenical Relationship:

The present research may facilitate and help the churches to recognize the sphere of ecumenical presence in the Naga folk dance, so that it may become an agent for promoting ecumenical relationships and unity between different Christian denominations in Nagaland.

b) Community Participation:

Naga folk dance has a boundless strength for promoting community participation among the people in the church and society. Community participation can take place by maintaining mutual understanding and relationship with one another in the community. Thereby, it may help them to reaffirm their communitarian identity and values. In addition, the research may further clarify and enhance the important role of the laity in ecumenical movement in the region.

c) Community Development Leading to Social Development:

Such a sphere of ecumenical presence in Naga folk dance need not be confined to the Church and for the purpose of unity alone. In this connection, the research may create a wider ecumenical awareness among people for working together on common interests of community development leading to social development such as, human dignity, quality of life, freedom, unity, peace and justice.

d) Promoting Tribal Soil and Culture as Ecumenical Resources:

Celebration of Naga cultural festivals and folk dances is closely associated with God, people and their land where they work on a daily basis. Land is the gift of God to people where they work and earn their livelihood. It is the place where they celebrate dances and festivals, and nourish their rich heritage of culture. In this connection, this research can create awareness among the people about the importance of caring and nurturing their culture, land and tribal spirituality as gift of God, so that they may remain as resources to promote ecumenical relationship and participation in the society.

e) Communal Harmony:

The research may facilitate in bringing closer not only Christians of different denominations but also people of other faiths towards mutual understanding, harmony and unity. In this connection, Networking and cooperation with other religions should be promoted in the context of common issues that will benefit all people. Moreover, it will provide new opportunities for co-operation with the people of other faiths on issues such as that of communication, communal harmony, peace and justice.

1.4. Literature Review

There are a number of writings on ecumenical initiatives and developments in North East India done by many church historians including those of the early missionaries. These works are mostly done, however, from a historical perspective and there is no particular emphasis on dance for the promotion of ecumenism with special reference to Nagaland, which is the interest area of this research. Therefore, only selected works of the preceding research, which are close to the present research, have been considered in this review. In this connection, the literature review of this section will be discussed on two main texts namely, Ecumenical texts and Communication texts.

1.4.1. Ecumenical Texts

Among these works, there are substantial writings done by F. S. Downs in the area of ecumenical initiatives and Church Union Movement in North East India. The following three articles entitled "Church Union in the North East India," "Church Union: Theological and Non-Theological Factors," and "Church Union: News and Views," were written in 1965 in which Downs points out to the fact that the present failure of the Church Union Movement in North East India is not due to theological factors such as the issues of episcopacy, baptism, etc., but due to non-theological factors such as geographical, denominational, linguistic, tribal and cultural differences, etc. Downs simply attributes its failure to indigenous factors as he looks at the ecumenical initiatives from a historical perspective, but does not recognize the presence of an ecumenical space within these factors such as myth, rituals, festivals, etc. In the article, "Tribal Ecumenism in North East India: The Christian Role in Solidarity Movement," (1989), Downs is of the view that tribal ecumenism is the development of a new consciousness and relationship among the villages of the same tribe, between the tribes and even with those outside the community who were once hostile to one another. In this process, Christianity has played a vital role in preserving a separate tribal identity through the introduction of comprehensive tribal institutions in the form of an ecclesiastical structure.

However, he does not show how such an exclusive ecclesiastical structure (such as the Naga Baptist Churches or Nagaland Baptist Church Council) might have created a negative attitude towards the idea of ecclesiastical pluralism (the presence of other Christian denominations). In addition, it is also argued that it is not only the local indigenous factors but also the theological factors and the affiliation of the Baptists with the mother church[16] that might have contributed to the denominational differences in Nagaland. In T. Likok's *A Picture of an Organic Church Union* (1970), the writer advocates spiritual unity that is union with Christ. According to him, the visible expression of spiritual unity can be manifested through Councils, Associations, inter-communion and Christian brotherhood. In this connection, he also shows positive attitude towards the idea of an organic Church Union. The work of Joseph Puthenpurakal entitled *Baptist Mission in Nagaland: A Study in Historical and Ecumenical Perspective* (1984), attempts to analyse and understand the present ecumenical situation in Nagaland through a study of the Baptist movement in the West and the teachings of the early missionaries.[17] He hopes that this analysis will be a preparation for the initiation of ecumenical dialogue between the Protestant and the Catholic Christians in Nagaland. In this connection, Downs says that dialogue and interaction between Protestants and Catholics in Northeast India may be possible only when Catholics understand the socio-cultural implications of their "intrusion", and Protestants learn to settle tribal solidarity with ecclesiastical pluralism.[18] J. Fortis Jyrwa's article on "Church Union Movement in North East India: A Historical Perspective," in Renthy Keitzar's (ed) *Church Ministry and Mission: Essays in Honour of K. Imotemjen Aier* (1988), highlights the whole period of Church Union discussion in North East India, which covers up to 1977. In his conclusion, he suggests re-examining seriously the non-theological problems with a view to explore and consider for a "Union" that is suitable to the Christian churches and the context in North East India. The recent work of Toshi Aier's "A Study of the Ecumenical Movement in North East India," *M.Th. Thesis* (2000), gives us an insight into the further development of the Church Union Movement in North East India up

16 The Baptist Church in Nagaland loyal to the Northern American Baptist Mission in terms of maintaining the structures they inherited from the mission. Consequently, it does not encourage them to have ecumenical relationship and wholehearted participation with Christians of other denominations. J. Fortis Jyrwa, "Church Union Movement in North East India: A Historical Perspective," in Renthy Keitzar (ed) Church Ministry and Mission: Essays in Honour of K. Imotemjen Aier (Guwahati: CBCNEI, 1988), pp. 71-72.

17 Downs rejects the assumption behind Joseph Puthenpurakal's hypothesis that the present hostile relationships are a continuation of the Western conflicts between the two groups. Downs views that for a meaningful dialogue between the Protestant and the Roman Catholic Christians in the North East India, the present conflict needs to be understood in terms of their indigenous rather than exotic factors. Downs, "Imported Substitution..." op. cit., pp. 73-74.

18 Ibid., pp. 79-80.

to 1998. He also agrees that because of the non-theological problems the church union's attempts in North East India have been unsuccessful. Both Jyrwa and Toshi Aier concentrated on similar topics and studied them from a historical perspective. Their concluding remarks show that the indigenous factors might have worked against the Church Union Movement in the Northeast India, but could not point out whether the ecumenical sphere as such could be identified by studying such factors for future ecumenical development in the regions.

1.4.2. Communication Texts

The following are the works of some communication scholars, which focused on Christian communication with ecumenical insights. William F. Fore's work on *Television and Religion: the Shaping of Faith, Values and Culture,* articulates that Christians need to be good stewards of the media especially that of the television, encouraging feedback, dialogue and avoiding commercial interest, so that it can be effective to advance the Kingdom values.[19] In this connection, Peter G. Horsfield's *Religious Television: The American Experience* also emphasizes that the religious use of television needs to do away with the commercialization and consumerization of religious faith and involve itself into contributing to the ongoing mission of the church.[20] The works of Fore and Horsfield affirm that the religious use of media needs to bring people together for contact, sharing, and participation with each other without any personal interest, which in itself has ecumenical significance in Christian communication. In addition, Horsfield says that the religious broadcasters need to be involved in action, which is ecumenically significant on behalf of the poor and the powerless, and on behalf of those who lack social and economic power to act on their own. In this connection, Edmund Arens' book on *Christopraxis: A Theology of Action*, gives a clear liberative perspective to Christian communication with a clear location of context toward ecclesial and universal solidarity.[21] Solidarity and unity of the Church is the first and foremost step to communicate the truth of the gospel to the oppressed and the suffering community in the society.

The above-mentioned survey of the previous researches show that they have mainly focused on the Church Union Movement in the North East India from historical perspectives, so far initiated by the high level of church leadership. Most of the works have subscribed to the fact that due to indigenous factors, the Church Union Movement has not been successful so far. In fact, both the theological and the indigenous factors have been working against ecumenical relations and

19 William F. Fore, *Television and Religion: The Shaping of Faith, Values, and Culture* (New Haven: SBS Press, 1987), p. 194.

20 Peter G. Horsfield, *Religious Television: The American Experience* (London: Longmans, 1984), p. 172.

21 Edmund Arens, *Christopraxis: A Theology of Action*, translated by John F. Hoffmeyer (Minneapolis: Fortress Press, 1995), pp. 150 -169.

against the Church Union Movement in the regions. In addition, the focuses of the previous researches on Christian communication were mainly on the religious use of media and advocacy from an ethical perspective. In my observation, the previous researches did not pay attention to the presence of communication sphere in the celebration of cultural festivals and folk dances,[22] which is important for the promotion of ecumenism among Christians of different denominations. Thus, it confirms the need for further researches that would incorporate wider ecumenical understanding, wider participation and initiatives of the lay people including the leadership of local churches towards the promotion of ecumenical relationship among the churches in North East India, especially in Nagaland.

1.5. Theoretical Framework of the Research

Folk dance is an important component in communication. In this connection, folk dance is a non-verbal form of communication which can play a vital role in human life. It can take place in various forms and demonstrate its artistic forms through bodily expression. In this connection, Collingwood says that "Body movement and gesture is central to all forms of expressions, even in rigidity and silence. Dance is the mother of all languages and is the primary form of communication."[23] The body movements and expressions in dance can demonstrate the interpersonal and group dimensions of communication. It may provide a communication space to articulate their aspirations, needs and communitarian values to others. Naga folk dance can be seen as one of the community media of communication in the society in bringing people together on a common platform promoting interaction, relationship and participation with one another. In this regard, Robert A. White is worthwhile to quote when he says that "Community media usually find a way to celebrate and perpetuate the most widely shared values of the community-the celebration of 'common sense', common virtues, and the humor of an ordinary life."[24] In fact, the people-based indigenous medium such as the folk dance can be a means of communication in promoting commonality, relationship and unity among the people.

1.5.1. Theoretical Understanding of Folk Dance as Communication

a) Interpersonal Communication: Dance has an element of interpersonal relationship and communication between two persons. Michael E. Roloff says

22 The analysis of the ecumenical texts shows that the present failure of Church Union Movement in North East India is due to indigenous factors as the texts dealt with the ecumenical initiatives from a historical perspective, but did not recognize the presence of an ecumenical space within these factors such as myths, rituals, music, dance, cultural festivals, etc.

23 R. H. Collingwood, The Principles of Art (London: Oxford University Press, 1974), p. 244.

24 Robert A. White, "Communication Creates Community: The Role of Community-Oriented Media," in Srinivas R. Melkote and Sandhya Rao, eds. In Critical Issues In Communication Looking Inward For Answer: Essays in Honor of K. E. Eapen (New Delhi: Sage Publication, 2001), p. 235.

that the interpersonal communication can take place between two people because they are willing to agree on the nature of the relationship.[25] In this regard, folk dance is basically people's dance. It has a capacity to bring people together and establish inter-personal relationship with one another in the community which may lead to a meaningful interpersonal communication among the people. Folk dance can bring people at interpersonal and face to face context for developing interaction with one another. This element of inter-personal communication is crucial in the study of dance in understanding how the celebration of folk dance can promote contact, interaction, relationship and participation with one another in the community. At this point, it may be seen as an ecumenical common sphere to enhance the ecumenical activities among the people in the community.

b) Group Communication: Dance has also a group dimension of communication. Basically, dance performance is a team work and group activity in which the each member has a part to play. In this connection, Sandeep Deshmukh states that the behavioral and cultural elements constitute group communication. Further, interaction between these two elements can produce the effect in the form of group communication.[26] In the study of the folk dance these two elements of behavioral and cultural life of a particular community will be useful in understanding the way they interact and convey messages and information to one another. Naga folk dance is a community dance. It means folk dance is itself a group activity in which all the members of the group are treated with equal importance and expected to engage and participate in coordination with one another.

c) Non-verbal forms of Communication: Dance is a universal language of communication in human life in the society. In fact, it is characterized by non-verbal communication in which the parts of the human body are instruments. In general, dance movements include all parts of the body, head, back, hips, feet, arms, fingers and the facial muscles which are brought into play with meaningful and rhythmic manner. In this connection, Stephanie S. Scott states that "Dance can be used to express the universal experiences of primary language such as joy or sadness and it can communicate the spiritual experiences of religious language."[27] The non-verbal forms of communication in folk dance can express and convey the psychological, emotional, religious, economical, social and political life of the people in the society. It is in such contexts that the non-verbal forms of

25 Michael E. Roloff, "Communication Strategies, Relationships, and Relational Change." In Gerald R. Miller, ed., in *Explorations in Interpersonal Communication: Sage Annual Reviews of Communication Research Vol. V* (Beverly Hills: Sage Publications, 1976), p. 182.

26 Sandeep Deshmukh, *Group Communication: Theory and Methods* (New Delhi: ANE Books India, 2008), pp. 62-63.

27 Stephanie S. Scott, "The Language of Liturgical Dance in African-American Christian Worship," in Journal of the Interdenominational Theological Center, Volume XXVII, Numbers 1 and 2, Fall 1999 / Spring 2000, p. 250.

communication such as symbolic objects and symbolic gestures that are employed in folk dance by the people will be useful tools in understanding the celebration of Naga folk dance. It may help the researcher to find out how the cultural forms of communication can bring people together on a common platform establishing contact, relationship and participation with one another which can be a sign of ecumenical progress.

1.5.2. Theological Backdrop of Folk Dance and Ecumenism

Ecumenism was nurtured and flourished in a meaningful way through communication channels. In this regard, theology of ecumenism is a study of ecumenism in relation to the demanding challenges of broken unity in the Church and the society at present, based on the concept of the unity of Christ. Emilio Castro says, "The ecumenical pilgrimage is a commitment to growth within the unity that already exists in God. The church is one, and our growth must be within this Trinitarian reality, in which the Holy Spirit makes us one with the triune God."[28] The unity of Christ derives from God the Father, and the Holy Spirit makes the unity of the church in Christ meaningful within the communion of the Triune God. In fact, theology of Ecumenism concerns itself not only with the personal reflection upon ones faith alone, but also with the unity of the church and also unity of the whole of God's creation in promoting towards peace, justice, freedom and development. In this connection, the church can be a place for promoting ecumenism. As such there is no space for ecumenical communication in the church. In this paradigm, folk dance can be considered as means of communication in promoting ecumenism in the church and society.

Naga folk dance can be seen as one of the means of communication in the community. It is the nerve centre of the people. In fact, one can say that it is a mirror of the people through which their way of life, behavior and the whole activities in the society can be seen, expressed and communicated. In addition, Naga folk dances are associated with the social, economic, political and religious life of the people in the community. In this connection, their community consciousness is strongly attached to the celebration of folk dance and cultural festivals that provides an ecumenical space to come together and strengthen their contact, relationship and communitarian identity. The researcher assumes that in the context of the existing problem of non-ecumenical spirit and denominationalism among the people in the church, the Naga folk dance as an important part of communication can enhance the ecumenical activities in the North East India in general and Nagaland in particular. It may bring people together on a common platform in celebration, establishing contact, relationship and participation with one another through the celebration of folk dances and festival which can be a positive sign of developing ecumenical communication, which is a major concern in this research. Further, it may pave way for doctrinal

28 Emilio Castro, *A Passion for Unity: Essays on Ecumenical Hopes and Challenges*, op. cit., p.1.

discussion with one another or focusing on wider ecumenism promoting towards community development, freedom, peace, and justice, which may happen sooner or later. The researcher assumes that this is going to be the church's mission vision.

1.5.3. Theoretical Concept of Ecumenism

The underlying theoretical concept of ecumenism outlines the visions and issues of ecumenism. Here, the researcher highlights the well-developed concept of ecumenical unity and action in the context of present ecumenical problems in the church and the society in relation to peace, justice and development. It is an endeavour to show that ecumenism is not only for the relationship, understanding, and unity of the church but also for the unity of the whole creation.

a) Ecumenism towards the Unity of the Church

The current ecumenical movement came into existence out of the conviction of the churches that the division of Christians is a disgrace and an obstruction to the witness of the Church.[29] In this context, it gives priority to the unity of the Church, so that Christians of different denominations can come together to a common platform with openness to speak out with one voice for the unity and development of the human community.[30] It has often been noted that the origin of the Ecumenical Movement lay in the missionary movement,[31] which made efforts to communicate the gospel of peace, unity, love and integrity not only within the churches but also in the whole inhabited world.[32]

b) Ecumenism towards Peace and Justice

The ultimate goal of ecumenical movement is not only for the unity of the Church but also (in its socio-political dimension) for peace, justice, development and unity of human community in the context of the many forms of oppressions, discriminations and exploitations against women, poor people and poor nations.[33]

---

29 James A. Scherer & Stephen B. Bevans, eds., *New Directions in Mission and Evangelization: Basic Statement – 1974 -1991*, Vol. I (New York: Orbis Books, 1992), p. 37.

30 WACC, Statements on Communication (London: WACC, 1997), pp. 6-7.

31 The modern ecumenical movement may be dated from the Edinburgh Missionary Conference of 1910, in which unity was emphasized as the key to successful global evangelization. Williams M. King, "Ecumenism," in Hans J. Hillerbrand, ed. The Encyclopedia of Protestantism, Vol. 2, D-K, (New York: Routledge, 2004), p. 636; However, this owed much to earlier movements, which prepared the way for the future ecumenical developments. F. L. Cross and E. A. Livingstone, The Oxford Dictionary of the Christian Church (Oxford: Oxford University Press, 1977), p. 528.

32 Joseph Mattam & Sebastian Kim, eds., *Mission Trends Today: Historical and Theological Perspectives* (Bangalore: St. Pauls, 1997), p.100.

33 T. V. Philip, *Edinburgh To Salvador: Twentieth Century Ecumenical Missiology* (New Delhi: CSS & ISPCK, 1999), pp. 92-93.

It is in the context of diverse socio-economic and political situations and divisions that ecumenism is envisaged.

Further, divisions are caused by globalization and plurality of cultural and religious differences. In addition, the relentless wars and tensions between nations, ethnic and communal conflicts, terrorism, ecological destructions are the realities that incessantly promote fears and uncertainties in the lives of the people. This situation demands socio-political peace and justice in the global community. In the context of the North East India, peace, justice and development are crucial not only for people's survival but also for maintaining their identity and human dignity. In such a situation social transformation is needed to advance a genuine *oikoumene.*

c) Dialogue as Ecumenical Communication

Dialogue itself is a powerful means of communication for building up ecumenical relations, promoting unity and harmony among people in the Church and society. Dialogue is not only for the unity of the Church but it also extends to people of other faiths towards achieving better understanding to realize communal harmony. In the present pluralistic context, where different religious communities are living together side-by-side, religious pluralism becomes a significant issue. At times communal disharmony and conflict occur due to misunderstandings between different religious communities and their exclusive attitude towards other religious faiths. In this regard, Christian communication with people of other faiths is meant for dialogical sharing, mutual understanding and learning from one another.[34] In addition, the Church needs to go beyond her institutional boundaries to build up dialogical communication, cooperation and coordination with people of other faiths, so that they may get opportunity to work together for common interests, such as peace, justice and development in the society.[35] Thus, it may help and benefit all sections of people regardless of religions, caste, tribe, and social status.

The goal and concept of ecumenism goes beyond the unity of the Church to include a wider ecumenism for the promotion of freedom, development, peace, justice, and peaceful co-existence among all God's creations. However, we need to go beyond the theoretical concept of ecumenism to explore whether there is any space for communication outside the church, to promote ecumenical relations between Christians of different denominations.

---

34 K. J. Thomas, *Ecumenism: A Call to Unity* (Bangalore: St. Peter's Pontifical Institute Publications, 2007), pp. 155-156.

35 John Joshva Raja & Samson Prabhakar, eds. *Introduction to Communication and Media Studies* (Bangalore: BTESSC/SATHRI, 2006), pp. 277-279.

1.6. An Overview of the Ecumenical Initiatives in North East India

In the light of the theoretical concept of ecumenism, the churches in Nagaland have not so far attempted any ecumenical initiative as such but have simply maintained ecumenical relationship within their own denominational group. For example, as a result of negotiations and consultations, all the Baptist churches and associations were brought together as a tribal ecumenical body under the umbrella of Nagaland Baptist Church Council (NBCC).[36] In addition, apart from maintaining ecumenical relations at the denominational level, there are no wider ecumenical initiatives taken by the churches in relation to freedom, peace and justice issues.

Though, there has been so far no positive outcome, since 1937, the Baptists, the Presbyterians and other churches in the North East India have been actively involved in the Church Union Movement under the leadership and initiatives of the North East India Christian Council (NEICC),[37] which is the most important ecumenical agency in the North East India. In addition, since the NEICC has been part of the National Council of Churches in India (NCCI), it has become an important link between the Christians of the North East India and those in other parts of the country. The Council of Baptist Churches in North East India (CBCNEI)[38] as part of the NEICC's initiated Church Union Movement has

36 The Nagaland Baptist Church Council (NBCC) is the central organization of the Baptist Churches in Nagaland. It was established in 1935 as the Naga Hills Baptist Church Advisory Board. But it was renamed as the Naga Hills Baptist Church Council on April 5, 1937. NBCC as such was reorganized later in1953 and yet functioned somewhat provisionally until 1960. After the inauguration of Nagaland as a separate State within the Indian Union, the Council was given a new name as the Nagaland Baptist Church Council. Alongla P. Aier, From Darkness to Light, op. cit., p. 104.

37 The initiative of the Welsh Presbyterian Mission has brought six mission organizations and two churches (the American Baptist Mission, the Santhal Mission of the Northern Churches, the Gossner Evangelical Lutheran Mission, the Co-operative Baptist Mission of North America (Mid-Mission), the English Baptist Mission (the south Lushai Hills), the Church of God, the Welsh Presbyterian Mission and the Church of India, (in Shillong on 23rd November 1937) to constitute the Assam Christian Council (ACC). The objective of this council was to share their common interests, mutual co-operation in matters of literary works, and to create and maintain Christian public opinion in the province. After three decades, the ACC was renamed as the North East India Christian Council (NEICC) in 1963. NEICC has been so far the most important ecumenical agency in the North East India. ACC Report, March 29 – 31, 1940, pp. 81-82; Also See, J. Fortis Jyrwa, "Church Union Movement in North East India: A Historical Perspective," op. cit., pp. 59-61; Toshi Aier, "Church Union Movement in North East India: A Reflection," in Akheto Sumi, ed. *Perspectives: Current Issues in Theological Thinking* (Mokokchung: Jongshinokdang Trust CTC, 2002), p. 141.

38 It was during the transition period in the late 1940s, when the American Baptist Mission had to hand over the authority to a local organization: two Baptist organizations such as the Assam Christian Convention and the Assam Baptist Christian Convention which came together and formed the Council of Baptist Churches in Assam on 9th January, 1950 at Golaghat. However, due to political structure of the region in the course of years, in 1954 it was reconstituted as

actively taken part in these Church Union consultations. During the early 1970s most of the Presbyterian churches and many of the smaller Baptist churches approved the plan of union and the Draft Constitution as a basis for official church union negotiations.

The second consultation of the CBCNEI held in August 1971, expressed that the Church Union plan of the NEICC was unacceptable mainly on theological issues in relation to baptism, centralized church government, the office of the Bishop, etc.[39] The Council requested the CBCNEI to give their alternative proposal in relation to their specific objections, so that the Council may improve the draft. However, in 1977, the CBCNEI expressed that they were not prepared to enter into negotiations, but that the door was open for future negotiations.[40] Since the CBCNEI is the largest single Baptist organization in North East India, the other Baptist organizations such as Baptist Church of Mizoram, the Tripura Baptist Christian Union, the North Bank Baptist Association and the Goalpara union also had to follow in accordance with the decisions of the CBCNEI in relation to the Church Union movement.[41] In addition, based on the decision of the NEICC annual session of 1986, the drafting committee's revised plan of union and draft constitution was distributed to all the affiliated bodies for consideration. However, the CBCNEI in its executive meeting in May 1998 discussed the plan of union and decided that it was not in favour of church union for certain technical reasons within the council.[42] Hence, the consultations for a united church of North East India came to a deadlock, which might have happened due to both theological and non-theological factors. According to Downs, the indigenous non-theological factors such as denominational, tribal, linguistic, and cultural differences might have worked against development and progress of the church union movement rather than theological factors.[43] However, Downs does not recognize the presence of ecumenical space outside the church in the celebration of cultural festivals and folk dances, which may be crucial for the promotion of ecumenism in the church. In addition, in relation to the ecumenical problem in the North East India in general and Nagaland in

---

the Council of Baptist Churches in Assam and Manipur (CBCAM) 1959. Finally, it was renamed as the Council of Baptist Churches in North East India (CBCNEI). CBCNEI is one of the largest national Baptist organizations in the country. There are six regional Conventions under the CBCNEI, namely: 1) Assam Baptist Convention (ABC), 2) Arunachal Pradesh Baptist Convention (APBC), 3) Garo Baptist Convention (GBC), 4) Kabir Anglong Baptist Convention (KABC), 5) Manipur Baptist Convention (MBC), and Nagaland Baptist Church Council (NBCC). See, The Baptist News, Vol 50, Nos. 1 & 2, Jan – Apr. 2000, pp. 1-2.

39 Downs, *Christianity in North East India*... op. cit., p. 163; See, J. Fortis Jyrwa, op. cit., p. 69.

40 Ibid., pp. 69-70.

41 D. Singson, "The Baptist Involvement in the Church Union Movement in India." M.Th. Thesis, 1975. p. 140.

42 Toshi Aier, op. cit., p. 150.

43 Downs, *Christianity in North East India*... op. cit., P. 155;

particular, theological factors need not be ruled out because they are still operative within the Christian denominations in the regions.

The earlier model of ecumenical dialogues and discussions at the universal, and the national levels were oriented rather top-down and centered within the sphere of the church under the high level church leadership and official representations.[44] Obviously, in the context of North East India, the high level church leadership (NEICC) directly initiated the church union movement in the region and led a number of discussions in relation to doctrinal and theological issues and problems, which were crucial to ecumenical discussions. Scholars have argued that the theological and local factors have contributed towards the present ecumenical tension and issues. Not much emphasis is made on the ecumenical presence outside the church's realm by the previous ecumenical researchers. The intention of the present research is to search for the existence of any ecumenical interaction of this kind. If so, the researcher wants to study as to how they create a space for understanding and for establishing contact outside the church. To specifically focus on the ecumenical sphere, the researcher has selected the 'Folk dance' of Nagas as a framework for this research and analysis.

1.7. Dance in the Old Testament

In the Old Testament, references of group and individual dances can be found. It also describes the use, purpose and benefits of dance among God's people. It shows that most of the Hebrew dances are communal or performed in a group.

a) Communal or Group Dance

In this connection, the Hebrew word for dance in the Old Testament has various forms, such as, *Machol*, *Mecholah*, and *Chul* (Chul being the infinitive) which are referred to as the circular group dance. These terms indicate the same group circular dances, and are translated by *Xopos* in the Greek Septuagint and *Chorea* in the Latin Vulgate.[45] In addition, these terms shows that dance was performed by a group circling and not solo dancers.[46] In Jewish circle dances, a wide range of individual movements were accepted and incorporated, but the priestly traditions in both the Jewish and Christian circle dances have tended to enforce standards of some individual grace or at least group harmony in such dancing.[47]

In the following passages of scriptures the Hebrew word *Machol* is used to denote a group circle dance. In Psalm 30:11-12, the Psalmist identifies the

44 O. L. Snaitang, *A History of Ecumenical Movement: An Introduction* (Bangalore: BTESSC/SATHRI, 2004), p. 166.

45 Doug Adams, *Congregational Dancing in Christian Worship* (Texas: The Sharing Company, 1980), p. 24.

46 Julian Morgenstern, "The Etymological History of the Three Hebrew Synonyms for 'To Dance,'" in American Oriental Society Journal, 36, 1916, pp. 321-332.

47 Doug Adams, *Congregational Dancing*, op. cit., p. 25.

presence of God and expresses happiness with a joyful dance. It shows, that giving thanks and praising the almighty God in dance and music was a normal form of worship in the temple. "Let them praise his name with dancing, making melody to him with tambourine and lyre" (Psalm 149:3). "Praise him with tambourine and dance; praise him with strings and pipe" (Psalm 150:4). In the above mentioned passages, the psalmist points out that communal dance and music had an important place in worship in the temple. In addition, in Lamentation 5: 15, it says, "The joy of our hearts has ceased; our dancing has been turned to mourning." This particular verse is found in the 5th section of "a prayer for mercy," which clearly shows that dance was a part and parcel of the Jewish religious life and worship.[48] These above mentioned dances are communal in character which were performed in community worship in the temple. In addition, several authors note the connection between *hagag* and dance. The usual translation of *hagag* is "feast," "festival" or "celebration," however, Gruber also underlines how this root can be translated into "dance in a circle."[49]

Mecholah is another word for a circular group or communal dance in Hebrew,[50] which is often found in the Old Testament. For instance, in Exodus 15: 20, the Prophetess Miriam, Aaron's sister took her tambourine and joyfully danced and praised God along with the women folk for His miraculous deliverance of the Israelites from the bondage of the Egyptians. In addition, the book of I Samuel shows that the use of dance had significance among the prophets in their worship. It was dance which took them to an ecstatic state by the spirit of God. The approval and need of such a dance and the transformation that it would bring is made clear from the advice given by Samuel to Saul (1 Samuel 10:10-13). *Chul* is another Hebrew word used for group dances. For instance, in the book of Judges, dance was a vintage festival[51] where women danced in a group during that time in the vineyard (Judges 21:21 & 23). This communal dancing in worship is true to the earliest prophetic practices, the later Talmudic and Midrashic vision of the people coming to God in the whole history of Hebraic practice.[52]

---

48 "The book of Lamentation is a collection of five poems lamenting the destruction of Jerusalem in 586 B.C. and its aftermath of ruin and exile. These poems are used by the Jews in worship on the annual days of fasting and mourning which commemorate the national disaster of 586 B.C." Francis Peter Barboza, *Christianity in Indian Dance Form* (Delhi: Sri Satguru Publications, 1990), p. 6.

49 Mayer I. Gruber, "Ten Dance-Derived Expressions in the Hebrew Bible," in Doug Adams and Diane Apostolos-Cappadona (eds), Dance as Religious Studies, p. 49.

50 Barboza, op. cit., pp. 6-7.

51 John L. McKenzie, *Dictionary of the Bible* (New York: Geoffery Chapman, 1975), p. 171.

52 Francis Peter Barboza, op. cit., p. 7.

Individual Dance

The survey made in the Scriptures indicates that most of the dances were communal or performed in a group. There are a few instances of individual dances in the Old Testament. The Hebrew word used for individual dances are *Karar* and *Raqad* translated *Opxounevos* in the Greek and *Saltatio* in the Latin which denote an individual circling and jumping.[53] The word *Karar* is mentioned only once where King David danced in the temple to honour the Lord (11 Samuel 6: 14-16). In addition, *Raqad* in Hebrew is found in many passages in the Scriptures that indicate the individual dance (1 Chronicles 15: 29; Job 21: 11; Ecclesiastics 3:4).[54]

According to the Old Testament, communal dancing has been popular and more in practice than the individual dance. It shows that throughout the history of the Jews the nature of the dance has been conditioned by the desire to include all the people in the community.

1.8. Dance in the New Testament

The New Testament continues with the Old Testament understanding of dance in terms of communal dance in worship and not in terms of the individual dance. For instance, the return of the Prodigal son to the father is accompanied by a group dance (Luke 15:25). Mathew 11:17, indicates a group dance since it is said, "We played wedding music for you but you would not dance." These instances show the importance of dance in the religious and community life of the people.

In the Old Testament, dance is indicated of joyous gathering of people as a community (Jeremiah 31:13; Lamentation 5:15). The same idea is found and continued in the New Testament. For example, Luke 6:23, "Rejoice and leap for joy," indicates a dance with joyful expressions and meaningful movements. In this connection, Doug Adams states that during the time of Jesus, dancing was a literal part of rejoicing and feasting in the community,[55] which is also an important part in the life of the church.

Throughout the Old Testament, God is envisioned as the one who is constantly leading and moving with the Israelites which can be seen as a divine dance for the deliverance of his own people. In the New Testament, the description of Jesus rejoicing in the spirit (Luke 10:21) gives us a picture of Jesus himself dancing, because at that time dancing was a part of Jewish worship and social life.[56]

The New Testament accounts make less direct references to dance. Unlike the Old Testament, there are no explicit calls for the people to dance as worship. Further, there is no mention of them not continuing to dance either—it is not

53 Doug Adams, *Congregational Dancing*, op. cit., p. 28.

54 Francis Peter Barboza., op. cit., 8.

55 Doug Adams, *Congregational Dancing*, op. cit., p. 90.

56 Ibid., p. 90.

condemned.[57] Although the New Testament does not make much of dancing as in the Old Testament, it makes more references to the importance of the body in worship. Its most significant contribution comes in the presentation of the Incarnation. In Jesus the word became flesh. The words and actions of Jesus are inseparable from each other. Jesus did not die for the spiritual part of persons but for the whole person.[58] Jesus' incarnation and communication with humankind, his creative and redemptive work, his suffering, death and resurrection can be seen as dancing for the salvation of all humankind (John 1:14). In this connection, he may be called as the Lord of Dance who danced and communicated his message in and through his body. The biblical understanding of dance indicates the importance of communal or group dance for the participation, welfare and benefit of the members of the community in worship. In this connection, dance can be seen as a vehicle of communication through which people can express and communicate their yearning, feelings and aspiration to God and one another.[59] It is still relevant in today's context of worship and participation not only for meaningfully expressing the Christian faith but also for promoting interaction, sharing, relationship, unity, peace and justice among the people in the church and society.

1.9. Method and Scope of the Research

The present research is based on the anthropological, sociological, group comparative and cultural analysis of the specific Naga way of life and behaviour in relation to folk dance and ecumenical relations. In this connection, assumptions are made and the outcome of the study will be the hypothesis for further thesis. In this research, some selected lay leaders, religious leaders and folk dancers who are active initiators and participants in the celebration of Moatsü festivals and dances of Ao Nagas are the primary subjects of this study. The research explores whether such celebration of festivals and folk dances allow people to establish contact, understand and develop relationship with one another. Can such a space be identified as a common ecumenical sphere and extended in the church towards promoting ecumenical unity between Christians of different denominations? Can such an ecumenical space enable them to work together for unity, justice, development and human dignity?

The study was carried out in social anthropological method,[60] which deals with the people's customs, social institutions and values, and the ways in which they

57 Doug Adams, *Congregational Dancing*, op. cit., pp. 27-28.

58 Carolyn Deitering, *The Liturgy as Dance and Liturgical Dancer* (New York: The Crossroad Publishing Company, 1984), p. 13.

59 Ronald Gagne, *Thomas Kane and Robert VerEecke, Introducing Dance in Christian Worship* (Washington: The Pastoral Press Washington, D.C., 1984), pp. 30-31.

60 M. N. Srinivas, Village Caste, *Gender and Method: Essays in Indian Social Anthropology.* (New Delhi: Oxford University Press, 2001), pp. 209-210.

are interrelated.[61] In addition, in India, social anthropology studies the primitives, the tribal and the backward segments of society living on a small scale and in small places with a comprehensive perspective including culture, ethnology, physiology and social system.[62] In this connection, the investigations are mainly carried out in the context of a living community, especially that of the Ao Nagas. In this connection, the researcher has used two qualitative anthropological methods[63] of participant observation and in-depth interview to investigate the way people relate, interact and establish relationship with one another during the celebration of Moatsü festival and its dances.

The process of establishing such a relationship between people through dance performances could bring together the study of communication and religion. In this connection, there are both theological and communicative dimensions in the study of folk dances in relation to ecumenical relations. It argues that close contact and engagement during the cultural performances of the participants is necessary for understanding the meaning of symbolic actions.[64] Both the methods, of participant observation and in-depth interview are commonly applicable to both religion and communication studies. They are often applied to groups as well as to individuals within a particular culture to investigate the various communicative symbols and meanings, and the nature of people's participation in such a communication process.

a) Participant Observation

Participant Observation has its roots in anthropology, which aims to gain a close association with a given group of people in their natural environment. In Participant observation, a researcher learns about a social group and its culture or

---

61 John Beattie, *Other Cultures: Aims, Methods and Achievements in Social Anthropology.* (London: Routledge, 1999), p. 16.

62 In European countries, social anthropology is the study of physical or biological aspects of humankind. In England, social anthropology is understood as ethnology or sociology. In USA, social anthropology concerns itself with the study of culture or it is essentially a cultural social science. In India, social anthropology in terms of Indian social science, studies the social system, culture, ethnology and physiology of the tribal and the weaker segments of society. S. L. Doshi and P. C. Jain, Social Anthropology. (Jaipur: Rawat Publications, 2002), pp. 11-12, 47. See also M. N. Srinivas, op. cit. p. 9.

63 The research will apply the qualitative research method to investigate and analyze the data. Arthur Asa Berger, *Media and Communication Research Method: An Introduction to Qualitative and Quantitative Methods* (Thousand Oaks: Saga Publications, 2000), p. 13. The advantages of using the qualitative research methods are that they can explore and appraise things that cannot be summarized by numerical analysis. In addition, the advantage of using qualitative method is characterized by subjective, exploratory, interpretive and descriptive research. *Susanna Hornig Priest, Doing Media Research: An Introduction* (Thousand Oaks: Sage Publications, 1996), pp. 4-5.

64 Universiteit Twente, the Netherlands, "Symbolic Interaction," http://www.tcw.utwente.nl/theorieenoverzicht/Theory/20clusters/Inte 09/09/2004. Browsed on 15-02-2005.

sub-culture through acting as a member of the group. It provides the opportunity to study people in a real-life situation, by becoming and acting as a participant and collecting the data from what is observed, by being an observer among the people.[65] Such a research usually involves a range of methods: informal interviews, direct observation, participation in the life of the group, collective discussions, and analyses of the personal documents produced within the group, self-analysis, and study of life-histories.[66]

In this process, gaining people's confidence may enable the researcher to get adequate information from them. Thus the process of observing and studying people's behaviour, identifying and understanding people's ways of interpersonal communication, group communication, social interaction, non-verbal communication and cultural signs and symbols may provide the researcher with useful data. It observes the relationship between what people say and what they do in order to discover the truth. The advantages of participant observation are that it helps the researcher to understand what is going on within the research study to determine which question to ask the informants and to gather useful insights about the group or people.

b) In-Depth Interview

In-depth interview is an open-ended conversational exploration of an individual's or family groups' worldviews in their own homes. It does not have a rigidly set structure, like a survey questionnaire but uses a particular set of questions that were being addressed.[67] In-depth interviews are useful in qualitative research method, which has been often used for data collection in media audience research.[68] Unlike a survey questionnaire method, in-depth interviews do not have a rigid set structure, thus it is sometimes called semi-structured interview.[69] The interview was conducted with a particular set of questions, followed by an open-ended conversation and clarifications in response to the informant's answers and interests, with a view to discover their worldview and attitudes. Since the responses were left open to the respondent, the interview was an unstandardised interview, which is mainly used in qualitative research.

Through this method, the researcher interviewed some selected individuals such as, lay leaders, religious leaders and folk dancers, personally in their respective places in order to find out the levels of their understanding, their idea, and vision on the promotion of ecumenical relationships and their actions in the society

---

65 Anya Peterson Royce, *The Anthropology of Dance,* op. cit., p. 18. Also See, Berger, op. cit., p. 161.

66 "Participant Observation," en.wikipedia.org/wiki/participant_observation, Browsed on 16-07-2005.

67 Barrie Gunter, *Media Research Methods* (London: Sage Publications, 2000), p. 99.

68 Ibid., p. 99.

69 Priest, op. cit., p. 26.

and the church. In this connection, the following tentative questions were asked: How does the celebration of cultural festivals and folk dances promote a space for communication among people? Do people recognize and experience such a space of contact and relationship outside the church? In what way can such an ecumenical space and interaction be extended in the church for the promotion of ecumenical relations between Christians of different denominations? Can we express such an ecumenical unity and work together for the promotion of peace, justice, development and human dignity in the society? In fact, an in-depth interview is useful in a situation where information cannot be obtained through mere observation.

The study specifically focuses on the question whether the ecumenical presence of unity and participation within the people's initiatives present in their folk dances could become a model for promoting ecumenical relations between Christian denominations for a wider ecumenical participation. The literature review was confined to the limited resource of materials available. The observation period was conducted during the three days cultural events of Moatsu festival. The samples were taken representing lay leaders, church leaders and folk dancers for the in-depth interview from the selected towns such as Mokokchung, Kohima and Dimapur, and villages such as Ungma, Chuchuyimlang and Changtongya, in Nagaland. In addition, as far as possible, samples were also taken from different tribes of those representing different Christian denominations in Nagaland. The study of participant observation was personally conducted only in three places during the celebration of Moatsu festival, such as Ungma, Chuchuyimlang and Mokokchung town.

1.10. Concluding Remarks

The present chapter dealt with the research problem of this study in relation to denominationalism and lack of communication among the Christians of different denominations in Nagaland. In this connection, it highlights a common ecumenical space, (which itself is a people-centered communication), that may be identified in the celebration of Naga cultural festivals and folk dances. Such a sphere for communication in folk dances goes beyond the existing WCC's concept of ecumenism which is church-centered ecumenism, to include all the community members and promoting towards mutual participation, sharing, and relationship. The research methods employed in investigation are discussed and analysed to see if such a common ecumenical sphere is available outside the church for the promotion of ecumenism in Nagaland. In this connection, the problem of Naga churches and denominationalism remains critical for it is the problem, which prevents them from coming together and sharing with one another. This will be taken up for discussion in the next chapter.

Chapter 2

Churches and Denominationalism

Denominationalism denotes a pattern of religious structuring and of ecclesial diversity that appeared in the modern, western world under conditions of religious pluralism, disestablishment, toleration and religious liberty.[1] Denominations facilitate and promote division of Church and society along ethnic, sectional, radical, economic and linguistic lines. In this context, it shows the need for expressing and working towards ecumenical relationship, unity, and participation among the Christian denominations based on tolerance, acceptance and respect for one another. In the preceding chapter, the research problem of this study in relation to denominationalism and the lack of communication was discussed. The research methods employed to investigate and find out if such a common ecumenical sphere is accessible outside the Church in the celebration of Naga festivals have also been dealt with. This proceeding chapter two deals with the growth and activities of the Naga churches in relation to the problem of denominationalism. It deals with the factors that led to the existence of denominationalism among the Christian denominations. It will also deal with the need for an ecumenical communication and relationship in which the leadership and participation of both the Church and the lay people will take place.

2.1. A Brief Historical Overview of the Growth of Different Churches in Nagaland

The beginning of the Christian faith in Nagaland was in 1872. Soon the Baptist missionaries established themselves there. The first Baptist Missionaries carried

1 Richard D. N. Dickinson, "Denominationalism," in Nicholas Lossky, Jose Migruez Bonino, John Pobee, Tom Stransky, Geoffrey Weinwright, Pauline Webb, (eds). *Dictionary of Ecumenical Movement*, (Geneva: WCC Publications, 1991), p. 265.

out their mission activities without any other denominations being present until the late 1940s.[2] It is obvious that since then, the intrusion and growth of other Christian denominations led to the existence of lack of communication among them.

After the Indian Independence, Catholic missions and other Christian denominations became active in the State. The Catholic Mission came to Nagaland in 1948 at the request of Akbar Hydari, the Governor of Assam, who sought their service in the Naga Hospital, Kohima. It was from 1952, under the leadership of Fr. Marocchino, that the growth of the Catholic Church started in the Angami area. However, in the same year, certain Lotha Baptist members from Lakhuti village developed some misunderstanding with the other Baptist church members. Reacting to this incident, they contacted the Catholic priest at Golaghat, and consequently, a Catholic Church was established in the same year despite strong opposition from the Baptists.[3] Today, the population of the Catholic Christians in Nagaland is 58,252 (2017)[4] and they are active, especially in the educational ministry.

Both the Ceylon Pentecostal Mission and the Assembly of God came to Nagaland after the Indian Independence. They did not work among the non-Christians but took away the existing Baptist Church members into their churches.[5] It created prejudices and a negative attitude towards each other among Christians of different denominations, especially towards the Baptists. The Revival Church, which is an indigenous church, emerged out of the existing Baptist Church during the revivals in 1948. This group of people was influenced by the teachings of the Ceylon Pentecostals and the Assemblies of God, and they resorted to the use of "tongues" and whole night prayers in the church. They also believed in a second baptism in order to speak in tongues. This new trend seemed to be contrary to the existing belief of the Baptists creating disorderliness in worship. As a result, the Baptist members did not allow them to use the church premises.[6] Consequently, they organized themselves as the Revival Church, which is now called the Nagaland Christian Revival Church. It shows that their separation from the Baptist Church was due to the new doctrinal beliefs and

---

2 "As an introduction, the author wishes to highlight that until the Indian Independence in 1947 except the Baptist denominations and traditional religions, no other religion or denominations existed or attempted to establish their presence among the Nagas." A. Bendangyabang Ao, *History of Christianity in Nagaland: Social Change*, 1872 – 1972, op. cit., p. 256.

3 David Syiemlieh, *A Brief History of the Catholic Church in Nagaland* (Shillong: Vendrame Institute Publications, 1990), pp. 121-122.

4 "Diocese of Kohima," http://www.dioceseofkohima.org, Browsed on 30-09-2019.

5 A. Bendangyabang Ao, *History of Christianity in Nagaland: A Source Material* (Mokokchung: Shalom Ministry, 1998), p. 247. Also See A. Bendangyabang Ao, *History of Christianity in Nagaland: Social Change* 1872 – 1972, op. cit., pp. 260-261.

6 *Ibid.*, p. 262.

practices. The Baptists accused both the Jehovah's Witnesses and the Seventh Day Adventists for taking away its members as they established themselves in 1960.[7] Though they are few in number, these groups of Christians mostly exist in Wokha, Kohima and Dimapur areas. In addition, there is a church of the Salvation Army (SD) in Dimapur under the leadership of its Pastor, Nitovi Sumi. The mission of the Salvation Army was established on 11th November 2003, which comprises four families with 50 members. The Church exists under the supervision of its central office in Mizoram, and its Head Quarters in London. The motto of the Church is to take care of the needy and help the poor people.[8] In this connection, further mushrooming of Christian denominations and churches in Nagaland may continue to enhance denominationalism through various forms of ecclesial activities.

2.1.1. Churches and their Ecclesial Activities

Presently, all the different churches are self-supporting and self-dependent. The percentage of the Christians constitutes 90% of the population in Nagaland. The State has a very high rate of church attendance in both the urban and the rural areas. Among Christian denominations in the State, the Baptists are the predominant group constituting more than 80% of the state's population. The other Christian denominations are: the Catholics, the Revivalists, the Pentecostals, the Assembly of God, Salvation Army, Church of Christ, etc. They constitute about 10 percent of the Christian population.[9] Catholics are found in significant numbers in parts of Wokha district and also in the urban areas of Kohima and Dimapur as well. The churches of these Christian denominations continue to grow in terms of not only increasing the number of members but also of expanding their ecclesial activities in Nagaland. Thereby, they consolidate themselves within their own denominational boundaries. It is observed that this tendency may rather nurture an exclusive attitude in them and may cause an elimination of other Christian denominations. Such attitudes are often expressed and maintained through their ecclesial activities. In this connection, it has been observed that the following are some of the important ecclesial activities are crucial through which their attitudes are beings expressed towards one another.

a) Worship and Prayer Meetings

In general, the understanding and practice of worship and prayer are exclusively meant for the members of the Church. The presence and participation of other Christians is not encouraged in the worship because of the fear of inviting an exclusive denominational communication. However, such prejudices and fear can be overcome if it is done with mutual respect towards mutual learning and

---

7 *Ibid.*, pp. 263-264.

8 Interview with Mr. Nitovi Sumi, Pastor, Church of Salvation Army, Supply Colony, Dimapur.

9 "http://en.wikipedia.org/wiki/Nagaland, Browsed on 01-10-2019.

growth. Further, the ministry of visitation is mainly done for its Church members for strengthening their faith. In this connection, such visitation and socialization can be extended to others for better understanding and for developing dialogue and interaction with one another.

b) Mission and Ministry

It is carried out for the expansion of the Church and its activities. There is no common Christian witness among different Churches towards promoting kingdom values of justice, peace, human dignity and development.

c) Celebration of Christian Festivals

It is felt that the celebration of Christian festivals such as Easter Sunday, Christmas and New Year should be an opportunity for all the Christians to share the gospel message and strengthen their relationship with one another. However, celebration of such Christian festivals is made an exclusive denominational celebration such that it prevents people from participating in the wider ecumenical fellowship with others.

The ecclesial activities are mainly carried out for the welfare, edification, fellowship and participation of their Church members and for strengthening their relationship in the Church. In addition, they do not provide space for communication through these activities for mutual inter-church participation, sharing and learning from one another. In this connection, Lotsüro states that Naga Christians need not emphasize on the denominational differences, but need to go beyond the exclusive boundary of their own Churches to make every effort to bring the Churches together in their common bond in Christ and his values.[10] If such ecclesial activities do not have space for other Christian denominations for fellowship and participation, then their ecumenical understanding and vision is at stake. It may continue to jeopardize their relationship and interaction with one another, which may be also linked with the Church's public relations and their communication activities.

2.1.2. Churches' Public Relations and their Communication Activities

The network of public relations is one of the Churches' important activities and ministries in Nagaland. In fact, Churches' public relation can play a vital role in relation to ecclesial activities in terms of strengthening and maintaining good relationship and mutual understanding not only between the members of the church concerned but also with sister organizations, other churches and the society. In this connection, J. N. Manakaran and S. D. Jeyakumar state that public relation is a planned and a sustained effort to establish and maintain mutual understanding between an organization and its public such as its members,

10 Angeline Lotsüro, *The Nagas: A Missionary Challenge.* (Shillong: Vendrame Institute Publications, 2000), p. 149.

supporters, employers, the government, sister institutions and the society.[11] In addition, it is supposed to clarify the opinion of the people, providing them with proper directions, creating awareness among them through various forms of communication such as interpersonal and group communication, Church newsletters and publications, audio-visual media, Internet, and New Media. Obviously, it needs to work towards establishing not only relationship, contact and unity in the Church, but also to work towards common interests of peace, justice, freedom, development and integrity of all creation.

i. Exclusive Denominational Communication

The term denominational communication refers to the public relational communication that happens within a particular church or denomination. It brings the members of the church in closer relationship and communication with one another through the publications of occasional Church newsletters, books, and audio-visual materials. However, such means of public relationship and communication is circulated and operated especially within the parameter of a church, which does not provide space to other churches promoting towards mutual participation, interaction and learning. Thus, it may be seen as an exclusive denominational communication.

In Nagaland, different churches put in a lot of efforts in public relations (CPR) and communication, bringing the members of the church in closer relationship and communication with one another. They do this through the publications of occasional Church newsletters, books, and audio-visual materials. However, such means of public relationship and communication is circulated and operated especially within the parameter of a church. The exclusive denominational communication may sometimes express the glorification of their traditions and doctrines. It is observed that the activities of the CPR need to go beyond the boundary of their local church to include the members of the whole community in terms of content and distribution, irrespective of their denominational and religious affiliation. It may provide a space for better understanding, interaction and participation among the members of the community. In this connection, the Church's public relation itself depends on the active communication with the whole community through both secular and religious media.[12] The Churches need to use these public relations and communication activities as instruments for promoting ecumenical relationship and participation among the members of different Christian denominations.

---

11 J. N. Manakaran and S. D. Jeyakumar, "Church and Public Relations," in Ebe Sunder Raj, SD Jeyakumar, and Varghese, eds. *Management of Christian Services in India,* Vol. I. (Chennai: Christian Institute of Management, 2004), p. 297.

12 Franz – Josef Eilers, ed., *Church and Social Communication: Basic Documents.* (Indore: Satprakashan Sanchar Kendra, 1996), p. 137.

ii. Lack of Ecumenical Thoughts in Christian Publications

The publications of theological and ecclesiological books can play an important role in communicating ecumenical thoughts to the readers as they are an important part of the activities of the churches' public relations and communication. Many Naga church leaders have so far written a lot of books in relation to various theological, ecclesiastical and societal issues, challenges and needs. However, less importance is being given to the need of ecumenism in the church. In this regard, Lotsuro points out that one of the serious lacunae in Naga Christianity is the absence of any ecumenical movement worth the name, clearly seen in the conspicuous absence of ecumenism in the publications of the theological and ecclesiological books.[13] It indicates that the Naga Churches need to make all efforts to focus on ecumenism and its vision, in writings and publications.

iii. Folk Media as Participatory Communication

The Churches have so far been engaged with the mass media and print media for their public relations and communication, but little importance has been given to traditional media such as folk music, folk dance, folk theatre and drama. They are the media of the people and accessible to people at all occasions, which do not need skilled training. They are participatory in character and foster space for interaction and exchange of feedback with one another. In this connection, Appavoo points out that the folklore, being the media of the people is an alternative media. Therefore, it is inexpensive, accessible, participatory, democratic, providing the community skills credible to the poor. These effective means of communication of the poor could challenge the existing unjust, exploitative and manipulative communication system.[14] Such traditional media may be used for the church's public relations and communication for communicating Christian messages, providing information, ideas and education. It may bring members of the community together on a common platform for the promotion of better understanding, learning, and interaction with one another in relation to the realities of denominationalism among the Churches.

2.1.3. The Ground Realities of Denominationalism among Naga Churches

Denominations are associations of congregations, though sometimes it might be said that congregations are localized subdivisions of denominations that have a common heritage. A denominational heritage normally includes doctrinal, experiential or organizational emphases, frequently including common ethnicity, language, social class, and geographical origin. The term "denomination" in general refers to anything distinguished by a name. In religious contexts, the designation applies traditionally to both the broad movements within Protestantism, such as

13 Angeline Lotsüro, op. cit., pp. 179-180.

14 James Theophilus Appavoo, *Folklore for Change*. (Madurai: Tamil Nadu Theological Seminary, 1986), pp. 65-68.

the Baptists and the Methodists. There are numerous independent branches of such movements that have developed over the years primarily because of geographical expansion and theological controversy.[15] Moreover, a true denomination need not claim to be the only legitimate expression of the church. The following factors may be seen as contributing to the existence of denominationalism among the Churches.

i. Denominational Structure

Denominationalism is one of the dominating factors that contribute to the prevailing problem of lack of communication among Christians of different denominations in Nagaland. It is also closely related to theological factors such as those connected with the issues of liturgy, worship, baptism, holy communion, etc., which are intrinsically related to the structure and functions of that denomination or church. It is largely based on the activities and teachings of the early missionaries. The early missionaries did not only introduce and teach Christianity but also taught the distinctiveness and structural aspects of the denomination. For instance, the American Baptists, the Catholic Mission, and the Pentecostal Mission, did just that.[16] Most of the Christians have thus become accustomed to the structures that they inherited from the missions. Here, we can find that the ecclesiastical differences are deeper than unity. As a result, it does not encourage them to have ecumenical relationship and whole hearted participation with Christians of other denominations.[17]

Further, Churches of these Christian denominations exclusively confine themselves to such ecclesial structures and try to remain loyal to the legacy of their own mission. Zacharias Mar Theophilus states that the churches swell in competition, struggle for existence and crave for expansion, and not yet ready for or interested in ecumenism.[18] It merely expands the gap between the different Christian denominations. In this connection, Elia Peter says that the churches must be willing to give up their rigid stands, which were perpetuated by the

---

15 D. G. Tinder, "Denominationalism," http://mb-soft.com/believe/text/denomina/hmt Browsed on 01-10-2019.

16 "There are problems because ethnic groups in the region have varying accounts of their origins, and the Christian missions have made the situation more complicated by creating separate and uncommon stories of religious origins and heritages as well. Each Church maintained its own independence in terms of administration, beliefs and practices and missionary outreach programmes while maintaining ecclesiastical ties with its parent bodies in Europe, North America or in the pacific region." O. L. Snaitang, "Development of the Ecumenical Movement in Northeast India. *"Indian Church History Review*. Vol. XXXVII Number 1, (June 2003), pp. 44-45.

17 J. Fortis Jyrwa, "Church Union Movement in North East India," p. 71.

18 Zacharias Mar Theophilus, "Ecumenical Vision for Today," in P. Jegadish Gandhi & K. C. John, eds. *Upon the Wings of Wider Ecumenism: Essays and Tributes in Honour of Rev. Dr. M. J. Joseph ECC*. (New Delhi: ISPCK/ECC, 2006), p. 5.

mission agencies.[19] Such an attitude may enable the churches to recognise each other's ministries and enable them to come to a common platform in communion with each other.

ii. Doctrinal Differences

One of the obstacles that have often disrupted ecumenical relations among the Christians of different denominations is doctrinal. It simply means the differences in doctrinal position and understanding in their faith and conduct. C.V. Theodore illustrates it, by taking the example of the doctrine concerning the Eucharist. Christian denominations have different views on it, pertaining to its memorial character and its concepts, some subscribing to the doctrine of consubstantiation and others to that of transubstantiation.[20] The second obstacle is that of the doctrine of Baptism, wherein there are two views and traditions, namely that of infant baptism and adult or immersion baptism. This had been an unending problem in ecumenical discussions. Thirdly, there are differences on the concepts of authority. For the Episcopal Churches, the authority is usually vested with a single person, whereas, for the Congregational Churches authority is understood as that of sharing with others, taking the voice of the congregation into account when making decisions.[21] More discussions on theological and doctrinal matters among the Christians of different denominations may not serve any purpose in terms of ecumenical relations among the Churches. Instead, efforts should be made to bring them together in joint celebrations and sharing.

iii. Cultural Differences

Cultural and linguistic differences have become barriers to ecumenical relations because people belonging to different ethnic groups and faiths find it hard to come together. When people fail to understand each other's cultural values and traditions such as their philosophy of life, worldview, and life style, they become uncomfortable and tend to distance themselves from one another, causing ecumenical barriers to communication. For many people in North East India where different tribal ethnic groups speak various languages, linguistic differences often happen to be a barrier to ecumenical communication between Christian denominations. In this connection, the present divisions among the Christian

---

19 M. Elia Peter, "Unity and Union: The Aspirations of the Indian Church in the Twenty first Century," in Brian Wintle, Emmanuel James, Jesudason B. Jeyaraj, Paul Mohan Raj, and Richard S. Gnanakan, eds. *Work Worship Witness: Essays Dedicated to a Vision and a Visionary.* (Bangalore: Theological Book Trust, 2003), p. 174.

20 C. V. Theodore, "The Pilgrims of Ecumenical Progress," in Vinod Victor, Leslie Nathaniel & P. Surya Prakash, eds., *Ecumenism: Prospects and Challenges* (New Delhi: ISPCK, 2001), p. 296.

21 B. J. Christie Kumar, "Baptists and CSI Union: Theological Foundations and Theological Aspirations," in Vinod Victor, Leslie Nathaniel & P. Surya Prakash, eds., *Ecumenism: Prospects and Challenges* (New Delhi: ISPCK, 2001), p. 283.

denominations in Nagaland need not be seen as those based on their tribal line and on their linguistic differences as such.

The Churches of different denominations are not separated by denominational location in a particular tribal area. In addition, the Churches within a particular denominational group still come together for fellowship and interaction irrespective of their cultural and linguistic differences. In this connection, it can be seen that during the inter-tribal meetings and Christian fellowship, participations and presentations of diverse ethnic and tribal groups are given importance and respected. The programme or meeting as such during inter-tribal gathering is always conducted in both English and Nagamese.[22] However, unless such cultural and linguistic differences are respected, it may become a barrier for establishing contact, relationship and unity among the people in the society.

iv. The Problem of Not Understanding Others

At present, the schism between different Christian denominations may be due to the lack of communication between Christian denominations. In this connection, it would be relevant to refer to Francis A. Sullivan who points out that from the early Church history we can understand that the divergence and schism between the Eastern Church of Constantinople and Western Church of Rome were due to different canonical traditions developed independently and also due to the lack of communication between the two Churches.[23] Today, the division between different Christian denominations in Nagaland may be due to an exclusive denominational communication. Owing to this reason or any other, Christians do not want to use ecumenical communication among themselves. In this connection, Lotsuro points out that one of the stumbling blocks for ecumenism is ignorance about other Churches, which is in fact, often the breeding ground for unsubstantiated prejudices and rivalries.[24]

Further, the negative attitude and prejudices towards each other, non-appreciation of the tradition and values of others, and doctrinal differences on faith and practices may also be considered as the contributing factors to the existing denominationalism. It continues to be a matter of concern for the Church because they refuse to acknowledge the values, traditions and practices of others. It shows that they are not willing to accept the new ideas and change with them. Instead, they prefer to maintain the values and practices of their own Church. In this connection, Lanunungsang says that the Christian denominations separate themselves from others because they refuse to acknowledge the good things and

22 In Nagaland, "English" is Recognized as an Official Language and "Nagamese" is used as a common language among the people.

23 Francis A. Sullivan, S. J., "Ecumenism as Communication," in Patrick Granfield, ed., *The Church and Communication* (Kansas city: Sheed & Ward, 1994), pp. 110-111.

24 Angeline Lotsuro, op. cit., p. 224.

positive aspects of other Churches and stress only on the differences and negative aspects of others.[25] Under these circumstances, the Churches in Nagaland need to come to a common ecumenical sphere to get to know each other better, to have fellowship and to build up mutual relationship with one another. Since all the Christian denominations are equally important, they shall give up the practice of making exclusive claims. In this way, they need to cooperate with one another in various specialized ministries, promoting ecumenism among its members in the Church.

2.2. Relationship among Different Churches in Nagaland

Nagaland is known as a Christian State. The growing number of Christian denominations in the State poses a number of ecumenical concerns, such as the generation of attitudes of indifference, exclusiveness and prejudice towards one another and lack of communication among denominations. However, the Churches have so far not given any serious thought on these concerns. Therefore, it is obvious that there is a crying need for an ecumenical relationship among these Christian denominations, which will be discussed in the following.

2.2.1. Present Scenario of Ecumenical Relationship among the Churches in Nagaland

The present condition of the ecumenical relationship among the Churches in Nagaland is crucial because they are more interested in developing their own denominations. They do not want to come together to get into dialogical communication and fellowship with one another. Further, they engaged themselves in denominational expansion rather than God's mission towards bringing unity, peace and justice among people.[26] In this connection, it is worthwhile referring to Hokishe Sema who states that the present situation of ecumenism among the Naga churches is getting worse because the churches are ambitious for expanding their own denominations.[27] In the context of the increasing number of churches and Christian denominations, inter-denominational rivalries occur among themselves. On and off, they accuse each other of sheep-stealing.[28] Such accusations and prejudices promote inter-denominational rivalries among themselves and widen the gulf between one another. As a consequence of the rivalry and competition, there is a growing sense of division among the Churches today.

25 Interview with A. Lanunungsang, Nagaland University, Lumami, May 12th 2006.

26 A. Wati Longchar, "Tribal Theology in Changing Context," Paper presentation in CISRS Golden Jubilee Convention, 12-14 February 2007, at Indian Social Institute, Bangalore. p. 7.

27 Interview of Hokishe Sema by the author, Footnote no. 103 in Chapter 4, in Angeline Lotsüro, *The Nagas: A Missionary Challenge.* (Shillong: Vendrame Institute Publications, 2000), p. 180.

28 A. Bendangyabang Ao, *History of Christianity in Nagaland: Social Change,* op. cit., pp. 260-261.

Among the Christian denominations in Nagaland, the Baptist group stands out with a majority. Such a situation is likely to create a feeling of a sense of superiority over other Christian denominations. Theophilus says that as the Churches are able to stand on their own feet, ecumenism doesn't seem to be essential.[29] Such an attitude may become an obstacle for building up an ecumenical relationship and interaction with other Christian denominations. On the other hand, other churches may have also a tendency to retreat to their own shells of denominational boundaries with reservations. With all these feelings and attitudes, they may choose to remain comfortable in their own respective Churches.

It is also observed that outside the Church, Christians from all the denominations live together and socialize with one another, but in the Church they do not find any space for ecumenical communication and fellowship with one another. Such strained relationships and gaps between the Christians of different denominations can be linked to the lack of understanding of the concept of ecumenism and willingness to change from within.

2.2.2. Ecumenism among Christians of Different Denominations: Conceptual Difficulties

The concept of ecumenism underlines both the need for the unity of the Church and the unity in action towards achieving peace, justice, participation, integrity of creation, and development among people in the society.[30] It also includes unity in initiating dialogical communication not only within the Christian community but also with various religious communities.[31] However, the concept of ecumenism is often understood by the Naga Churches in terms of unity in Christ and unity of the Church within a limited boundary of the Church.

The terms "unity in Christ" or "spiritual unity" needs to be understood in terms of unity of all believers together with the unity of the truth of Christ. However, it has often been taken as a unity of all believers in Christ, also unity and participation within a particular denominational group at the Church association and at the council levels. In this connection, it is worth referring to T. Likok who says that spiritual unity itself is union with Christ, which can be manifested through Councils, Associations, inter-communion and Christian brotherhood.[32] At this point, I want to make a case, that since, the concept of ecumenism is to go beyond the unity of the Church in Christ to include other Christian denominations, endeavouring towards wider ecumenism in relation to other religious faiths, and fostering peace, justice and integrity of creation,

29 Zacharias Mar Theophilus, op. cit., p. 5.

30 Emilio Castro, *A Passion for Unity: Essay on Ecumenical Hopes and Challenges.* (Geneva: WCC Publications, 1992), pp. 83-87.

31 Konrad Raiser, op. cit. pp. 54-57.

32 T. Likok, *A Picture of an Organic Church Union.* (Impur: Author, 1970), pp. 2-8.

then, the Naga Churches' understanding and practice of ecumenism is irrelevant. Incidentally, their understanding and practice of ecumenism does not have space for contact, communion and relationship with other Christian denominations and therefore is inadequate. Is it because they do not want to recognize and accept the goodness in others? Do they really understand that the concept of ecumenism is an act of Christians coming together on a common platform promoting unity in diversity of different Churches and fostering common interests, peace, justice, and development in the society? Is this because they have a fear that if they come together in communion and fellowship with other Christian denominations they may lose their own denominational or religious identity?

2.2.3. Ecumenism and Religious Identity

The concept of ecumenism is closely associated with the coming together of Christians on a common platform for sharing, interaction and participation with one another. It is always intended to achieve a common consensus of unity that is represented by the members of various Christian denominations that subscribe to a common religious identity. In addition, it is expected that the more they come together, the more important questions of identity arise. Regarding this, S. J. Samartha states that a religion seeks to give people within a community a sense of identity and belonging through shared faith in dogmas and doctrines, rituals, symbols and liturgy, in patterns of relationship, and code of conduct.[33] Sometimes, such religious identity can become a barrier to ecumenical communication with other Christian denominations because they do not want to identify themselves in communion with others in favour of their own identity. It is also observed that the reason why the Naga Christians do not want to use ecumenical communication could be because they do not want to lose their own denominational identity. In addition, ecumenism can be accused of abolishing confessional identity and leading to an arbitrary pluralism and relativism. Owing to such fears and misunderstanding, they do not give importance to ecumenism and ecumenical communication. With regard to this, Cormac Murphy-O'Connor says, "Every denomination wishes to have its own identity and not be absorbed in a faceless, bigger whole."[34] But the truth is that the more they come closer, the more they can ward off such a fear, and understand each other.

i. Unity in Diversity

Ecumenical communication seeks to bring closer the Christians of different Churches to communicate with one voice. Further, it does not encourage surrendering one's own denominational identity in favour of a collective identity of different Churches. It does not seek to achieve uniformity by allowing the loss

33 S. J. Samartha, *One Christ – Many Religions: Towards a Revised Christology*. (Bangalore: SATHRI, 1992), p. 52.

34 Cormac Murphy-O'Connor, "Unity on a Knife edge." *The Tablet*, 20/11/2004, p.14.

of anyone with denominational identity, but to develop unity in diversity. At this point, unity in diversity simply means unity in communion with one another, unity in participation, and unity in action for the common interests. In this connection, it is relevant to refer to Macquarrie who points out that diversity in religion is simply difference – difference in belief, in liturgy, in spirituality, in the application of moral principles, in vocation and so on.[35] From its very inception, the Christian Church has been characterized by unity and diversity. However, diversity has often turned into division in the Church. Further, it leads to breaking down of communication between Christians of different denominations and the spirit of pride, exclusiveness and prejudice takes control. Unfortunately, they do not want to identify with others because they do not want to lose their own identity. At this point, it is well to remember what Wesley says, that the Church must establish a forum for understanding and openness, a platform for dialogue, a readiness to mould and correct its view as needed.[36] In fact, the Church needs to be willing to recognize each other's religious identities in terms of respecting the diversity of nature, creation, colour, creed, and conviction. It may bring the Christians of different denominations into meaningful interaction and participation with one another, thereby strengthening their religious identity and tribal identity as well.

2.2.4. Tribal Solidarity and Denominationalism

The idea of unity in diversity is relevant not only to the Naga religious life but also to their socio-cultural life and contexts. Here, it briefly highlights the formation of the tribal identity. Before the advent of Christianity, Nagas living in villages in a particular geographical area were somehow related to each other in terms of preserving and practicing similarities in myth, religion, social customs, and language.[37] For instance, the Ao Nagas have traditions about the common origins of the various clans of the tribe, and have practices of various cultural values and traditions, which give them a sense of unity and solidarity among them.

Despite the seeming solidarity, the Nagas did not have a structural expression of tribal solidarity. There was often inter-village and inter-tribal hostility and warfare.[38] In this connection, Downs states that to a certain extent, the British administration contributed to the development of tribal solidarity, first, through the very structure and operation of administration, resulting in the cessation of warfare between the villages of different tribes; secondly, through the development

35 John Macquarrie, *Christian Unity and Christian Diversity*. (London: SCM Press LTD, 1975), p. 2.

36 Arun Kumar Wesley, *Millennium Miscellany: Essays on Current Theological Issues*. (Bangalore, Asian Trading corporation, 2003), p. 92.

37 Frederick S. Downs, "The Christian Role in Tribal Solidarity Movements in North East India," in *Bangalore Theological Forum*, Vol.XX, Nos.1-2, Jan-June 1988.

38 M. Horam, *Naga Polity*, (New Delhi: B. R. Publishing Corporation, 1975), pp. 25, 61.

of a tribal consciousness towards the preservation of their traditional ways of life in North East India.[39]

Further, Christianity played a central role in strengthening a sense of tribal identity in the North East India, firstly, through the creation of written forms of their standard languages, secondly, through its educational works, thirdly, through its theology in which Christianity was proclaimed as relevant to the whole tribe and fourthly, through its ecclesiastical structures.[40] However, it is noted that such contributions of tribal solidarity in the hill areas have promoted denominationalism. For instance, in Nagaland, Tripura, South Mizoram, and Garo hills, the Baptists are the dominant Protestant Christian community since the American Baptist Mission specifically concentrated their work in these regions. In addition, in North Mizoram and in Khasi hills, Presbyterian Christians form the predominant group since the Welsh Presbyterian mission concentrated their work in these areas.[41] It could be possible that the geographical isolation of a particular Christian mission might have reinforced denominationalism among the Christians.[42] In these regions, these Christian denominations did not want the presence of other Christian missions because the majority of these tribal communities had already become Christians, and owed their allegiance to different Christian missions.

In Nagaland, the activities of the Baptist mission were prevalent without the presence of other Christian denominations for more than eighty years. Positively, Christianity has been one of the powerful agencies integrating the people within the tribes of the Nagas and with others, bringing them in close association with one another.[43] However, it shows that the concentration of the American Baptist Mission in isolated Naga inhabited geographical area might have created such an attitude of denominational exclusiveness among the people. Previously, there was a general understanding and feeling among the Baptists that all the Nagas should be Baptist Christians.

i. Denominational Identity among Different Churches

Today in the context of the existing different Christian denominations in the state, such a feeling and attitude among the Baptist Christians have greatly changed. Instead, the growing consciousness of denominational identity has been strongly felt and noticed among the Christians of different denominations. O. L. Snaitang points out that Christianity has contributed to unifying people, but it

---

39 Downs, "The Christian Role in Tribal Solidarity Movement in North East India," op. cit., pp. 6-7.

40 *Ibid.*, pp. 9-15.

41 Downs, *Christianity in North East India: Historical Perspectives*. op. cit., p. 164

42 Lionel Caplan, *Religion and Power: Essays on the Christian Community in Madras*. (Madras: CLS, 1989), pp. 5-6.

43 Downs, *Christianity in North East India: Historical Perspectives*. op. cit., p. 165.

also contributed to disunity through denominational identities, different rituals and an uncommon history of origins.[44] It has promoted competition among the Churches that simply serve to expand their activities. It is observed that in the context of the denominational rivalry and competition among the Christian denominations in Nagaland, ecumenical communication and participation has become the need of the hour among them. In this connection, Joseph Edakkudan says that the ecumenical relationship and fellowship could be the most enviable thoughts of the Nagas in the Church and the society as well.[45] At this juncture, the Church leadership needs to play a vital role in providing a common space for encouraging a better understanding and participation among the members of the Church.

2.3. Church Initiatives of Ecumenism in Recent Years

In North East India in general, and Nagaland in particular, the underlying importance of ecumenical relationship in the church is not an option but crucial in the context of the present ecclesial fragmentations due to denominationalism. We can also see the apparent social fragmentations and degeneration because of economic globalization.[46] In such contexts, Churches need not remain as mere spectators, but need to become active participants and harbingers of unity, peace and justice, not only in the Church but also in the whole of God's creation. Church initiative in ecumenism can be seen through gestures of coming together of different Churches with mutual understanding, making interaction, initiating fellowship and sharing with one another.

2.3.1. Church Leadership

The Church leadership of each Christian denomination in Nagaland has so far brought together their local Churches and units of the denominations and has organized themselves into Church associations or Council of Churches. Thereby, they enjoy an ecumenical relationship and participation within their own denominational groups. Ecumenism is not supposed to be exhausted within a denominational group, but needs to be extended and shared with other Christian denominations. However, such a desirable goal of ecumenism has not been given importance at the level of Church leadership in terms of making attempts to bring the Christians of different denominations for interaction and sharing.

---

44 O. L. Snaitang, op. cit., p. 52.

45 Interview with Joseph Edakkudan, SDB, Society of Don Bosco, Christ the King, Kohima, 10th May 2006.

46 Lap-yan Kung, "Globalization and Ecumenism: A Search for Human Solidarity, with Reference to Pentecostalism/Charismatism in Hong Kong." *Asia Journal of Theology,* Volume 17 Number 2 (October 2003), pp. 381-382.

i. Church Leadership towards Peace and Justice

In relation to the issues of working towards peace, justice, harmony and integrity in the society, the churches often show a propensity to involve and participate autonomously without any connection and association with other Churches. In this connection, most of the churches have taken up projects related to community health care, education, and development programmes for the welfare of the poor and needy in the society. In the context of the socio-political problem in North East India in general, and Nagaland in particular, the Nagaland Baptist Churches Council (NBCC) has involved and taken initiatives in bringing reconciliation, peace, harmony, and unity not only between the underground factional groups but also among the people of the land. Keitzar points out that the most significant contribution of the NBCC is the reconciling role that it played in the restoration of peace and normalcy in the strife-torn Nagaland.[47] Despite all these efforts, ecumenical co-operation of all the churches for the purpose of achieving common interests and goals still remain to be achieved fully.

ii. Church Leadership on Common Witness

The term common witness simply means the witness that the churches, even while separated, bear together, especially through joint efforts, by manifesting whatever divine gifts of truth and life they already share and experience in common.[48] In this connection, the Joint Working Group (JWG) of Roman Catholic Church and WCC[49] encourages all the churches to enter into more cooperative ways of being in mission together and to refrain from proselytizing others' members.[50] Despite differences and diversity among the Christian churches, they can jointly carry out some common interests or mutual responsibilities, which may strengthen

47 The Council also struggled and achieved the imposition of total prohibition of liquor in Nagaland through demonstrations, protests, fasts and indefinite hunger strike and held negotiation with the State government. Renthy Keitzar, *Triumph of Faith in Nagaland.* (Kohima: NBCC, 1987), pp. 17-20.

48 "In the Protestant origins of the ecumenical movement, a limited understanding of common witness had been conveyed by other words, such as "co-operation," "united ministries," "joint mission." Tom Stransky, "Common Witness," in Nicholas Lossky, Jose Miguez Bonino, John Pobee, Tom Stransky, Geoffrey Wainwright, and Pauline Webb, eds. *Dictionary of the Ecumenical Movement.* (Geneva: WCC Publications, 1991), p. 197.

49 "The Joint Working Group was established in 1965 by the Roman Catholic Church and the World Council of Churches as their consultative forum. The Joint Working Group is a clear sign that both the Roman Catholic Church and the World Council must work together in the one ecumenical movement." "The History of the RCC-WCC Joint Working Group," in *Joint Working Group between the Roman Catholic Church and the World Council of Churches: Seventh Report* (Geneva: WCC Publications, 1998), pp. 24-30.

50 In 1961 the WCC's New Delhi assembly condemned proselytism as "a corruption of witness." Birgitta Larsson and Emilio Castro, "From Mission to Mission," in John Briggs, Mercy Amba Oduyoye and Georges Tsetsis, eds., *A History of the Ecumenical Movement* Volume 3 1968-2000. (Geneva: WCC Publications, 2004), p. 144.

their ecumenical relationship and participation. The Church leadership may facilitate their members to jointly carry out shared Christian responsibilities such as prayer, reading the Bible, common celebration of Christian festivals and other important events together with the translation, production and distribution of Bible editions, involvement in socio-political concerns to support peace, justice and human dignity.[51] The Church leaders need to come forward to work together for a specific purpose, for the interest of the people in the church and society.

However, Christian witness is often restricted within each denominational understanding, beliefs and practices in relation to faith, worship, and ethical issues. For such reasons and others, the Christian denominations can find it hard to come together to carry out mutual responsibilities in co-operation with one another. In this connection, Stransky says that the common witness has limits because of difficult, even contradictory, understanding of the revealed content of the faith regarding worship (e.g. Eucharistic sharing), faith (e.g. Authority in and of the Church), personal and social ethics, such as abortion, and women's rights in the Church.[52] Nevertheless, mutual respect, understanding and dialogical communication between the Church leaders of different churches, including the participation of people may overcome such differences and diversity within the Christian denominations.

2.3.2. Lay Leadership

Since the era of the missionary activities in Nagaland, when no theologically trained leaders were available, committed lay people have actively taken part not only for the advancement of the gospel but also for fulfilling the need for taking leadership in various important positions in the Church. They took up responsibilities and led the Church with their leadership. In this connection, it is well to remember Longkumer who states that the growth of the Church in Nagaland in general, and in Ao churches in particular, was in a large measure due to the active involvement of the laity in Christian ministry.[53] They carried out the work and activities of the mission of the Church under the supervision of the early missionaries for more than eighty years. Even after the missionaries had left the Naga soil, they carried on the responsibility of the Church. In addition, on the occasion of the departure of the last missionary, namely, R. F. Delano, on February 8th, 1955, all the responsibility in the Ao Church was handed over to the Church and to its evangelist L. Kijung Ao, a theologically untrained person.[54] For many years, the lay leadership was quite prominent in the Church in bringing

51 Tom Stransky, op. cit., p. 199.

52 Stransky, op. cit., p. 199.

53 Nuklu Longkumer, *The Growth of the Baptist Churches Among the Aos of Nagaland.* (Changtongya: Changtongya Baptist Church: 1988), p. 35.

54 *Ibid.* p. 24.

people together for experiencing ecumenical fellowship and relationship with one another.

Since 1940s, lay leadership has been slowly replaced by theologically trained persons in the Church, especially for full time pastoral ministry of the Church. At present, though the full time ministries are handled by theologically trained people, still, lay ministry is given importance in the Church. In local churches, all the decisions are taken by the deacon board under the chairmanship of the pastor which consists of lay people in the Church. Moreover, lay leadership and participation can be seen in evangelism, Sunday school duties, and taking various responsibilities not only in the local churches, but also at the Church council and association levels. It recognizes and uses its members from those specialized in various fields as they are important in the ministry of the Church. Regarding this, Monteiro says that a participatory Church respects the dignity of every member and restores equal discipleship, where all live fulfilling their proper vocation and performing their respective roles.[55] Thus, it may rediscover the potentiality of laymen and women in the Church and empower them to become co-workers in the ministry, so that communion and fellowship in the Church may be strengthened through their involvement and participation.

2.3.3. Lay Participation

Lay leadership and participation in the life and ministry of the Church is important for communicating the Christian message and improving the ecumenical relationship, fellowship and communion in the Church. It is the responsibility of all the members in the Church including men, women and children. It goes beyond the hierarchical and patriarchal structure of the Church to include the active participation of both laymen and women not only in worship but also in the various forms of ministry in the Church.

i. Participation in Worship

Active participation in worship includes the laity and the clergy, men and women, young and old and others, which will result in forms of worship more clearly related to Christian life, ecumenical relationship, and mission in the world, more expressive of the equality of all in Christ.[56] All the members of the Church, both men and women have different gifts, and they are expected to use their varied gifts to communicate the gospel for edification and strengthening of their fellowship in the Lord.

---

55 Evelyn Monteiro, *Church and Culture: Communion in Pluralism*. (New Delhi: ISPCK, 2004), p. 201.

56 Ernest L. Unterkoefler and Andrew Harsanyi, *The Unity We Seek: A Statement by the Roman Catholic/ Presbyterian-Reformed Consultation*. (New York: Paulist Press, 1977), p. 36.

a. Participation through Music and Songs

Music and songs play an important part in worship not only for communicating the Christian message, but also for motivating and inspiring people to worship God meaningfully. In this connection, the Naga Church music is being dominated by the western music as it was taught by the early missionaries. Western music can also be used in the Church as it had been part of the Church for many years.[57] In this regard, the members of the church, especially the musicians including the young people can play a significant role by leading the worship songs, praise and worship and presentation of songs during the time of worship and fellowship. Further, Christian folk music is always preferable for effective communication in worship. Today, there are many local folk musicians in the Church. They can promote Christian folk music and songs in the Church. The musicians who have the expertise in folk music as well as in western music respectively may be instrumental in promoting the quality of Church music. Since music is ecumenical in character, it can bring people together in a common bond by expressing the message of togetherness and unity. It should break down barriers and build bridges between people.[58] Music can also bring people together irrespective of gender, colour, status, and denominational affiliation to promote the message of love, unity, and brotherhood among people in the Church and society. Thus, the church should be open to welcome different genre of music that strengthens and promotes the corporate worship with wider ecumenical spirit.

b. Participation through Dance

Dance is a timeless medium of communication in the Church and society. It was given an important place in Christian tradition of worship and liturgy.

According to Arokiasamy, dance traditions in India developed to enhance worship.[59] In this connection, it is observed that dance movements have been used in different churches in Nagaland. Often, the participation of people during the worship, such as dancing during the time of revival meetings and crusades, praise and worship, presentations of invocative dance and choreography has been meaningful. The Church needs to encourage its members and provide more avenues for participation in the Church. In addition, the Naga folk dance, which is getting popular outside the Church among the people, can also be a means of

---

57 A Temjen Jamir, *Popularisation of Folk Music in Christian Worship* (Mokokchung: Author, CTC, 2001), p. 80.

58 Hannibal Cabral, "The Role of Music in Religious Communication: Implications for a Theological Curriculum," in Michael Traber, ed. *Communication in Theological Education: New Directions.* (New Delhi: ISPCK, 2005), pp. 164-167.

59 F. Arokiasamy, "Classical Indian Dance: Understanding its Significance for our Liturgy and Catechetic," in *Word and Worship*, NBCLC, Bangalore, Vol.38, July-August 2005, no. 4. p. 246. Also see, Arun Kumar Wesley, "Dancing in the Aisle: Towards a Form of Worship in Drama," in *Masihi Sevak*, Volume XXV No. 2, July 2000, pp. 69-70.

communication for promoting ecumenical relationship and participation among the people both in the Church and in the society.

Folk dance is by nature inclusive, has a capacity to go beyond tribal solidarity and identity from within the limited geographical boundary of denomination and tribal region, to relate and participate with other Christian denominations. In this connection, it is well to remember Doug Adams who says that such a community dance can play a vital role in fostering a sense of equality between worshippers of all ages and all denominational and ethnic backgrounds.[60] In fact, folk dance is an integral part of Naga culture, which can act as a unifying factor in an ecumenical and multicultural situation. In addition, it may encourage people towards ecumenical relationships with one another in the light of the wider ecumenical understanding and participation.

c. Participation through Drama

Drama is one of the means of communication in the Church through which lay people, especially the young people can participate and express the Christian message and ideas, transfer information, and create awareness among the people. Drama and play has an ecumenical overtone because it can provide an ecumenical sphere for people to develop mutual interaction, critical reflection, entertainment, and fellowship with one another. Drama and dance provide a sphere where people not only identify or relate themselves with the characters displayed, but their eyes and ears can also be opened to critical imagination.[61] The biblical and non-biblical events, and dance drama with biblical and ecumenical themes can be enacted. In fact, through this, people can make tremendous contributions and promote participation in script writing, producing and acting out the story. Drama can provide the space for counseling, dialogue, and interaction between different cultures, religious groups and communities. It may thereby, motivate people for bringing about change and development in Church and societies.[62] Thus, drama can enable a wider participation of the people in the Church and society.

ii. Participation through Service

The role of the Church in communicating the Christian message need not necessarily take place inside the Church alone, but also outside the Church through sacrificial services in all aspects of life in the community. The ministry of service in the society in various fields has been done by laymen and women of the Church.

---

60 Doug Adams, "Dancing and Community," Chapter 2, Congregational Dancing in Christian Worship. N. Aurora, IL: The Sharing Company, 1976, excerpted from pp. 15-40. (Cited in PAST 207/307, p. 317).

61 John Joshva Raja & Samson Prabhakar, eds. op. cit., p. 309.

62 *Ibid.*, p. 311.

a. Participation through Educational Ministry

The Church has a mission to communicate the Christian message and to promote an ecumenical relationship among people through the educational ministry. Regarding this, Wati Longchar states that education had not only brought together a sense of oneness among the people of a single tribe, but had also promoted inter-tribal relationship.[63] In Nagaland, there are a number of schools and educational institutions being run by different churches. In terms of management of the institution, both the Clergy (full time workers) and the members of the Church get the opportunity to coordinate and work together. These educational institutions are ecumenical in character in terms of recruitment of teachers and enrollment of students. Moreover, in such Christian institutions, the churches need to employ committed and competent workers for both the teaching and the non-teaching staff. These educational institutions are meant not only to provide quality education but also to impart Christian values, which may enable the students to read the Bible and Christian literature.[64] The educated people of the Church have been involved and are making significant contributions through these institutions. According to Cyril, educational ministry should aim at bringing transformation in the society by driving away the darkness of competitive structures that breed ambitions, selfishness, hatred and divisions and promote love, freedom, sincerity and justice among people.[65] It could bring people together, both teachers and students, irrespective of social status and religious affiliation for the purpose of learning and growing together towards achieving unity and transformation in the Church and society.

b. Participation in People's Health Service

Health and wholeness of life is God's gift from God. Health service is an important part of the Church's ministry. Healing ministry has been always done in the Church through visitation of its members and praying for the sick. In this connection, George Koshy says that it communicates the love and compassion of God demonstrated in the life and ministry of Jesus Christ to the people inside and outside the church.[66] In Nagaland, different churches put their efforts for the promotion of health by organizing and conducting health seminars and health camps from time to time in the locality. In such programmes, doctors, nurses, and those who are competent in this field are invited to offer their services to

63 A Wati Longchar, "Christianity among the Nagas," in F. Hrangkhuma, ed. *Christianity in India: Search for Liberation and Identity.* (New Delhi: CMS/ ISPCK, 1998), p. 254.

64 George Koshy, "Involvement of the Congregation for Transformation," in R. Mohanraj, ed. *Communicating for an Alternative Humanity.* (Chennai: The Department of Communication of the Church of South India, 2003), p. 80.

65 S. M. Cyril, "Education for Transformation of Society," in L. Stanislaus, ed. *Education as Mission* (New Delhi: ISPCK, 2004), p. 183.

66 George Koshy, op. cit., p. 81.

the people. The Church needs to encourage and make use of the service of these people for the purpose of community health care.

c. Participation for Justice and Development

Participation for the welfare of the common people can be one of the practical means for communicating the Christian message in the society. Periannan states that development in a community where human rights, dignity, collective and emotional security, are actualized and integrated by the word of God, there is immense scope for maintaining the dignity of each and every individual.[67] It is a ministry that identifies with the poor and the needy in the community. It is the duty of the Church to try to bring about a just society through participation in the developmental activities and by encouraging its members to get involved in the struggles of the people for justice.[68] In Nagaland, more than 80 percent of the people live in rural areas. Most of the people are still living under poor living conditions, without proper self-sustenance of life. The socio-economic development activities and programmes are not only done by the State government, but also to a great extent, by the churches in Nagaland in coordination with the help of the Church Associations and Councils. In this connection, Nagaland Baptist Churches Council (NBCC) also coordinates and organizes a number of developmental programmes for the welfare of the people.[69] Churches are also playing a significant role in this field through the participation and involvement of its members of the Church. Laymen and women have to serve the society in order to extend help to the needy, promote justice and transform the existing orders into more righteous and useful ones.[70] Such a participation and involvement can not only communicate the message of universal brotherhood and love, but also helps to empower people to make them self-reliant.

2.3.4. Towards an Ecumenical Communion of Churches

The mystery of the communion that exists between Christ and his Church – the believers, is rooted in the Trinitarian communion of the God-Head. It is this communion that demands all Christians to be in communion and fellowship not only with one another, but also with those of different churches and other

67 Sebastian Periannan, "Communication Theology for Formation and Mission," in Joseph Palakeel, ed. *Towards a Communication Theology*. (Bangalore: Asian Trading Corporation, 2003), p. 189.

68 S. M. Cyril, op. cit., p. 81.

69 In the year 2000, NBCC has created a new department called the Nagaland Development Outreach (NDO), which centers in Dimapur. Its main objectives are to assist the churches in their material development, to generate self-employment avenues, to give education and conduct awareness programmes on the related topic by conducting and organizing lectures, seminars and training camps, especially for the educated unemployed youth in the churches as well in the community.

70 Thangasamy, op. cit., p. 95.

religious communities. Monteiro states that every ecclesial community is rooted in the Trinitarian communion from where the inspiration and sustenance comes for Christians to be in communion with one another and with the different Christian churches, religions, and cultural and ethnic groups.[71] In such a context of religious and cultural plurality and diversity, the churches in North East India in general, and in Nagaland in particular, need to recognize one another and remain open to each other for communion and fellowship.

The starting point of the communion of churches is from within, with the work of the Spirit of the Triune God. Based on the work of the Spirit, the communion of the churches is to be started from what the churches have actually in common, that is the revealed truth of the unity of Jesus Christ.[72] The external factors such as, the doctrinal, theological and denominational differences among churches have always remained obstacles to attaining the communion of churches. In this connection, it is worth quoting Joseph Edakkudan who says that we always point out what divides us and not what unites us. Instead, we need to point out what unites us and leave out what divides us.[73] In fact, communion of churches necessitates mutual understanding among the churches, without prejudice to the autonomy and rights of each Church in terms of respecting their particular theology, liturgical and spiritual traditions, and cultural-creativity.[74] Such an act of openness, mutual respect, acceptance and recognition of each other's legacies of diversity may be identified as the expression of a true communion of the Church.

Churches need to come together on a common ecumenical space to get into mutual participation of people in prayer, songs, liturgical dances, and Eucharist, through which they may be reciprocally enriched and may learn from one another. It may promote dialogical communication between the different Naga churches, which is based on a spirit of openness, willingness to listen to each other and a desire to respect and understand others in their differences and diversity. Dialogical encounter may provide a context for the exploration of new patterns of mission. Proclamation and witness can be improved through dialogue, within and among the churches as well as beyond the boundaries of Christian community.[75] In addition, communion of churches need not limit itself to the parameter of the

---

71 Evelyn Monteiro, op. cit., p. 198.

72 Bernard Leeming S. J. *The Vatican Council and Christian Unity: A Commentary on the Decree on Ecumenism of the Second Vatican Council, Together with a Translation of the Text.* (London: Darton, Longman & Todd Ltd., 1966), pp. 134-135. Also see, John B. Chethimattam, *Towards a Theology of Intercommunion.* (Bangalore: Dharmaram Publications, 2001), pp. 267, 275.

73 Interview with Joseph Edakkudan, SDB, Society of Don Bosco, Christ the King, Kohima, 10th May 2006.

74 Monteiro, op. cit., p. 201.

75 Birgitta Larsson and Emilio Castro, op. cit., p. 146.

participation of different churches, but also extend it to make it participatory involving all the members in the Church.

2.4. Concluding Remarks

This chapter has so far taken for discussion the existing problem of denominationalism in Nagaland in the light of the growth and activities of different Christian denominations in the land. It shows that the ecclesial activities including the churches' public relations are being functioned and used mostly for the purpose of an exclusive denominational communication, which enhances only their denominational identity. In addition, denominationalism is nurtured because of the traditions of denominational and doctrinal structures inherited from the early missionaries. In this connection, the present scenario of strained ecumenical relationship between Christian denominations indicates that they feel comfortable within their own denominational group. They do not want to come together on a common platform for ecumenical communication, participation and fellowship with others.

Furthermore, they have a fear that they may lose their denominational identity, since the concept of ecumenism is not understood. It indicates the need for ecumenism among the Christians of different denominations in which the participation of both the Church and lay leadership will be significant. In addition, with the traditional media of folk dance, folk music, and folk drama, made accessible and by promoting participatory media for people in the community, it is possible to bring interaction, participation, harmony, changes and transformation among the people in the Church and society. In the next chapter three, the theological understanding of ecumenism and ecumenical communication will be discussed. It will be dealing with the relationship between ecumenism and culture to show that the cultural performances have an important part to play for the promotion of ecumenism in the Church and society.

Chapter 3

Theological Understanding of Ecumenism and Ecumenical Communication

The present chapter will go into discussion on the theological understanding of ecumenism and ecumenical communication. It will deal not only with the unity of the Church, but also with the unity of the whole humankind including the integrity of the whole of God's creation. In addition, it will try to explore the possibility of establishing a common ecumenical sphere that can be established during the celebration of Naga cultural festivals and folk dance, going beyond the traditional model of unity and dialogue within the Church. In this connection, the relationship between ecumenism and culture will be discussed, underlining that such a celebration of cultural performances may be potential not only for bringing people together irrespective of the denominational affiliation, but also for promoting contact, participation, unity, peace, justice, etc., in the Church and society.

3.1. The Meaning of 'Ecumenism'

The word "Ecumenical" or "Ecumenism" is derived from the Greek word *"Oikoumene"* which means 'the whole inhabited world'.[1] The word in its turn is a combination of two Greek words "*Oikos*" meaning "household" and "*meno*" means "to live". The Greeks used it in a universal, non-theological, popular and

1 Colin Buchanan, "Ecumenical Movement," in J. D. Douglas, ed., *The New International Dictionary of the Christian Church* (Grand Rapids: Zondervan Corporation, 1978), p. 327. Also see, F. N. Norman Goodall, *The Ecumenical Movement: What it is and What it Does*, Second edition. (London: Oxford University, 1964), p. 3; http://www.britannica.com/eb/article-67623/Christianity.

even in an inclusive sense to describe the earth and human inhabitance.[2] Thus, in secular Greek, *Oikoumene* is a geographical term for the inhabited parts of the earth. The word and what it stands for has played an important part in Greek, Roman and Christian civilizations.[3] It shows that it was from this concept of the whole inhabited world that the idea and endeavour of ecumenism and ecumenical movement was started for the promotion of unity, peace, justice, human dignity and development in the Church and the whole of God's creation. Thus, the idea of ecumenism is not limited to Church unity alone but extends to the unity of the people of other faiths, and that of the whole creation towards freedom, peace and justice. Konrad Raiser says, "The goal of the ecumenical movement could not be the unity of the Church in its narrow sense but must be the unity of humankind in justice and peace."[4] Therefore, the unity of the Church needs to be expressed through witness and service with a wider ecumenical understanding of unity for the new human community and for the whole creation in justice and peace.

Oikoumene is an important concept in the New Testament as we find phrases like the Kingdom of God, all the nations – in the entire world, the world to come and so on. Oikoumene is used in Mt.24: 14; Acts 11:28; Heb.2: 5; Rev.16: 14. God is the creator and source of '*Oikoumene*', the universal ecumenical community. Muthunayagom` states that Yahweh's creative and redemptive action is the dynamic force behind the formation of an ecumenical community.[5] The historical fact is that the Ecumenical Movement was started as a Church unity movement to bring about unity and fellowship between Christian churches.[6] In this connection, it is worth remembering what Konrad Raiser says, "The goal of the ecumenical movement could not thus be the unity of the Church in its narrow sense but must be the unity of humankind in justice and peace."[7] Today, the unity of the churches must result in the witness and service of humankind in the world since churches play the role of the servant in this world.

3.2. Theological Understanding of Ecumenism

The theological understanding of ecumenism is rooted in a vision of achieving unity embracing all inhabited earth. In this connection, ecumenical movement has come into being for the unity of all churches. In recent times, this unity

2 O. L. Snaitang, *A History of Ecumenical Movement: An Introduction,* op. cit., p. 11.

3 Norman Goodall, op. cit., p. 3.

4 Konrad Raiser, *Ecumenism in Transition: A Paradigm Shift in the Ecumenical Movement* (Geneva: WCC Publications, 1991), p. 8.

5 Daniel Jones Muthunayagom, "A Look at Ecumenism from a Biblical Perspective," in Vinod Victor, Leslie Nathaniel & P. Surya Prakesh, eds., *Ecumenism: Prospects and Challenges* (New Delhi: ISPCK, 2001), p. 353.

6 P. Jegadish Gandhi & George Cheriyan, eds., *Ecumenical Perspectives in Asia Beyond 2000* (Chennai: ACISCA, 2000), p. x.

7 Konrad Raiser, *Ecumenism in Transition,* op. cit., p. 8.

is conceived as a means to achieve the unity of all humankind, irrespective of religion, race, sex, or political ideology, including the integrity of all God's creation. Thus, justice and peace, political, economic, social and cultural aspects of life, are all integral to ecumenism.[8] Today, the concept and practice of ecumenism is broadened to incorporate all aspects of human life, including the whole of creation.

3.2.1 Theological Insights of Ecumenism

Ecumenism is a movement for the unity of all Christians, including the integrity of all God's creation. The source of Christian unity derives from the unity of the triune God.[9] Since Christ is not divided, the Church is expected to live in communion and union with the Lord and with one another. In this connection, it is worthwhile quoting Pope John Paul II who states that "Christian unity is our heart's desire."[10] However, due to the division of the churches based on the problem of different theological understanding and expression of the gospel, the unity is being endangered. Theology constantly strives forward to express its faith in a manner which will preserve the shared experiences of God, guarding against deviations affecting the truth of God and his salvation.[11]

Theology is a means of expressing and communicating the experiences of the believer's faith and belief in God. It is also necessary for the sharing and edification of the community of believers in the Church. Theology does not only concern itself with the individual's faith affirmation, but is also concerned with the unity of the Church or the Christian community. In this connection, God's concern for the unity is not only for the unity of the Church alone but for unity of all humankind including people of other faiths, and the integrity of all creation. Thus, the theological understanding of ecumenism tries to show that unity, justice and peace need to be promoted in all the realms of God's creation. Such Kingdom values can be promoted in the Church and society not only through dialogical communication, participation and involvement, but also through the celebration of cultural festivals and folk dances among the people in the community.

---

8 M. A. Thomas, *Towards Wider Ecumenism* (Bangalore: ATC, 1993), p. 193.

9 "The WCC is a fellowship of churches which confesses the Lord Jesus Christ as God and Saviour according to the Scripture and therefore seeks to fulfill together their common calling to the glory of the one God, Father, Son and Holy Spirit." Visser't Hooft Willem, "The Basics: Its History and Significance," in *Ecumenical Review*, Vol. 37, no. 2, 1985, p. 173.

10 John Paul II, Homily in the Basilica of St. Paul, Rome, on January 25th, 1993, in *Osservatore Romano,* English Edition, (*OR*), no. 4, January 27, 1993, p. 1.

11 Nicholas Lossky, "Theology, Ecumenism," in Nicholas Lossky, Jose Bonino, John Pobee, Tom Stransky, Geoffrey Wainwright and Pauline Webb eds., *Dictionary of Ecumenical Movement* (Geneva: WCC Publications, 1991), p. 986.

i. Theology of Ecumenism

Theology is a necessary means of communication, especially for establishing broken unity, and so it necessarily implies finding out the meaning that each gives to the same word.[12] In addition, theology is necessary for the communication of the believers' faith, for the sharing of the experience of belief, and for the teaching and learning of the community of believers. The sole criterion for theology of ecumenical communication is God himself, and Jesus Christ, the image of the Father, bearer of the Spirit who, while revealing himself so, cries "Abba Father" in the heart of all believers. Thus, it implies total humility and intellectual honesty, and willingness to be guided into all the truth by the Spirit of truth.[13]

The theology of ecumenism concerns itself not only with the personal reflection upon their faith, but also with the unity of the church as a community of believers. It is a study of ecumenism in relation to the demanding challenges and needs in the Church and the society at present, based on the concept of the unity of Christ. From the very beginning of the Christian Church, one of the main concerns in the Christian community has been maintaining unity. This unity has always been endangered by the complex theological problem of understanding and communicating the gospel of Jesus Christ in the contexts of contemporary challenges.[14] According to Evans, ecumenical theology is concerned with unraveling mutual misunderstandings among Christians which have occurred in the past; these, as we have seen and shall see again, constantly threaten to occur or recur in the present and in the future.[15] In fact, the truth of the unity of Christ needs to be read and expressed in the historical contexts. Ecumenical theology can be neither blind to the variety of contexts of the present world nor deaf to the witness of all times to the apostolic faith. It is a renewed awareness of the Church's responsibility for all, in that it exists for the life of the world.[16] In this connection, the needs to be stated are that, the unity of the Church in Christ is closely linked with the unity and integrity of God's creation in terms of promoting peace, unity, justice, freedom and development in all the realms of creation.

3.2.2. Communicating Towards the Unity of the Church

Christian communication is Christ's own communication,'[17] which means Christ is the foundation stone of Christian communication. Christian communication is sharing and exchanging the gospel message with a view to bringing Christian

12 *Ibid.* p. 987.

13 *Ibid,* p. 988.

14 *Ibid.* pp. 986-987.

15 G. R. Evans, *Method in Ecumenical Theology: The Lessons So Far.* (Cambridge: Cambridge University Press, 1996), p. 22.

16 Nicholas Lossky, op, cit., p. 987.

17 Gaston Roberge, *The Faithful Witness: On Christian Communication* (Anand: Gujarat Sahitya Prakash, 1999), p. 25.

people together to communicate with one another in the spirit of unity. Christian communication goes beyond evangelism and sharing of the gospel, to include ecumenical vision based on the gospel values. It aims not only at achieving Christian unity but also towards freedom, justice and holistic development for all people.

The present ecumenical movement came into being out of the conviction of the churches that should there be division among Christians it would be a scandal and an impediment to the witness of the Church.[18] *WACC's Statements on Communication* affirms that ecumenical relations and the search for unity are the responses to a divine command. As it says, "The Churches do not exist for their own sakes, but for the sake of the Kingdom. For this reason, the Christian communicator gives preference to ecumenical communication so that Christians of different denominations can speak with one voice, thus, bearing witness to the one body of Christ."[19] The Scripture clearly points out that all are one in Christ, Christ is not divided and therefore, there should be no schism in the body of Christ, the Church. Based on this biblical truth, ecumenical communication gives priority to the unity of the Church, so that Christians of different denominations can come together to communicate with openness and speak out with one voice for the needs of the human community.

The issue of ecclesiastical unity is crucial in the context of the churches in Northeast India in general, and in Nagaland in particular, where the aspiration of ecumenical relationship is still an unfinished task, and it calls forth the Christian communicators to fulfill this need. In addition, in the light of building up a relationship and fellowship between churches, ecumenical dialogue has been used as an effective means of communication among them. So, where divisions and differences among churches are found, such ecumenical dialogue could bring them closer and build interactions towards achieving the required goal.

i. Dialogue as Ecumenism

Dialogue is a common form for building up ecumenical relations. It is a process of making human relationships and it is an expression of human community through which human aspirations of unity and fellowship can be fulfilled. Such a process demands, acceptance, respect, honesty and patience towards others. Dialogue has been an effective method of communication to bring unity and relationship between different Christian denominations. According to Konard Raiser, ecumenical dialogue is a deliberately guided conversation between representatives of different churches for achieving unity, sharing efforts of

18 James A. Scherer & Stephen B. Bevans, eds., *New Directions in Mission and Evangelization: Basic Statement* – 1974 -1991, Vol. I (New York: Orbis Books, 1992), p. 37.

19 WACC. *Statements on Communication.* (London: WACC, 1997), pp. 5-6.

overcoming divisions.[20] Such dialogues have taken place between churches at national and universal levels. From the very beginning of the modern ecumenical movement, bilateral and multilateral dialogues have been used side by side.

ii. Bilateral Dialogue

In bilateral dialogues, churches of two parties were allowed to discuss and concentrate on particular issues that have divided them, inherited from the past. This method is used here to overcome divisions in the churches, so that closer unity may be achieved with each other.[21] In addition to this, consultations between churches have two features. Firstly, this being an official inter-church dialogue, the respective church authorities authorize selected representatives to whom the results are directly submitted. Secondly, they are concerned with doctrinal matters such as that of authority in the church, the Eucharist, the ministry, and ecclesiology.[22] Therefore, bilateral dialogue can be an indispensable instrument of the ecumenical movement towards a visible unity. It may lead the churches to find out their commonalities and enable them to build new relationships.[23]

iii. Multilateral Dialogue

In multilateral dialogue, churches of more than two parties are involved in ecumenical conversations. It focuses on the central theme the Christian faith, which is mostly shared by the dialogical partners, to find agreement in confession and interpretation. Most churches have in fact discovered that in and through multilateral dialogues, worthwhile relationships could be cultivated in all directions. Quite a few multilateral church unions have taken place at the national levels, such as the Church of South India (CSI) in 1947, and Church of North India (CNI) in 1970.[24] In addition, such multilateral dialogues and fellowship of the churches provide opportunities to focus their attention on common interests for the welfare and development of the people in the society. Multilateral dialogue

---

20 Dialogue method has been used in the encounter between Christians and people of other faiths, and also in Christian efforts to reach responsible solutions to social and political conflicts. Raiser, op. cit., p. 14.

21 At the time of reformation, there were such bilateral religious conversations between Catholics and Lutherans, Lutherans and Anglicans. Even in the 20th century such bilateral dialogues have taken place between Anglicans and Orthodox, Anglicans and Old Catholics, Lutherans and Reformed Churches. Nicholas Lossky, Jose M. Bonino, and John Pobee, eds., *Dictionary of the Ecumenical Movement*, 2nd Edition (Geneva: WCC Publications, 2002), p. 310.

22 *Ibid*, pp. 310-311.

23 Melanie A. May, "The Unity We Share, The Unity We Seek," in John Briggs, Mercy Amba Oduyoye and Georges Tsetsis, eds. *A History of the Ecumenical Movement,* Volume 3 1968-2000. (Geneva: WCC Publications, 2004), pp. 94-95.

24 Nicholas Loosky, Jose M. Bonino, and John Pobee, eds. op. cit, p. 322.

in many ways encourages the churches to face common tasks in a common world in terms of proclaiming the gospel and serving the needy among the humankind.[25]

3.2.3. Communicating Towards Wider Ecumenism

The theoretical concept of ecumenism goes beyond the unity of the Church to include all humankind, of different religious communities and the entirety of God's creation, In this regard, Theophilus points out that a wider ecumenism includes the cooperation and participation of the Church, religious communities, people of faiths or of no faith, so that the divine purpose of the reconciliation and transformation of all humanity and creation may be accomplished.[26] Such a wider ecumenism is important for all people who inhabit the world, which is necessary in Asia, especially in India, the land of many religions, culture, and languages.[27] This may lead to the creation of a larger human community irrespective of caste, tribe, colour, religions, culture, or languages, resulting in a peaceful co-existence where harmony, justice, human dignity and development may prevail in the society.

i. Dialogical Communication in a Multi-Religious Context

Christian witness among people of various faiths has caused a lot of tension in the last few decades. The reason for promoting inter-faith dialogue is to promote peace and harmony. It aims at bringing people of other faiths together with a view to understand each other and to live together in peace. Arles says that in the context of religious pluralism, ecumenical missiology is challenged to be more sensitive and open to the people of other faiths; promoting inter-faith dialogue will bring about religious harmony and national integration.[28] In the Indian context where different religious communities are living together side-by-side, accepting the reality of religious pluralism becomes a significant issue. At times communal disharmony and conflict occur due to misunderstandings between different religious communities and their exclusive attitude towards others. In this regard, the WACC's *Christian Principles of Communication* strongly affirms that the Christian communicators need to acquire sensitivity not only to the peoples

25 *Ibid.*, p. 322.

26 Zacharias Mar Theophilus, op. cit., p. 6.

27 Rosario Gomez, "Towards a Wider Ecumenism," in R. Mohanraj, ed., *Communication for an Alternative Humanity* (Chennai: The Department of Communication of the Church of South India, 2003), p.16.

28 Siga Arles, "Ecumenical Missiology" Challenges from an "Evangelical Perspective," in Lalsangkima Pachuau, ed., *Ecumenical Missiology: Contemporary Trends, Issues and Themes* (Bangalore: UTC, 2002), p. 53; See Gideon Goose, *Bringing Churches Together: A Popular Introduction to Ecumenism*, Revised and Enlarged Edition (Geneva: WCC Publications, 1993), pp. 133-134.

of other faiths and ideologies, but also to people caught in situations of religious discriminations in different parts of the world.'[29]

Christian communication with people of other faiths need not be in a manner of self-justification, but in a way of dialogical sharing, mutual understanding and learning from one another. In this connection, the WCC's interim document recognizes and accepts dialogue with people of living faiths and ideologies as one of the major concerns of the ecumenical movement.[30] However, inter-faith dialogue is not to make converts, it is not a forum where partners in dialogue come to total agreement, nor is it a sphere to find a new universal religion. Conversion should be left to the personal conviction and decision of individuals.

The advantage of ecumenical communication is that it has the potentiality to bring closer not only Christians of different denominations but also people of other faiths towards mutual understanding, harmony and unity. However, the disadvantage is that it is a risk-taking job; unless the communicative partners focus on common interests it may create tensions as well. Samartha states that courage for dialogue in a multi-religious context needs the courage to be, to go, to meet, to take risks, to hope, to trust in the power of Jesus Christ and the guiding presence of the Spirit.[31] In this connection, Eilers suggests that the Church needs to look beyond her institutional boundaries. Networking and cooperation with other religions should be promoted in the context of common issues that will benefit all people.[32] Moreover, it will open up new opportunities for co-operation with the people of other faiths on issues such as that of communication, peace and justice.

ii. Communicating Towards Development and Social Justice

WCC's vision of the ecumenical movement has a socio-political dimension in which not only the unity of the Church and that of the people of other faiths through dialogical communication, but also peace, justice, development are advocated in the context of oppressions, discriminations and exploitations of all forms.[33] It is in the context of diverse socio-economic and political situations that people are divided. These divisions are caused by globalization and non acceptance of plurality of cultural and religious differences. Philip Potter says that development efforts so far have been powerless to redress the gap between the

29 WACC, op. cit., p. 32.

30 S. J. Samartha, *Courage for Dialogue: Ecumenical Issues in Inter-religious Relationship* (Geneva: WCC Publications, 1981), p. 36.

31 *Ibid,* p. 62.

32 Franz-Josef Eilers, ed., *Church and Social Communication in Asia,* op. cit., pp. 24 -25.

33 T. V. Philip, *Edinburgh To Salvador: Twentieth Century Ecumenical Missiology*, op. cit., pp. 92-93.

rich and the poor between and within the nations.[34] In such a situation social transformation is needed to advance genuine *oikoumene*. The following issues are interrelated to each other in the ecumenical discussions.

a. Ecumenism as Promoting Economic Justice and Progress

The realities of economic liberalization and globalization characterized by competition, domination and discrimination challenge the global economic justice. Further, globalization is not simply an economic issue. It is cultural, political, ethical and it is an ecological issue. Increasingly, Christians and churches find themselves confronted by the new and deeply challenging aspects of globalization faced by a vast number of people, especially the poor.[35] In this context the poor become poorer while the rich become richer at all levels, and the gap between the haves and the have-nots widens. R. Devadoss says that in the context of globalization, the Church with ecumenical concerns needs to enter into a meaningful partnership with the dalits, adivasis, women and the victims of globalization, to intervene and alter equations, relationships and structures, which degrade people.[36] In this connection, Christians and churches should reflect on the challenge of globalization from a faith perspective, so that the unilateral domination of economic and cultural globalization may be resisted.[37] The Church and all Christian Communicators need to opt for the poor for their emancipation and development. According to Sadananda, humanitarian services, economic and social development, people's participation in collective action, awakening of indigenous people, the dalits, the tribals, women and children to self-identity – all these different aspects of justice can contribute to create a community based on peace and justice.[38]

b. Ecumenism as Promoting Ecological Justice

Economic justice is closely related to ecological justice. We perceive that the challenges of ecology and crisis arising out of deforestation, energy shortage, global warming, acid rain, ozone depletion, importability of water, impurity of

---

34 "Several years of involvement in development aid have convinced us that a purely economic growth concept, working automatically for development should be replaced by a process aimed at economic and social justice, self-reliance, and people's participation in establishing goals and priorities and making decisions regarding economic growth as a means to the end of a globally just society." Philip Potter, *Life in all its Fullness* (Geneva: WCC Publications, 1981), p. 84.

35 Diane Kessler, ed., *Together On the Way* (Geneva: WCC Publications, 1999), p. 183.

36 R. Devadoss, "Ecumenism: A Framework for Praxis," in Vinod Victor, Leslie Nathaniel & P. Surya Prakash, eds. *Ecumenism: Prospects and Challenges* (New Delhi: ISPCK, 2001), p. 246.

37 Diane Kessler, ed., op. cit., p. 183.

38 John S. Sadananda, "Peace and Justice – Commitment for Sahodaya and Sarvodaya," in P. Jegadish and K. C John, eds., *Upon the Wings of Wider Ecumenism: Essays and Tributes in Honour of Rev. Dr. M. J. Joseph, ECC.* (New Delhi: ISPCK & ECC, 2006), p. 170.

air and infertility of soil, are the result of the distorted, uncontrollable power that the humans exercise on nature. Ecological crisis is ultimately a crisis of wholeness, separating humans from the web of environment.[39] In this regard, K. C. Abraham states that ecology is ecumenism on a new basis. We need to evolve a discourse on ecumenism with the clear focus on ecology. Ecology of ecumenism calls for unity that is rooted in our common belonging to the earth.[40] Our relationship with nature can be the main concern in evolving a new paradigm for ecumenism, which may promote ecological justice and peaceful co-existence with all God's creation. According to Samartha, a harmonious relation between humanity and nature is necessary to support peaceful relation between human beings in community.[41] It is imperative for all the religious communities to join hands to work together for protecting and saving the mother earth, which itself will be an act of promoting ecological justice in the community.

c. Ecumenism as Promoting Justice for Women

Attempts to promote the role and status of women in the Church and society are part of the ecumenical agenda,[42] where women are denied the exercise of their rights but made to experience discrimination and unequal treatment from their male partners. In this connection, violence against women, commodification and commercialisation of women are crimes against them. According to V. M. Kurian, the conditions of women have become deplorable in the era of globalization. Though feminisation of work has started, differences in the earnings between male and female workers have increased.[43] Ecumenical communication aims at giving a voice to women so that they may articulate their own experiences and thereby make a meaningful contribution to Church and society.

---

39 A. Pushparajan, "Eco-Vision for Social Amity," in P. Jegadish Gandhi and K, C. John, eds., *Upon the Wings of Wider Ecumenism: Essays and Tributes in Honour of Rev. Dr. M. J. Joseph, ECC.* (New Delhi: ISPCK & ECC, 2006), pp. 131-133.

40 "We use ecology in a broader sense; it is a worldview, a new value system and a pattern of relationship between humans and humans and nature and humans. In this sense, today, we talk about social ecology and political ecology. Following this clue I would like to suggest a discussion on ecology of ecumenism. Certainly ecumenism is rooted in a vision of unity embracing all inhabited earth." K. C. Abraham, "Ecology and Ecumenism: A New Paradigm," in P. Jegadish Gandhi and K. C John, eds., *Upon the Wings of Wider Ecumenism: Essays and Tributes in Honour of Rev. Dr. M. J. Joseph, ECC.* (New Delhi: ISPCK & ECC, 2006), p. 18-19.

41 "Human beings are guests of mother earth and stewards of her abundant resources; they should not act as strangers and exploiters of her gifts." S. J. Samartha, op. cit., *Courage for Dialogue*, p. 122.

42 Siga Arles, op. cit., p.53.

43 V. Mathew Kurian, "Life and Death through Globalisation: The Indian Experience," in P. Jegadish and K. C John, eds., *Upon the Wings of Wider Ecumenism: Essays and Tributes in Honour of Rev. Dr. M. J. Joseph, ECC.* (New Delhi: ISPCK & ECC, 2006), p. 233.

d. Ecumenism as Promoting Peace and Justice

The incessant wars and tensions between nations, ethnic and communal conflicts, terrorism, ecological destructions are the realities that continuously promote fears and uncertainty in the lives of the people. Further, humanity is threatened by unjust social order as much as it is threatened by a nuclear war. Such unjust social structures cause widespread poverty, hunger, ignorance and disease and various forms of exploitation.[44] Denial of peace and justice to the people in the society is a violation of human dignity. In this connection, it is well to remember that Justice, Peace and Integrity of Creation (JPIC) was conceived in the Vancouver WCC Assembly in 1983, to be the priority, in the programme. It was shaped in the context of the rapid alarming growth processes that endanger people, all living creatures, the future and that of the mother earth. Human beings are under a serious threat of nuclear war, stockpiling of destructive weapons, and militarism. In addition to this are the problems due to global unjust economic order, social discrimination, oppression and the misuse of science and technology. The JPIC programme, together with churches seeks to provide a theological affirmation and reflection on these three concerns, while encouraging to resist and to fight against these demonic powers of destruction.[45] It shows that war and violence are the consequences of the ultimate failure of communication. This situation demands socio-political peace and justice in the global community. In addition, Gomez says that conflict resolution and reconciliation are the two tasks attributed to the promotion of peace and harmony in the community.[46] In this connection, it is worthwhile quoting Philip Lee who says that Christians are called to promote the true meaning of global ecumenism – not the post Reformation ecumenism aimed at reuniting all Christians, but an ecumenism aimed at bringing together all the people inhabited in the world to act in solidarity to bring about their physical and spiritual salvation.[47]

In the Indian context, especially in the North East India, peace, justice and development are crucial not only for people's survival but also for maintaining their identity and human dignity. Ecumenical communication that reflects Christian principles of communication needs to create awareness and inculcate

---

44 John S. Sadananda, op. cit., p. 168.

45 O. L. Snaitang, *History of Ecumenical Movement*, op. cit., pp. 217-221; Also See Ans J. Van der Bent, *Vital Ecumenical Concerns: Sixteen Documentary Surveys* (Geneva: WCC Publications, 1986), pp. 116-117; Also see, Ulrich Becker, "Ecumenical Formation," in John Briggs, Mercy Amba Oduyoye and Georges Tsetsis, eds. *A History of the Ecumenical Movement,* Volume 3 1968-2000. (Geneva: WCC Publications, 2004) p. 187.

46 "Real conflict resolution will have to be done in three phases: (1) A restoration of justice and reconciliation; (2) A solution to the problems that gave rise to the conflict and (3) Healing of memories." Gomez, op. cit., p. 23.

47 Philip Lee, 'Communicating is Peace: WACC's Mission Today.' *Media Development* Vol. LIV 1/2007, p. 52.

education among people to articulate their own needs. In mutual participation, the people and the Christian communicators should strive for advancing people's needs and aspirations.

3.3. Theological Understanding of Ecumenical Communication

The term *ecumenical communication* means 'to bring people together on a common ecumenical sphere' to promote the values of faith, unity, relationship, peace, justice, love, integrity, and living as a community not only among the Christian people but also in the whole inhabited world in the context of the present realities. In this connection, the act of people coming together, sharing and communicating towards achieving common interests, irrespective of their geographical, cultural, religious and denominational differences can be seen as ecumenical advancement. In addition, from a biblical point of view, we can say that the term "ecumenical communication" is God's communication obligated to all Christians transcending all human barriers to promote the kingdom values in all the realms of his creation.[48]

The theological understanding of ecumenical communication is closely linked with the vision of ecumenical missiology. Ecumenical communication and ecumenical missiology are the two sides of the same coin and they are not identical. It has often been noted that the origin of the Ecumenical Movement lies in the missionary movement, which attempted to communicate the gospel of peace, unity, love and integrity not only within the churches but also in the whole inhabited world.[49] According to Gomez, the word *oikoumene* means the global community or a larger human community that we want to construct. The communication we use to construct such a community is called the ecumenical communication.[50] Ecumenical communication is intended not only to build a larger human community, but also to communicate and promote the Kingdom values of peace, justice, relationship, development and participation in all realms of life. In this connection, Russell Rollason points out that the goals of ecumenical communication are the promotion of justice, participation and peace, as revealed in the Bible and in the living Christ.[51]

---

48 Emilio Castro, *A Passion for Unity: Essays on Ecumenical Hopes and Challenges*. (Geneva: WCC Publications, 1992), p. 83

49 Joseph Mattam & Sebastian Kim, eds., *Mission Trends Today: Historical and Theological Perspectives* (Bangalore: St. Pauls, 1997), p. 100.

50 Gomez, op. cit., p. 17.

51 Russell Rollason, "Behold all Things New: Ecumenical Communication as a Sign of the New World Information and Communication Order," in T. K. Thomas, ed., *Ecumenical Communication in Asia* (Singapore: CCA, 1981), p. 61.

3.3.1. Ecumenical Communication: A Life-long Task of all Christians

From a biblical perspective ecumenical relations and unity are not an option but an imperative because it comes from the heart of the Triune God as revealed by Jesus. Communion and unity are given in Christ Jesus because he is the source of the unity. He prayed for the unity of his disciples - as he is one with the Father. The Canberra Assembly of the WCC had described it thus: "The Holy Spirit as promoter of *koinonia* (II Cor. 13:13) gives to those who are still divided, the thirst and hunger for full communion."[52] Further, it affirms and supports the wish and prayer of Christ that whoever believes in him may be one. The fundamental principle of unity promotes relationship, sharing, equality, justice and human dignity for all people. In this connection, Traber says, "Cultivating an ecumenical spirit should be the life-long-task of all Christians and all churches. In the deepest theological sense, churches and Christians have no option but to be genuinely ecumenical."[53] To live an authentic Christian life is to live in better ecumenical relations and interactions with all men and women as God's children, which is an inevitable task for all Christians. It affirms the biblical principle of one body, one Spirit, one Hope, one Lord, one Faith, one Baptism, one God, and Father of all, who is above all and through all in all. (Eph.4: 4-6). Thus, Christian communication opposes any form of non-communication that divides people destroying relationship and community life.

3.3.2. Ecumenical Communication Towards Communion and Integrity

The word *Oikoumene* is also referred to as communion, which means fellowship and relationship among human beings. The purpose of God's ecumenical concern is to have communion, union and fellowship among all living beings in the entire inhabited world. The entire household of God's creation is the place where God personally communicates with all humankind irrespective of gender, caste, tribe, status, religion, and denomination. God's communication with all human beings is intended to bring about Kingdom values of fellowship, unity, peace, justice, integrity and living as a community in the whole of His household of creation. Therefore, ecumenical communication brings into being life, integrity and living as a community to the whole creation. At this point, from a biblical point of view, we can say that the term "ecumenical communication" is God's communication obligated to all Christians that transcends all human barriers to promote kingdom values among the Christian people and in the whole inhabited world in the context of the present realities.

---

52 WCC, "The Unity of the Church as *Koinonia*: Gift and Calling," in *Ecumenical Trends*, Vol. 20, no. 3, 1991, p. 42.

53 Michael Traber. "Ecumenical Relations in Communication." *Media Development*, 27/1, 1980, p. 1.

3.3.3. Ecumenical Communication Towards Unity and Service

Ecumenical communication demands unity of hearts, commitment and self-sacrifice towards ecumenical relations among the Christians of different denominations. Thereby, they can come together to speak out or communicate the truth, that is, to practice ecumenical communication from a common platform for the welfare of the people. According to Traber, Christian Communication should be ecumenical – that the churches should speak with one voice to articulate people's needs and aspirations.[54] Thus, the objective of ecumenical communication should not be that of self-interest, with denominational and institutional interests. It needs to aim at achieving unity and coordination among Christians of different churches as well as among those of the wider human community, where everyone is respected, accepted and treated with a sense of oneness, commonness, belongingness and communion.

To achieve the objectives of ecumenical communication, churches and their leaders need to commit themselves to the use of folk media, group media as well as mass media as effective means of interdenominational communication. In fact, it is intended to promote a positive attitude and openness towards others, and to create a better atmosphere for mutual understanding of one another. Such an attitude may help Christians to grow in ecumenical awareness, relations and participation with one another.

i. Ecumenical Communication as Solidarity with Others

Ecumenical relations and communication demand witness and practical involvement for the welfare of others. Surya Prahash says that the goal of ecumenical efforts is not for the sake of unity, but for the sake of common witness ("that the world may believe") and common service.[55] In this connection, Arens argues that a Christian witness involves solidarity of both practical and active assistance and healing of sick, the poor and outcasts with the purpose of removing their socially imposed excommunication.[56] Thus, on behalf of the poor, Christian witness is supposed to denounce all forms of injustice, corruption, violence, and discrimination being committed to the innocent people and making comprehensible and accessible the transforming power of Christ to them. Such a Christian witness is supposed to be ecumenically relevant to the poor and the suffering community.

---

54 Michael Traber, "Ecumenical Relations in Communication." *Media Development*, 27/1, 1980, p. 2.

55 P. Surya Prakash. "Towards Understanding 'Ecumenism' of the Church," in Vinod Victor, Leslie Nathaniel & P. Surya Prakash, eds., *Ecumenism: Prospects and Challenges*. (Delhi: ISPCK, 2001), p. xviii.

56 Edmund Arens, op. cit., pp. 57-58.

ii. Ecumenical Communication as Self-giving and as Sacrifice

Edmund Arens affirms that witnessing is the disciples' action in the face of Jesus' life, death, and resurrection that demands self-giving love and sacrifice for the sake of Christ and others.[57] Following the footsteps of Jesus, working for solidarity and unity of the Church is of utmost importance in order to communicate the truth of the gospel and to work towards the solidarity of the oppressed and suffering community in the society. It may require even suffering on behalf of others, so that they may experience a sense of freedom, self-respect, and belongingness. According to Eilers, Christian witness is a common witness of self-giving service for others and sometimes it might call for a prudent political involvement to defend the dignity of the people.[58] In fact, critical Christian witness is a way of the cross and involves suffering for the benefit and development of others.

3.3.4. Mass Media and Ecumenical Communication

There are some communication scholars however, who believe that the churches could use mass media in order to promote co-operation and unity among churches. Richard Adler says that there are ecumenical relationships in communication. Christian publications, radio programmes, cassette ministries, audiovisual productions, all of which should be made participatory and accessible to all Christians and churches, for these could promote such relationships. However, if the churches and Christian organizations attempt such projects together they can promote co-operation, coordination and facilitate unity among churches.[59] David Wanless argues that the reason why churches fail in ecumenical communication is because its leaders have failed to understand the nature and power of the media.[60] Traber comments that "media can serve as an ecumenical rallying-point for the churches, such unity of purpose could promote co-operation among the churches."[61] Media have a great role to play towards ecumenical communication in promoting not only unity and co-operation, but also fostering peace, justice, and development in the churches and in the society. In this connection, Richard Adler mentions the financial constraints and demands of media personnel.[62]

---

57 *Ibid.,* p. 89.

58 Franz-Josef Eilers. *Communicating in Ministry and Mission: An Introduction to Pastoral and Evangelizing Communication.* (Bangalore: ATC, 2003), p. 111.

59 Richard Adler, "Ecumenical Co-operation in Papua New Geuinea." *Media Development*, 27/1, 1980, pp. 4-5.

60 David Wanless, "Wasted Opportunities in Ecumenical Communication." *Media Development*, 27/1, 1980, pp. 19-20.

61 Micheal Traber, *Media Development*, 27/1, 1980, op. cit., p.1.

62 Richard Adler, op. cit., 5.

3.3.5. Language as Ecumenical Communication

Language gives us hope, a common vision, mission and concerns, and an ecumenical spirit that becomes the source of the ecumenical communication. John Coventry argues that language opens onto communion, and that the expression of this communion becomes sacramental. Thus language, which entails a shared worldview, provides the basis for ecumenical communication.[63] Thus, language provides an ample ground and opportunity to live and communicate ecumenically for the betterment of the whole human community. Religious language itself is the creative Word of God, which has both divine and human elements.

From a theological point of view, humans communicate because God has communicated and continues to communicate with them. Thus, they share in God's creative power in using language.[64] Language provides a point of contact and mutual interaction with one another and thereby builds up communion and a human community. Religious language is inclusive and universal in its character. For instance, 'Kingdom of God' is not simply a concept, but a symbolic language of hope for all people. Kingdom values such as love, sharing, unity, freedom, justice, peace, equality and living as a community have ecumenical overtones and are addressed to all peoples. Thus, all Christians are called to celebrate the language of God's Kingdom with ecumenical responsibility towards one another. Because of ecumenical awareness among Christians, today, they have learnt to use inclusive language, for instance, gender-friendly language, religious-friendly language, which encourages ecumenical communication and relations among Christians as well as with those of other faiths.

In WCC's theoretical understanding of ecumenism and ecumenical communication, culture has been given an important part in terms of understanding and expressing the gospel meaningfully in the context of the people, especially in the third world countries. However, it has not so far been given a close attention to the exploration of an ecumenical space that may be found in the celebration of the cultural festivals and folk dances, which itself is given main focus in this study. At this point, it may be important to discuss the relationship between ecumenism and culture, with a view to explore and understand the existence of such an ecumenical space in the celebration of cultural performances.

3.4. Relationship between Ecumenism and Culture

As mentioned earlier, culture and ecumenism are closely related to one another, though they are not identical. Culture is basically a learned behaviour, belief,

---

63 John Coventry, "Ecumenical Communication." *The Way*. 12:2, 1972, pp. 134-141.

64 Paul A. Soukup, op. cit., p. 32.

attitude, values and ideals, generally shared by members of a community.[65] In this connection, culture can be understood in terms of everything that the people possess, think, and how they behave in a particular way, which can preserve and express their religious and cultural identity.[66] Cultural expressions may provide people an opportunity to strengthen their ecumenical relationship and unity through their mutual participation and sharing with one another in the Church and community. In this connection, Paul Tillich's view of relationship between religion and culture may clarify the understanding of relationship between ecumenism and culture. He says that there is an essential relation between religion and culture that "culture is the form of religion and religion is the substance of culture" which is realized in the Spiritual Community.[67] According to Tillich, substance is different from content. It signifies the meaning, the spiritual substantiality, from which alone the form receives its meaning.[68] It shows the essential relatedness of each cultural expression to its religious ground.

In the words of Tillich, culture is the expression of religion in which art, poetry, drama, music and dances can play an important role for communicating and promoting unity and integrity of the whole of God's creation.[69] In addition, religion in itself is the essence of culture in terms of preserving and exhibiting various cultural symbols, art forms, festivals and ceremonies, not only for the purpose of communicating the religious message, but also for promoting participation, interaction, peace, justice, unity among people in the Church and the society as well.[70] In this connection, it underlines an ecumenical appeal that

---

65 Carol R. Ember and Melvin Ember, *Cultural Anthropology*, 7th Edition, (Englewood Cliffs, N. J.: Prentice Hall, 1993), p. 18.

66 According to Gary Ferraro, Culture means everything that people *have*, and it refers to material possessions; everything that people *think*, referring those things they carry around in their heads, such as ideas, values, and attitudes; and everything that people *do* referring behaviour patterns, expressions, and performances. Gary Ferraro, *Cultural Anthropology: An Applied Perspective,* (Saint Paul: West Publishing Company, 1992), p. 19.

67 "Spiritual Community has been used to characterize sharply that element in the concept of the church which is called the "body of Christ" by the New Testament and the "Church Invisible or Spiritual" by the Reformation." Paul Tillich, *Systematic Theology*, Volume III (Chicago: The University of Chicago Press, 1963), p. 158 & 162. Tillich's famous essay on 'a theology of culture' expounds his view that religion is the substance of culture and culture is the expression of religion. J. Heywood Thomas, *Paul Tillich: Makers of Contemporary Theology.* (Atlanta: John Knox Press, 1965), p. 48.

68 Victor Nuovo, ed., *Visionary Science* (Detroit: Wayne State University Press, 1987), p. 27.

69 J. Heywood Thomas, *Tillich: Outstanding Christian Thinker* (London: Continuum, 2000), p. 36.

70 "It (art) is cultural because it is not attached to a specific ritual activity; and religious, because it evokes questioning as to the absolute to the limits of human existence. This is equally true of painting, of music and poetry, of philosophy and science. That which is valid in the intuition and knowledge of the world is equally valid in the practical shaping of law and custom, in morality and education, in community and state. Wherever human existence in thought or

the Church as a religious institution has been powerfully called back out of its self-chosen ghetto, out of its disregard for culture, to do its tasks for the world.[71] In addition, there is a vision which might overcome the ruthless situation of denominational rivalry and make the Church again a uniting power, reconciling the broken world with God by overcoming its splits and separations, yet doing this from within reality and never by the authoritarian means of the church and political power.[72] It indicates that ecumenism can be seen intrinsically as part of both the religion and culture. Therefore, it follows that the ecumenical endeavour promoting unity, peace, justice, and integrity of God's creation can be seen as a part of religious activity with culture as an integral component. Thus, ecumenism and culture compliment each other.

In the whole understanding of culture, the ecumenical values of interaction, unity, sharing, relationships, and participation, are implicitly and explicitly present. In this regard, the concept of ecumenism also advocates and respects people and their culture, especially, for those who belong to the third world countries who are being dominated by the developed countries with their dominant ideology.[73] By such an endeavour the suppressed will be able to survive and articulate, expressing their needs and aspirations in the language and media of their culture. Cultural expressions and behaviour, especially non-material culture, such as language, folk music, drama, and folk dances, can keep the people active, lively, and innovative in the community. At this point, one can say that ecumenism can be seen in culture in terms of providing space outside the Church for communicating and interacting with one another. In addition, both ecumenism and culture are closely connected for communicating and promoting unity, sharing, fellowship, and participation among people in the Church and society.

3.4.1. Ecumenical Communication and Cultural Performances

Cultural performances are meant to define, communicate, and celebrate the collective and individual identities of members of a particular folk group or of the community. Cultural performances include the presentation and celebration of folk dance, folk music, and folk drama. During cultural performances, the cultural values, beliefs, aesthetics and identities of folk groups or community are put on display for themselves and for other folk groups, which pave the way for

action becomes a subject of doubts and questions, wherever unconditioned meaning becomes visible in works which have only conditioned meaning in themselves, there, culture is religious. Through the experience of the substantially religious character of culture, I was led to the border of culture and religion, which I have never deserted." Paul Tillich, *The Interpretation of History,* Trans. by Rasetzki and Talmey (New York: Charles Scribner's Sons, 1936), p. 49.

71 Walter Leibrecht, *Religion and Culture: Essays in Honour of Paul Tillich* (New York: Harper and Brothers Publishers, 1959), p. 17.

72 *Ibid.*, 17.

73 W. A. Visser 'T Hooft, ed. *The New Delhi Report: The Third Assembly of the World Council of Churches 1961,* (London: WCC Publications, 1962), p. 98.

interaction and learning with one another. The act and manner of these cultural performances can be seen as an ecumenical communication as they not only bring people together to display their artistic talents, but they also enable them to interact, express and communicate their common interests for the development and integrity of the society. They tend to occur at a specified time and place, and are different from normal everyday life.

3.4.2. Ecumenical Characteristic in Cultural Performances

Cultural performances have a lot of ecumenical characteristic, such as unity, interaction, fellowship, participation, contact, and learning. They are essential not only for strengthening the identity of a community or folk group, but they are also indispensable for retrieving their communitarian values. These noble virtues and characteristics can transcend all human barriers of oppressive values and discriminative social structures, to establish and construct a larger human community and build the integrity of all creation. The following are the ecumenical characteristic found in cultural performances:

i. Unity and Solidarity

The heart of ecumenism itself is unity in all realms of God's creation. As mentioned earlier, it promotes not only the unity of the Church, but also the integrity of all creation. In addition, it encourages unity in action namely that of extending sacrificial service for the people in the society. In this connection, it is well to quote Emilio Castro who says that Christians are called to present the witness of a united Church which can symbolize, anticipate and serve to bring about reconciliation and unity of all humanity and the whole of creation.[74] Such ecumenical characteristic of inclusiveness, unity, integrity and solidarity are intrinsic to cultural performances. Cultural performances and celebration of dances and music are always the means of promoting unity and social solidarity in society. In this connection, R. N. Sharma states that dancing is a means of not only uniting individuals into a harmonious whole, but also a means to maintain social solidarity.[75] At this point, dance can be seen as a powerful medium of communication for promoting interaction, unity, peace, justice and human dignity among the people in the Church and society.

The celebration and cultural performances of Naga folk dances, their music, songs, and drama, have inclusive and communitarian characteristic in which the community members and other folk groups are given the opportunity to be part of the celebration. According to Among Chang, when it is the celebration of cultural festivals and folk dances it is always a time for revitalizing friendship

74 Emilio Castro, *A Passion for Unity: Essays on Ecumenical Hopes and Challenges*. (Geneva: WCC Publications, 1992), p. 1.

75 R. N. Sharma, *Social and Cultural Anthropology*. (Delhi: Surjeet Publications, 2005), p. 58.

and relationship within the members of the community and with others.[76] Cultural performances have an important place in the community in terms of strengthening relationship and unity among the members of the community through their mutual participation with one another. Further, it motivates people to be sensitive to the needs and development of others in the society.

ii. Fellowship and Sharing

Cultural performances can bring people together, provide space for achieving reconciliation and strengthen relationship between individuals and groups of people in the community. Thereby, it may lead to a meaningful fellowship and sharing in which all the participants and the community members are equally respected and accepted. In this connection, it is well to note Hekhevi Achumi who says that dance performances can not only bring people together on a common platform but they can also establish reconciliation, unity, relationship and fellowship with one another.[77] They create a sense of openness and friendliness among the members in enabling them to express their emotions of joy, sorrow, good and bad memories. It is also a time for sharing their emotional feelings, and a time for sharing in table fellowship with one another that expresses their ongoing ecumenical journey of experiencing communion and fellowship with God and with one another. The Church's ecumenical endeavours aim to achieve wholeness and reconciliation into *Koinonia,* that is, communion and fellowship with God, with people, and communion with creation as a whole.[78]

iii. Cooperation towards Justice and Development

WCC's ecumenical concerns support and encourage the cooperation, participation and common witness of different churches in terms of sharing their resources of mission, inter-church aid and development for the purpose of liberation of the poor. Through this cooperative undertaking, different churches, religious orders and individuals may help the poor in different parts of the world achieve economic development, justice and self-reliance.[79] In addition, it can encourage not only inter-religious dialogue, but also provide space for practical cooperation between different religions based on respect and openness towards each other for

---

76 Interview with Mr. Among Chang, Asset. Director, Art & Culture, Government of Nagaland, Kohima, Nagaland, May 8th 2006.

77 Interview with Mr. Hekhevi Achumi, Public leader, Dimapur, Nagaland 4th May 2006.

78 Hans S. A. "Unity and Witness in an Ecumenical Context," in Vinod Victor, Leslie Nathaniel and P. Suryaprakash, eds., *Ecumenism: Prospects and Challenges.* (New Delhi: ISPCK, 2001), p. 29.

79 " As a matter of fact, significant ecumenical development right from the successful holding of the World Missionary Conference and to the rise of the International Missionary Council, the life and Work Movement, the Faith and Order streams of the WCC, have in many ways been developments that could be dubbed as co-operative ecumenism." O. L. Snaitang, *A History of Ecumenical Movement: An Introduction*, op. cit., pp. 150-151.

expressing their solidarity to the people in the society.[80] In this connection, such ecumenical characteristics of cooperation towards justice and development can be seen in the Naga cultural performances of folk dances and music as well.

Cultural performances serve not only the purpose of entertainment and socialisation, but also that of mutual co-operation and community participation among different villages, between different groups of people and between families and individuals for the welfare and development of the people in the society. Cultural performances can motivate people towards building human community that goes beyond the local community to include other communities. They promote and strive towards communitarian values of love, peace, justice, and development for each member in the community.

iv. Dialogical Communication

Dialogue has been promoted at various levels for the purpose of establishing ecumenical relationship in the Church and society. In this regard, Siga Arles states that the goal of dialogue has varied between dialogue for developing communal harmony and national integration, better perception and appreciation of each other's faiths and the attempt to learn multifaceted (multidimensional) godliness.[81] Cultural performances of folk dance and music while enabling people to experience unity, solidarity and fellowship with one another, can also provide space for establishing interaction and dialogical communication between participants and people in a person-to-person context.

At this juncture, one can say that the celebration of the Naga cultural festivals and folk dances can provide a common ecumenical space for communication and participation which is not available within the Church. In this connection, Mhonrao Kikon points out that in the Church, Christians of different denominations cannot come together and talk with each other, but outside the church, the celebrations of cultural festivals and dances could provide them space to meet each other where they can discuss and talk about the things in relation to individual and community life.[82] Here, people may talk about their feelings, personal experiences, aspirations, common problems, common interests, beliefs and practices of traditions and values. Such a space for dialogical communication can clarify their doubts and misunderstanding, and can help them to strengthen their friendship, relationship and cooperation with one another. In this regard, Samuel Meshack states that dialogical communication points towards acceptance,

---

80 Lukas Vischer, "Major Trends in the Life of the Churches," in John Briggs, Mercy Amba Oduyoye and Georges Tsetsis, eds. *A History of the Ecumenical Movement Volume 3 1968-2000.* (Geneva: WCC Publications, 2004), P. 42.

81 Siga Arles, "Glimpses of a Transit Missiology," in Brain Wintle, Emmanuel James, Jesudason B. Jeyaraj, Paul Mohan Raj, Richard S. Gnanakan, eds., *Work Worship Witness: Essays Dedicated to a Vision and a Visionary* (Bangalore: Theological Book Trust, 2003), p. 329.

82 Interview with Mr. Mhonrao Kikon, Dobashi, Wokha, 3rd May 2006.

humility, forgiveness, reconciliation, justice and love.[83] Thus, a true communion and ecumenism in true relationship can come out of acceptance, forgiveness, mutual understanding, reconciliation and love which are the components of true communication.

3.5. WCC's Ecumenical Concerns on Ecumenism and Culture

The concept of ecumenism goes beyond the unity of the Church to give importance to people's culture in terms of supporting their cultural values and identity, which is part of human dignity. The relationship between gospel and culture has been an important theme in ecumenical conversations. In this connection, WACC's *Statements on Communication* affirms that it supports people's basic culture and the need for cultural identity, which are part of the dignity of the human person.[84] It also respects all people including their cultural traditions, values, practices and behaviour, especially those in developing countries who are being challenged by the dominant culture or cultural groups.

The question of cultural identity was dramatically posed by Vatican II's instruction that the mass should normally be said in the vernacular.[85] It indicates that the Christian message should be expressed and communicated in the culture and language of the people, which can make it meaningful and relevant. The Bangkok Assembly 1973 stated that "Culture shapes the human voice that answers the voice of Christ. Many Christians who have received the gospel through Western agents continue to ask the question "Is it really I who answers Christ?...." How can we responsibly answer the voice of Christ without copying foreign models of conversion that are imposed and not truly accepted?[86] In fact, most of the early missionaries who worked in the third world countries had a negative attitude towards local culture. They were insensitive to other cultures and regarded them as "primitive" and "pagan." Thereby, they discouraged other cultures and propagated the gospel within the format of the western culture. In most cases, the gospel was not made relevant, it was not understood in the context of the people.

There were however, some who laboured tirelessly to preserve the local culture while communicating the gospel to the people. In this connection, L. Kijung states that in 1871, in Sibsagar, E. W. Clark, one of the early American

83 Samuel Meshack, "Communication, Ecumenism and Theological Education," in Samuel W. Meshack, Eberhard von de Heyde, eds., *Communication of the Gospel: In the Context of Globalisation, Religious Pluralism and Nationalism.* (Chennai: Gurukul Publications, 2002), p. 229.

84 WACC, *Statements on Communication*, (London: WACC, 1990), p. 10.

85 Birgitta Larsson and Emillio Castro, "From Mission to Mission," op. cit., p. 139.

86 Bangkok Assembly 1973: Minutes and Report of the Assembly of the Commission on World Mission and Evangelism of the World Council of Churches, December 31, 1972 and January 9-12, 1973, WCC, 1973, p. 73.

missionaries in Nagaland, and Godhula, an evangelist, wrote a Christian folk song and the Lord's Prayer in Ao Naga language with the help of Subongmeren and some other village elders from the Dekahaimong village.[87] There are two other Christian folk songs available, composed by the missionaries in those early days. For sometime they used those songs effectively in communicating the gospel to the people and they really shared their great interest in Naga folk songs.[88] However, later on, when the early missionaries found out that the Naga folk songs such as the warrior song, love song, and feast of merit, were rather dangerous to be used, as they stimulated the people to go for war, and created enmity, and immorality, they strongly opposed the use of folk songs by the Christians.[89] Consequently, the use of Naga folk songs, dances and cultural practices were discouraged in the church and society. It shows that in many cases, the early missionaries, especially in the developing countries, despite their positive efforts and attempts were not sympathetic to the local culture while presenting the gospel to the people. Because of this reason in addition to others, people could not understand and express the gospel meaningfully in their own context.

The Canberra assembly in 1991 has brought a renewed urgency into the ecumenical exploration of gospel and culture with a view to relate the gospel to contemporary attempts and to understand the faith in its context.[90] It indicates that the WCC's ecumenical concerns support and respect the local culture in terms of communicating and promoting the kingdom values of peace, justice, unity, development and human dignity by the people themselves through various means of cultural expressions such as folk dance, folklore, folk music, and folk drama. This shows that the traditional means of communication are powerful and effective especially in the developing countries not only in terms of bringing people together for interaction and participation with one another, but also communicating information, ideas and messages including Christian message in the Church and the society.

3.6. Theoretical Understanding of Dance

Dance in all cultural traditions has some rhythmic body movements which are accompanied by musical instruments, beating of drums or songs. Dancing is the art of composing steps with grace, precision and facility to the time and bars given in the music, just as music itself is simply the art of combining sounds and modulations so that they afford pleasure to the ear.[91] According to Young, dancing

87 L. Kijung, *Nokinketer Mongchen* (*The Place of Warrior*) (Guwahati: Christian Literature Centre, 1972), p. 27.

88 Temjen Jamir, op. cit., p. 38.

89 Interview with L. Kijung, Former Executive Secretary, ABAM, Mokokchung, June 7th 1993.

90 Birgitta Larsson and Emillio Castro, "From Mission to Mission," op. cit., p. 140.

91 Jean-Georges Noverre, *Letters on Dancing and Ballets,* Trans. By Cyril W. Beaumont (London: C. W. Beaumont, 1951), p. 3.

or dance consists of rhythmical movements of all parts of the body in accordance with some format of individual or concerted action which is expressive of emotion or ideas.[92] Amongst the primordial people dance has always some accompaniment of musical instruments or beating of drums by which the rhythm is emphasized. In this connection, creating a dance can include movements of human bodies with their capabilities and limitations, space and time within which bodies move to music, and other audible accompaniment, while scenery, costumes, and other paraphernalia tailored to the dance function, add to the nature of the occasion and the audience.[93] All these tools and factors can contribute not only to the understanding of dance but also may help in creating dance in the community for mutual interaction, participation and learning from one another.

Further, dance can be an individual or a group activity, which may be performed spontaneously or conformed to a preconceived idea or tradition. According to Richard Kraus, dance is an art performed by individuals or groups of human beings, in which the human body is the instrument and movement is the medium. The movement is stylized, and the entire dance work is characterized by form and structure.[94] In this connection, body language such as gestures and body movements is a basic means of expression and non-verbal communication. Dance in the North East India in general and Nagaland in particular, is a community dance which plays an important role in the society. Solo dance is very rare in the region. In this regard, it would help taking a look at the different kinds of dances and their roles and functions ritual dance, dance for entertainment and merry-making, dance as a means of communication and dance for social unity and integrity.

a) Ritual Character of Dance

Firstly, dance has a ritual character in relation to observance of various religious and social events in the community. In this connection, dance is always associated with community events and activities in relation to agriculture, harvest, birth, marriage, death, hunting, etc. In this regard, dance can be seen as a means of religious worship, as a form of ritual and with direct means of communication with the gods.[95] Every year during the observance and celebration of such ceremonies, festivals and community events, appropriate dances to the occasion will be performed. It can be observed that during the celebration of cultural festivals, dances of all kinds related to various community events are displayed.

92 Alexander Bell Filson Young, "Dance," in *The Encyclopedia Britannica*, Fourth Edition, Volume 7, Damascus to Education. (London: The Encyclopedia Britannica Company, Ltd., 1929), p. 14.

93 Kealiinohomoku, op. cit., p. 273.

94 Richard Kraus, *History of the Dance: In Art and Education* (Englewood Cliffs: Prentice-Hall, 1969), p. 13.

95 *Ibid.*, p. 12.

This brings the community members into closer contact with each other. Thus it not only has an important place in the community, but it also plays a vital role in terms of bringing people together for mutual participation and sharing.

b) Dance for Entertainment and Merry-making

Secondly, dance is always a means of merry-making, of celebration of life and enjoyment for the community members. It may be a form of popular entertainment, appealing to a broader audience than when it represents an art form with a high level of aesthetic worth.[96] It enables people to pour out their emotions by expressing their feelings of joy and sorrow. Such entertainment and enjoyment through the performances of dance may be instrumental in bringing the hearts of the people closer. In addition, dance can serve as a therapy in offering a form of physical and emotional release and rehabilitation.[97] Thereby, it may pave the way for experiencing healing and enjoying fellowship and interaction with one another in the society. The meaning of the dance to the dancers and their emotional involvement and attachment is very important.

c) Dance as a Means of Communication

Thirdly, dance apart from being a means of social entertainment and enjoyment, is a means of communication in the community. Dance can communicate and express all the community events and activities in relation to social and religious life in a meaningful way. Janesick says that dance is a type of dramatic storytelling, which has always fulfilled a basic need in society, expressing happiness, sadness, fear, joy and wishes.[98] It provides a common sphere for people to express their feelings and emotional experiences – intuitive perception and elusive truth,[99] while allowing them to exchange their ideas, information and message with one another. In this connection, it is worthwhile to remember Hanna when she says that dance is a part of cultural communication systems through which information and ideas can be conveyed to oneself and to others.[100] In fact, dance can motivate and encourage both the dancer and audiences with new insights and inspiration. Consequently, it may promote mutual understanding, sharing and relationship among the people in the society.

---

96 *Ibid.*, p. 12.

97 *Ibid.*, p. 12.

98 Valerie J. Janesick, "The Dance of Qualitative Research Design: Metaphor, Methodology and Meaning," in Norman K. Denzin and Yvonna S. Lincoln, eds. *Handbook of Qualitative Research.* (Thousand Oaks: Sage Publications, 1994), p. 217.

99 John Martin, "From the Dance: Dance as a Means of Communication," in Roger Copland and Marshall Cohen, eds., *What is Dance?: Readings in Theory and Criticism* (Oxford: Oxford University Press, 1983), p. 22.

100 Judith Lynne Hanna, op. cit., pp. 25-26.

d) Dance for Social Unity and Integrity

Fourthly, dance can be seen as a means of reaffirming social unity. For instance, peace-making dances and festival dances can provide a sense of social unity as a pleasurable accompaniment. In society, people want to be associated with one another and long for a sense of group fellowship and interaction. Dance provides people with a sense of satisfaction, unity and belongingness in the society.[101] It is through the performances of dances during the celebration of festivals, that the community members get the opportunity to come together on a common ecumenical sphere, through which they strengthen their friendship and relationship with one another. The sentiments of unity, harmony and friendship are primary functions of dance performances which can be experienced by the people during the celebration.[102] It may create and promote social solidarity and integrity among the people characterized by mutual or joint participation in singing, dancing, sharing and interaction with one another. In addition, it may enable them to focus their concern on common interests for the welfare and development of the people in the society.

3.7. Concluding Remarks

The theoretical understanding of ecumenism shows that ecumenism is not only concerned with the unity of the Church, but also with the wider ecumenism, which is the unity of the whole humankind including the unity and integrity of the whole creation. The objective and concept of ecumenism needs to go beyond the unity of the Church to include wider ecumenism for the promotion of freedom, development, peace, justice, and peaceful co-existence among all God's creations. In this connection, the present concept and practice of ecumenism is characterized by a church-centered, top- down model. It is always initiated by the high level church leadership that does not include the participation of the local churches and common people as well.[103] While using the theoretical concept of ecumenism, however, in such present ecumenical initiatives, we also need to go beyond the traditional models of unity and dialogue especially within the Church exploring whether there is any ecumenical space for communication outside the Church, to promote ecumenical relations between Christians of different denominations and also for the unity of the whole creation. In this connection, one can see a close relation between ecumenism and culture in terms of promoting contact, participation, relationship, and fellowship with one another in the community. In addition, in a developing country, especially in Nagaland, cultural performances of folk dances and music are powerful means

101 Alexander Bell Filson Young, op. cit., pp. 14-16.

102 Paul Spencer, "Introduction: Interpretations of the Dance in Anthropology," in Paul Spencer, ed., *Society and the Dance: The Social Anthropology of Process and Performance* (Cambridge: Cambridge University Press, 1985), pp. 14-15.

103 O. L. Snaitang, A *History of Ecumenical Movement*, op. cit., pp. 166-167.

of communication among the people, which may create an ecumenical sphere for the members of the community irrespective of their background, be it status, colour or religious affiliation.

The concept of ecumenical communication brings to light the obligation on all Christians. In this effort, creating a larger human community is crucial in which the Kingdom values of unity, peace, justice, love, and human dignity, can be promoted. In this connection, the mass media can be effective tools for promoting ecumenical communication, if the churches are able to provide adequate financial assistance, employing media workers for the same purpose. However, in reality, communication media have certain limitations as they provide mostly a one-way traffic communication with minimal feedback. As such, there are less opportunities for people's active participation. Thus it may not often serve the needs and aspirations of the people.

In the context of the developing countries, interpersonal communication, group media, folk media and alternative media of communication will be more effective for disseminating and exchanging ideas, information, Christian message and awareness education to one another. Thus, we need to rediscover and revitalize certain people-based indigenous communications, such as folk dance and music which are already available with the people, especially among the Nagas for they would be effective for creating an ecumenical common space for promoting participation and unity among the people in the Church and the society. In fact, they can facilitate more interactive and ecumenical communication towards promoting ecumenical relations and cooperation among Christians of different denominations. In the next chapter, folk dance in Naga culture will be taken up for discussion in which the different types of Naga folk dances, their functions and their basic understanding in their culture will be given importance. In addition, it will consider and show that the celebration of the Naga cultural festivals and folk dances can provide a cultural space for communication, participation and relationship among the people in the society.

Chapter 4

Naga Folk Dance as a Medium of Communication

The theological understanding of ecumenism and ecumenical communication has been discussed in the preceding chapter in which it is highlighted that such an understanding needs to go beyond the traditional model and practice of unity and dialogue within the Church, to include other ecumenical spheres, outside the Church in the community that can be created through the celebration of the cultural festivals and folk dances. In chapter 4, a discussion on the basic understanding of folk dance in Naga culture will be taken up, dealing with the various Naga folk dances, their meaning and functions that are operational in society. In this regard, the celebration of the Naga folk dances as a means of communication in society, how it may strengthen relationships and build a cohesive life for the people in the community will be highlighted.

4.1. Concept of Dance

Dance might have started as an experience of joy when an individual or a group of people shout and jump for joy over the birth of a new child, or the celebration of a festival. It is assumed that the community turned the jumps into a dance and the shouts into a song.[1] In this connection, Lois Ellfeldt states that the mythological origins of dance include instances of supernatural visitation, disguised teachers, dream-trance experience, or happenings at the eclipse of the sun and moon. Further, in terms of social origins, it may have evolved as expressions of communal

1 Alexander Bell Filson Young, "Dance," in The Encyclopedia Britannica. Fourteenth Edition, Volume 7, Damascus to Education. (London: The Encyclopedia Britannica Company, Ltd., 1929), p. 14.

life, joy, fears, hope for the future, and mimicry of animals.[2] At this point, one can understand that dance might have started through various expressions of human life and activities in the community.

a) Dance as a Performing Art

Unlike painting, sculpture, and architecture which can be available to the observer or audience in a finished form, the performing art such as dance, drama and music can be available to the audience in performance. In this regard, Ellfeldt points out that dance as an art form, as a performing art, serves a purpose beyond the immediacy of entertainment or spectacular display, recreation or therapy, celebration of national festival, or projection of personal resolution of personal skill.[3] Further, in this connection, when the dancer's imagination, idea, emotion, thought and skill are converted into this perceptible form or dynamic image, the work of dance art can be made available for public viewing. It can create and provide a common platform for interaction and participation among the people in the community. Such a performance of dance movement can be seen as the formulation, the interaction, dynamics, and rhythm of the movement which result in a symbolic image that is presented for the spectator‘s perception.[4] In this connection, one can say that the symbolic images in dance performance is a non-verbal language or body language which can be used not only for communicating information, attitude, ideas and messages to one another but also for promoting contact, relationship, learning and participation among the people in the society.

b) Dance as Non-Verbal Language

Dance is a non-verbal language in which the human body is the instrument. It is a means of communication in the society. In this regard, dance is a sequence of synchronized and rhythmic movements of the body and limbs, usually to the accompaniment of vocal or instrumental music, the beating of drums, or the clapping of hands.[5] Folk dance always has some accompaniment by which the rhythm is emphasized. Every dance has its own song or music, which is played or sung by the performers themselves or by the onlookers.

Dance movements employ all parts of the body, head, back, hips, feet, arms, fingers and even the facial muscles are brought into play. In this connection, Collingwood notes that body movement and gesture is central to all forms of expressions, even in rigidity and silence. It is the centre of all languages and is

---

2 Lois Ellfeldt, *Dance From Magic to Art.* (Dubuque: Wm. C. Brown Company Publishers, 1976), p. 12.

3 *Ibid.,* p. 186.

4 Ibid., pp. 186-187.

5 Alexander Bell Filson Young, op. cit., p. 14.

the primary form of communication.[6] Through these dance movements, the content of a particular dance is expressed and conveyed. In addition, through the attachment of meaning to movement, dance can be used to express the universal experiences of primary language such as joy or sadness and it can communicate the spiritual experiences of religious language.[7] These dance movements and gestures can be seen as a non-verbal language in dance which can convey a lot of messages to others. In this connection, must be understood by the group of people concerned, whether participants in the dance or as audience, so that the full potential of its function and purpose may be realized and achieved for the benefit and welfare of the people in the community.[8]

4.1.1. Relationship between Dance and Music

Although dance can be recognized and experienced as an independent art, the discussion of dance would be incomplete without some reference to music. In fact, dance and music are intrinsically related to each other. In this connection, music is said to have come from dance, from the rhythmic impulses of the human, and to have taken from dance its rhythmic form and structure. Because of its transient phase and its melodic and harmonic qualities, music is the most important of all the partners of the dance.[9] In fact, music and dance have rhythm as the basis of their movement, and, because of its temporal phase, music is able to express abstract aspects of the movement. Music can contribute guidance to dance creation. Through rhythmic structure, music can guide the rhythmic form of movement-responses and offer the setting for an idea.[10] In this regard, a musical composition may be used as the source of inspiration for a dance, and its structure may influence the structure of dance form related to it. Further, dance needs to be understood and developed independently of music, so that it may not lean too greatly upon music and retain its own vitality. In fact, dance can depend upon the dancer's own concepts to impel and control its movements.[11] Music can be used as an accompaniment to dance which may bring about a musical resemblance to the

---

6 R. H. Collingwood, The Principles of Art. (London: Oxford University Press,1974), pp. 244-245.

7 Stephanie S. Scott, "The Language of Liturgical Dance in African-American Christian Worship," in Journal of the Interdenominational Theological Centre, Volume XXVII, Numbers 1 and 2, Fall 1999 / Spring 2000, p. 250.

8 Sally Murphy, "Why Dance? A Functional Perspective," in Dance: The Study of Dance and the Place of Dance in Society, Proceedings of the VIII Commonwealth and International Conference on Sport, Physical Education, Dance, Recreation and Health, Conference '86 Glasgow, 18-23 July, (London: E.& F.N. Spon Ltd., 1986), p. 95.

9 Margaret N. H'Doubler, *Dance: A Creative Art Experience* (London: The University of Wisconsin Press, 1972), pp. 153-154. Also see, Judith Lynne Hanna,To Dance is Human: A Theory of Nonverbal Communication. (Austin: University of Texas Press, 1979). pp. 18-19.

10 Margaret N. H'Doubler, op. cit., p. 156.

11 *Ibid.*, p. 157.

meaning of the dance, rhythmically and emotionally. In this connection, Steve Reich points out that music and dance are basically related to each other and they must share the same rhythmic structure which will determine the length of the music and dance as well as when changes in both will occur.[12] The relationship between dance and music is natural and close, if it is understood and used rightly, it may be of mutual benefit and help for the community. As mentioned earlier, in Naga tradition music is associated with dance which is attached to the praises of God and can demonstrate a harmonious movement of dance and interaction among the people in the community. It may thus become not only a means of social entertainment and enjoyment for the members of the community but also can promote interaction and participation among the people in the society.

a) Dance for Social Entertainment

Dance is a means of enjoyment and entertainment for the members of the community. It enables people to express their happiness, sorrow, fear, or joy. It is also a channel for conveying wishes to one another. Such an entertainment comes through their mutual participation and attachment with one another. Further, occasions that are primarily social and recreational in nature usually provide opportunity for the general participation of all who attend, with the additional stipulation that they enjoy themselves.[13] In fact, within every individual in a community there is a conflict of desires. At the same time, there is a wish to outstand and a longing for a sense of group fellowship. Dancing provides the emotional satisfaction of getting expression to all these.[14] In addition, the dancer can display oneself to the best advantage and can do so in harmony with every other.

b) Communication Role of Dance

Dancing is a means of enjoyment, however, it is more than enjoyment and merry-making. In every society or community, dance has an important place as a means of communication. It provides people with a common platform to share and express information of different nature and messages through the various community events and cultural festivals. Dance can help members of the community to engage themselves with others and articulate their experiences, and share information and ideas meaningfully.

Dance is a communicative behaviour. Human beings communicate by both verbal and non-verbal behaviour, including dance. In this connection, it

12 Steve Reich, "Notes on Music and Dance," in Roger Copeland and Marshall Cohen, eds., What is Dance?: Readings in Theory and Criticism (Oxford: Oxford University Press, 1983), pp. 336-338.

13 Anya Peterson Royce, *The Anthropology of Dance* (Bloomington: Indiana University Press, 1977), p. 81.

14 Alexander Bell Filson Young, op. cit., pp. 14-15.

is worthwhile to quote Hanna when she says that dance is a physical instrument for feeling and thought and is sometimes a more effective medium than verbal language in revealing needs and desires of the people in the community.[15] Janesick states, dance as an art engages and develops human experience with a sense of meaning.[16]

Dance is thus a powerful agent of communication in communicating information, ideas, meaning to one another by all patterns of behaviour such as movements, posture, attitudes, and interactions between persons, the use of space, clothing, paraphernalia and the entire environment of the dance event.[17] In fact, dance systems use gestures, dynamics of human movements and theatrical devices such as costumes and equipment to convey message and information. In addition, movements in dance become standardized and patterned symbols, which the members of a society may understand as these symbols are intended to represent experiences in the external and psychic world.[18] Those signs and symbols, content, mode, and structure that are embedded in the dance event are indispensable for communicating and exchanging messages with one another. Through this medium of communication, people can learn and promote their cultural values, beliefs, attitudes and behaviour a group shares. It may also promote participation, interaction and relationship among the people in the community.

d) Dance for Relationship and Unity

Dance is a social activity which has a tradition of popular appeal.[19] The purpose and contribution of dance needs to be directed towards the continued well-being of a society in terms of promoting interaction, sharing, relationship and unity among the people. In this connection, Sally Murphy suggests that when dance is an integral part of everyday life and normal behaviour, then one may understand and learn about his or her culture or society in its fullest which also may be helpful for promoting cooperation and unity in the society.[20] For instance, social dance and performance dance are expressed in a variety of codes and bodily aesthetics which communicate not only information and ideas, but also bring people together for sharing, interaction, and learning from one another in the community.

---

15 Judith Lynne Hanna, op. cit., p. 4.

16 Valerie J. Janesick, "The Dance of Qualitative Research Design: Metaphor, Methodolatry, and Meaning," in Norman K. Denzin and Yvonna S. Lincoln, eds., Handbook of Qualitative Research. (Thousand Oaks: Sage Publications, 1994), p. 210.

17 Joann Marie Wheeler Kealiinohomoku, *Theory and Methods for an Anthropological Study of Dance* (Ann Arbor: University Microfilms International, 1981), p. 118.

18 Judith Lynne Hanna, op. cit., p. 4.

19 Helen Thomas, *Dance, Modernity and Culture: Explorations in the Sociology of Dance* (London: Routledge, 1995), p. 3.

20 Sally Murphy," Why Dance? A Functional Perspective," in *Dance: The Study of Dance and the Place of Dance in Society*, op. cit., p. 95.

Dancing can be seen as a means of reaffirming social unity that may happen on all occasions which are socially important in relation to birth, marriage, death, initiations, hunting, building of a communal house, and peacemaking. Dance as an art serves as a bridge between the experience of the individuals and the community. In other words, dance forces us to think about how human beings are related to each other in their respective work and community.[21] Dance in general and folk dance in particular, brings people together on a common platform to express their solidarity with one another. Thereby, it strengthens relationship and unity among the people in the community.

4.1.2. Dance as a Symbolic Ritual

Dance can be seen as a symbolic ritual or a symbolic way of life of people that expresses the essence of their community life, cultural values, traditions and practices. According to James Carey, dance is a process of mapping space that transforms vacant space of social life into a featured environment, which he calls as "ritual dance."[22] Ritual dance is related to daily activities of environment in a given space. Dance is capable of mapping a particular space in a situation to clarify and bridge it by providing guidance and understanding. The movements of dance can provide suitable steps of certain descriptions about a particular space of our world-view depending upon where we live in relation to social, political, cultural, religious and economic life.

Dance is often an integral part of religious life of a people in society. It is frequently used as a form of worship and reverence. Most of the tribal dances are associated with festivals, events and ceremonies. Through the celebration of these dances, they worshiped God and invoked his blessings for the whole community members. Dance, which has both the vertical and horizontal dimensions, may be seen as the symbolic ritual that may guide the behaviour of the people in the society. In fact, one may understand the symbolic representation of the space even while learning the dance that may guide one's behaviour. Thus, dance can be seen as a symbolic form of communication in terms of both expressing people's way of life, their religious experiences, and also bringing them together for fellowship, learning, and unity. Dance has an important place in the Christian Scriptures. In fact, Christians can experience God and understand him in dance. In this connection, the biblical understanding of dance may highlight that the sacred

---

21 Valerie J. Janesick, "The Dance of Qualitative Research Design: Methaphor, Methodolatry, and Meaning," in Norman K. Denzin and Yvonna S. Lincoln, eds., Handbook of Qualitative Research, op. cit., p. 217.

22 "The map stands as a representation of an environment capable of clarifying a problematic situation. It is capable of guiding the behaviour and simultaneously transforming undifferentiated space into a configure – that is known, apprehended, understood – space." James Carey, op. cit., p. 27.

dance has been part of the Christian life in expressing and communicating their faith as a community of believers.

4.2. The Basic Understanding of Dance in Naga Culture

Dance has been understood as purposeful and intentionally expressed, with rhythmical non-verbal communicative body movements that are culturally patterned and endowed with aesthetic values.[23] In fact, dance derives from human movements and consciousness and therefore, Naga folk dances can be seen as the rhythmic movements and expressions of their way of life. Their purpose and intention, associated with their social, religious and cultural environment are expressed through varied dance movements. In this connection, it is worthwhile to quote Fraleigh who says that dance is an activity in human nature as moving beings and it is communicated in its environment and culture.[24] Dance can be found almost in all the recognized societies, serving the needs of the people in various specified contexts and situations. However, the form it takes and the meanings attached to it may broadly differ from society to society, as it is largely conditioned by each cultural milieu and practice.

4.2.1. Folk Dance as Non-Material Culture

The term *culture* from the Latin *cultura* stemming from *colere*, meaning "to cultivate," generally refers to patterns of human activity and the symbolic structures that give such activities significance and importance.[25] Culture can be understood as learned human behaviour patterns and perceptions which can be shared and exchanged with one another in the society. In this connection, Edward B. Tylor defines culture as "that complex whole which includes knowledge, belief, art, morals, law, custom, and any other capabilities and habits acquired by man as a member of a society."[26] Here, culture can be seen as the way of life, codes of manners, dress, language, habits, arts, beliefs, institutions, rituals, norms of behavior such as law and morality that are passed down from generation to generation. It can provide space for communication, interaction learning, and participation among the people in the society.

Further, anthropologists most commonly use the term "culture" to refer to the universal human capacity to classify, codify and communicate their experiences symbolically. In this regard, Raymond Williams points out that

23 Judith Lynne Hanna, *To Dance is Human: A Theory of Nonverbal Communication*, (Austin: University of Texas Press, 1979), p. 19.

24 Sondra Horton Fraleigh, 'Family Resemblance,' in Sondra Horton Fraleigh and Penelope Hanstein, eds. Researching Dancing: Evolving Modes of Inquiry (Pittsburgh: University of Pittsburgh Press, 1999), p. 3.

25 http://en.wikipedia.org/wiki/Culture Browsed on 10-02-2008.

26 Edward B. Tylor, *Primitive Culture: Researches into the Development of Mythology, Philosophy, Religion, Art, and Custom*. (London: John Murray. 1871). p. 1.

culture is manifested in music, dance, literature, lifestyle, painting and sculpture, theatre and film and similar things.[27] It indicates that culture refers not only to consumption of goods and material objects, but also to immaterial things such as art, science, moral system, music, dance and drama which give them meaning and to the social relationships and practices among the people in the society. In fact, culture is continuously evolving products of people[28] interacting with each other. At this point, one can say that culture is a powerful means for human survival, social interaction, communication, participation, and learning for the members of the society, promoting social relationship and cultural identity among them. Culture can be classified into two, such as the material culture and the non-material culture.

i. First, **material culture** refers to the physical objects, resources, and spaces that people use to define their culture. These include homes, neighborhoods, cities, schools, churches, synagogues, temples, mosques, offices, factories and plants, tools, means of production, goods and products, stores, and so forth.[29] In this connection, Thomas Menamparampil points out that the material culture includes everything that people have, which refers to material possessions such as housing, crops, cooking pots, beds, hoes, plows, handicraft, clothes, tools, and other human products.[30] All of these physical aspects of a culture can help to define its members' behaviors and perceptions in the society. Further, they can communicate the living situation, habits, practices, rituals, and the way of life of the people.

ii. Second, **non-material culture** refers to the non-physical ideas that people have about their culture, including beliefs, values, rules, norms, morals, language, organizations, and institutions.[31] In this connection, Gary Ferrao states that the non-material culture includes everything that people think in their heads such as ideas, values, and attitudes. It also comprises the behaviour patterns which

27 Raymond Williams, *Keywords: A Vocabulary of Culture and Society* (New York: Oxford University Press, 1983), pp. 87-93 and 236-238.

28 "Culture is a powerful tool for survival, but it is a fragile phenomenon. It is constantly changing and easily lost because it exists only in our minds. Our written languages, government, buildings, and other man-made things are merely the products of culture. They are not culture in themselves. For this reason, archaeologists cannot dig up culture directly in their excavations. The broken pots and other artefacts of ancient people that they uncover are only material remains that reflect cultural patterns-they are things that were made and used through cultural knowledge and skills." http://anthro.palomar.edu/culture/culture. htm Browsed on 03-02-2006.

29 "Sociology: Material and Non-material Culture." cliffsnotes.com/WileyCDA/CliffsReviewTopic Browsed on 07-02-2008.

30 Archbishop Thomas Menamparampil, *The Challenge of Cultures: Cross-Cultural Relationships, Conflicts, Inculturation* (Bombay: St. Pauls Publications, 1996), p. 25.

31 cliffsnotes.com/WileyCDA/CliffsReviewTopic/Material-and-NonMaterial-Culture.topic. Browsed on 07-02-2008.

mean everything that people do in the society.[32] In addition, music, drama, dance, and language, can be seen under the category of non-material culture. Therefore, the celebration of Naga cultural festivals and folk dances can be considered as an integral part of their non-material culture. Such a non-material culture has an important place in the society and it plays a vital role in terms of socializing with one another, communicating information, and integrating people into a harmonious social life.

4.2.2. Functions of Folk Dance

Dance may function in a number of different ways both between and within the societies. Although dance often performs a number of functions simultaneously within a society, some functions will be more prominent than others. Folk dance as a medium of communication plays various important functions in the society maintaining and expressing the emotions, ideas and way of life of the people. In this connection, it is worthwhile to remember Richard Kraus when he says dance is commonly performed to musical or other rhythmic accompaniment, and has as a primary purpose the expression of inner feelings and emotions, although it is often performed for social, ritual, entertainment, or other purposes.[33] Dance may also remain as a means of popular entertainment in the society. In addition, the function of a dance can be seen in its cultural context, found in their rituals, art forms, games, etc. identifying their basic aesthetic intention embodied in the movement.[34] For instance, the height and suddenness of jumping are aesthetic properties that could be intended in any dance movement, such as their war dance, ritual dances, and festival dances. It could be the total context that establishes its purpose and communicates a particular message to the people in the community. The functions of these dances could be psychological, social, religious, political and educational, playing vital roles in the society.[35]

i. Psychological Function

The psychological function of the dance can enable people to release their emotional tensions to enjoy life meaningfully in relation to others. Hanna states that dance is psychological, involving cognitive and emotional experiences affected by and affecting an individual's personal and group life.[36] It may serve as an outlet for self-expressiveness and personal creativity. In this connection, Anya Peterson Royce points out that dances serve the very important function of

---

32 Gary Ferraro, *Cultural Anthropology: An Applied Perspective*, op. cit., pp. 18-20.

33 Richard Kraus, op. cit., p. 13.

34 Sondra Horton Fraleigh, 'Witnessing the Frog Pond,' in Sondra Horton Fraleigh and Penelope Hanstein, eds. Researching Dance: Evolving Modes of Inquiry (Pittsburgh: University of Pittsburgh, 1999), p. 193.

35 Ibid., pp. 292-293.

36 Judith Lynne Hanna, op. cit., p. 4.

psychological release or outlet. It also serves as a means of knowing and coping with socially induced tensions and aggressive feelings. It is one of the most effective vehicles for psychological release because its instrument is the human body.[37] Human movements cannot be separated from their emotional feelings, for the inner feelings are enacted and expressed through such movements. Regarding this, Fraleigh points out that there are various forms of feelings of the humankind that may be manifested in and through human movements. They are beautiful, expressive, and soothing.[38]

Folk dance is almost a universal language among the indigenous people in general and among the Nagas in particular, providing them with an outlet for expressing emotions of joy and sorrow in addition to being a source of exercise and recreation. In this connection, Richard Kraus states that 'dance offers an important social and recreational outlet, both as a means of restoring oneself physically, and of finding social acceptance within group participation.'[39] It also has a capacity of bringing the whole community on a common platform promoting an opportunity for mutual sharing of such emotions with one another. Thus, it goes beyond the premises of enjoyment and merry-making to play a vital integrating role in the society.

ii. Social Function

Dance has an important place in the society as a means of bringing people together for mutual participation and fellowship with one another. In this regard, dance can be seen as a social behaviour. Social life is necessary for human mastery of the environment in which dance reflects and influences patterns of social organization in relation to relationships between individuals in groups and among groups.[40] In this connection, Kealiinohomoku points out that dance is social in that it is usually manifested by a group or for a group. Dance experiences are interactive, and even audiences are rhythmically compelled by empathy.[41] Most societies have dances that are considered appropriate to particular ages, kinship, friendship, ethnic background, etc., that enhance their social relationship.[42] Dance can play a significant function in enabling the participants in articulating and reinforcing their social relationships, thus building unity among the members of the society.[43]

Consciously or unconsciously, Dance remains a means of reaffirming social unity, occurring on all occasions which are socially important, such as attainment

---

37 Anya Peterson Royce, *The Anthropology of Dance*, op. cit., p. 81.

38 Sondra Horton Fraleigh, 'Family Resemblance,' op. cit., pp. 10-11.

39 Richard Kraus, *History of the Dance*, op. cit., p. 12.

40 Judith Lynne Hanna, op. cit., p. 4.

41 Joann Marie Wheeler Kealiinohomoku, *Theory and Methods for an Anthropological Study of Dance* (Ann Arbor: University Microfilms International, 1981), p. 170.

42 Anya Peterson Royce, op. cit., p. 80.

43 Gary Ferraro, op. cit., p. 293.

of puberty, death, initiation, and during group activities such as hunting and fishing, building of a communal house, peace-making, etc.[44] There are also dances associated with war and raid, with sowing, harvesting and rain-making, courtship and marriage. Many of these dances have religious and economic motives and all serve to foster a sense of solidarity in the community. Thus it preserves and strengthens their cultural values and identities in the society.

iii. Religious Function

Dance has a religious function that helps people to communicate with supernatural forces through various methods and expressions. In most societies, people witness to the practices of dance as a religious activity right down to the present day. In addition, dance had and still continues to have an important part as a ritual of most of the world religions.[45] In primal religious tradition, people express their religious feelings and emotions through dance.[46] The fundamental purpose of religious rites and rituals is to express something to God and to get something done. In this connection, Douglas Kennedy points out that the religious aspects of dance generally has as its purpose communication with the unseen forces which provided food, promoted fertility, regulated the weather, gave good fortune in warfare, and thus controlled tribal welfare and human survival.[47] At this point, dance can be seen as a means of worship of God. The aroma of sacrifice, the humble petitions and the expressions of a sacred dance are believed to prevail upon them.[48] In this connection, the Nagas perform a ritual of rain making to invoke rain for the crops. However, the ceremonies vary from tribe to tribe and from village to village. Some observe the ritual ceremonies with movements of dance and music, and some follow a simple ritual ceremony. For instance, during this festival of the Aoling Monyu of Konyak Nagas, the people worship their traditional God, known as 'Wangwan' which means the Spirit of blessing or God of blessing, invoking his blessings for the whole year.

iv. Political Function

In most cultures, dance has been used in various religious and political contexts, for achieving its specific purpose. Dance is a powerful medium that can express political values and attitudes, showing allegiance to political leaders, and

44 Alexander Bill Filson Young, "Dance," in The Encyclopedia Britannica, Fourth Edition, Volume 7, Damascus to Education, (London: The Encyclopedia Britannica Company, Ltd. 1929), p. 14.

45 J. G. Davies, *Liturgical Dance: An Historical, Theological and Practical Handbook* (London: SCM Press LTD, 1984), p. 4.

46 Gary Ferraro, op. cit., pp. 292-293.

47 Douglas Kennedy, *England's Dances* (London: G. Bell & Sons, Ltd., 1950), pp. 31-32.

48 Henry H. Presler, *Primitive Religions in India: A Textbook on the Primitive Religious Type among India's Tribals*, (Bangalore: Christian Literature Society, 1971), p. 108.

controlling behaviour.[49] It plays a political behaviour and function in expressing its political values and meaning in the life of the people in the society. Dance is a forum for articulating political attitudes and values. It is a forum for training which carries over to important positions in other spheres of life, and acts as a vehicle of control, adjudication, and change.[50]

Naga folk dance plays a vital political function in the society in terms of articulating and promoting political values and attitudes. In this context, dance is used as a means of reciprocal communication without any selfish motive behind it. For instance, a warrior dance bringing the head of the vanquished to the village[51] is honoured by the whole community members for his great achievement. Similarly, during the feast of merit, the rich donor is praised and honoured by the members of the community, in return for his great contributions to the society. In both cases, they are given praises and honour with befitting songs and dances, politically and socially recognized by the society. Through these dance rites and performance the people express and communicate support for their leaders. Thus, they become influential leaders among the people in the society. In addition, the celebration of such festivals and dances has also been linked with the worship of God, giving thanks and asking his blessings for the whole community members in general, and for the individual and the family members in particular.

v. Educational Function

Dance is often used as a means to educate: "to draw forth," *to educe* (or lead forth as a river). Dance may be a vehicle for drawing out individual responses to movement of creative dance and establishing group cohesiveness (folk forms).[52] In this connection, if dance is to educate people, it must be emotional, intellectual, spiritual and physical in developing and capitalizing every possible resource, selecting and integrating the contribution into a totality. It serves as a means of education, in the sense that it is taught to achieve the specific purposes of education within a given society, just as art, music, or theater are taught as cultural forms.[53] Dance can function as a means of giving education and free opportunity to every child for experiencing the contributions it can make to his developing personality and his growing artistic nature.[54] It may help every individual person

49 Garry Ferraro, op. cit., p. 292.

50 Judith Lynne Hanna, op. cit., p.4.

51 "By taking a head from another village, it was believed that a new injection of vital and creative energy would come to the aggressor's village when he did so. This was valuable for human and animal fertility. It stimulated the crops to grow better, especially, when the head that was that of a woman with long hair." Verrier Elwin, Nagaland (Guwahati: Spectrum Publications, 1997), p. 11.

52 Sondra Horton Fraleigh, op. cit., p. 10.

53 Richard Kraus, op. cit., p. 12.

54 Margaret N. H'Doubler, op. cit., p. 59.

not only educating and developing him or her in all round development in terms of disciplining, training of one's energies and attaining of skill in execution, but also can enable him or her to contribute towards betterment and welfare of the members of the community. In addition, it may also promote their cultural identity, values and practices in the society. In this connection, it is worthwhile quoting Lois Ellfeldt when he says that 'if by education we mean meeting and increasing the potential of the student, helping him to find relationships, encouraging him to broaden his views, and providing opportunities for enrichment and creativity, then the dance experience will stress the process of searching, learning, experimenting, improvising, organizing, creating, and sharing, rather than simply performing as the end product of the dance.'[55]

There is a transmission and exchange of communitarian values in the educational process of dance. Folk dance can be seen as being transmitted from one generation to another by continuous immersion rather than by formal education. It plays as a medium of education, learning and entertainment in the society. In this connection, Eilers says that dance, drama, mime, etc., can convey educational, moral and social messages to the people in the society.[56] Educationally, dance passes on the cultural traditions and values, and beliefs from one generation to the next.[57] In the Naga society, folk dance is still considered as one of the media of education and learning among the people through which they can preserve their own identity and also maintain, and continue their customs, mores, values and practices with one another from one generation to the next.

Dance in general, and folk dance in particular, can exert various significant functions in the socio-cultural, political and religious life of the people. In this connection, it can promote interaction, participation, unity, religious favour and development in the society. It indicates an emerging perspective of folk dance in ecumenical communication for the promotion of peace, justice, unity and development in the society. The Naga folk dances are associated with their cultural festivals and important social events, portraying their customs, behaviours and social life.

4.2.3. The Place of Folk Dances in Naga Festivals

The love of dancing is a universal passion among the tribes in every part of the world.[58] The Nagas are very fond of dance and music, which are close to their hearts. They celebrate feasts and cultural festivals with dances. The performances of such dances continue for hours with steps slowing down or quickening moving

55 Lois Ellfeldt, op. cit., p. 115.

56 Franz-Josef Eilers, *Communicating Between Cultures: An Introduction to Intercultural Communication* (Indore: Satprakashan Sanchar Kendra, 1993), p. 129.

57 Gary Ferraro, op. cit., p. 293.

58 W. Robinson, *A Descriptive Account of Assam, to which is Added a Short Account of Neighbouring Tribes* (London: Oxford University Press, 1841), p. 395.

round and round, forward and backward, rocking and curving and turning, as human figures seem to merge in one graceful serpentine line.[59] Folk dance is an adequately articulated, integral part of the Naga festivals. The indispensable ingredient of Naga festival is that the people enjoy vigorous dances in colourful costumes. Since Naga dance is a community dance, it is a social necessity, and everyone needs to know dancing. That is why Nagas are called born dancers.[60] Celebration of folk dance makes the festival vivacious and full of life. During the festival, both men and women wear their best traditional dresses. For this purpose they work hard throughout the year, which strengthens their skilled labour such as weaving, and handicrafts (appendix I B). Each festival and ceremony has its own appropriate dances and meanings that make the celebration complete and significant.

4.2.4. The Different Types and the Meaning of Naga Folk Dances

Etymologically the term "dance" in Ao Naga language is *Tsüngsangba,* and it comes from two words *Tsüng* (mystery), meaning the mystery of God (Tsüngrem) in relation to rain, thunder, sun, moon, etc., and *Sang* (praise) which means the praise of God in relation to the whole created order. In addition, it has another meaning in its roots *Tsüng* (leg) and *Sang* (movement or stretch). In combination of these two 'root meanings,' if we take it literally, *Tsüngsangba* (dance) means the praise of God with movements of feet. This harmonious movement of dance and communication among people and praise to God has in itself an ecumenical significance.

Folk dance itself is people's dance, originated by the people themselves for the purpose of entertainment and recreation. In this connection, Lois Ellfeldt says that folk dance is a communal, sharing, participation activity in which the people all join.[61] It is closely associated with folk song, folktales, language, habits, weather, environment, food, and politics. It also strengthens their social relationship and participation with one another in the community. There are different types of folk dances associated with festivals, and with events such as birth, marriage, harvest, death, hunting, etc. Naga folk dance itself is a community dance that includes everyone in the community and promotes communitarian values. In this connection, Quiggin states that many folk dances have religious and economic motives and they foster the sense of solidarity in the community.[62]

59 M. Horam, *Nagas Old Ways and New Trends* (New Delhi: Cosmos Publications, 1988), p. 52.

60 R. R. Shimray, *The Origin and Culture of Nagas,* (New Delhi: Published by Mrs P. Shimray, 1985), p. 134.

61 Lois Ellfeldt, *Dance From Magic to Art* (Dubuque: Wm. C. Brown Company Publishers, 1976), p. 119.

62 Alison Hingston Quiggin, "Dancing," in Chambers' Encyclopedia. New Edition. Volume IV, Confirmation – Educational Psychology. (London: George Newnes Limited, 1959), p. 361.

The Nagas have a variety of folk dances, and the style varies from one tribe to another. There are different types of dances, such as, festival dance, war dance, feast of merit dance, mimic dance, etc. They are associated with their cultural festivals and other community events. Each type of dance has its distinctive character, form and meaning attached to it. It plays an important role in communicating meanings, ideas, and serves the needs of the people in the society. During the celebration of cultural festivals and dances both men and women can dance together or separately. Since the dance in Naga culture is a community dance and it is part of their life, it is customary for them to dance together in groups. During the festival, they do dance in circles, semicircles, lines and other formations in accordance with the format of each dance (see appendix I B). The following are the important dances of the Nagas, taken for discussion below.

i. Festival Dance

All the folk dances have their specific purposes and objectives, which are associated with particular actions, or events or places. Festival dances are usually performed during the observance of various festivals all through the year. Sometimes a festival dance is interchangeably used with the seasonal dance as it takes place during a particular season or occasion. During the fore-parents' time, each and every type of folk dance was performed according to the appointed time and purpose. However, today all the different types of folk dances including the festival dances are displayed and performed only during the celebration of various Naga festivals and on important occasions. The researcher wants to discuss a few selected festival dances of the Nagas here.

a) Merry-making Dance

It is a seasonal dance which is usually performed during the celebration of cultural festivals. This dance is popular among the Ao Nagas. Moatsu is one of the major festivals of the Ao Nagas that marks the retreat of spring and the beginning of summer, which is celebrated from May 1-3 every year. According to Sangyusang, during this festival, as a part the tradition of celebration, people take out a procession wearing their traditional attires and headgears with *daos* and spears in hand dancing on the street from one end of the village to the other. This dancing procession is known as Sangbangtur. The dancers will move forward and backward turning in different directions according to the rhythm. The dance does not have a song but goes along with the rhythmic beating of the drum. There is another type of this dance, which is accompanied by songs, either a love song (Sungonaro ken) or songs of praise of others.[63] This festival is intended to appease the deities and to get blessings conferred on their good crops. During this

63 Interview with S. Sangyusang Pongen, Ungma village, on May 14th 2006. Also See, G. K. Ghosh, *Tribals and Their culture in Manipur and Nagaland*, Vol. III (New Delhi: Ashish Publications House, 1995), p. 49.

occasion, boys and girls called *Zunga* of different age groups, rejoice themselves in singing and dancing and merrymaking.[64] This dance is performed spontaneously with all the movements coherently. The meaning conveyed through this dance is, let us move together and dance.

b) Aoling Dance

Aoling dance is another festival dance of the Konyak Nagas, which is performed during the celebration of the Aoling Monyu festival. It is observed from April 1-6 as Aoling Festival. The celebration of the festival and dance is associated with their agricultural operation.[65] This festival marks the end of the dry season with sowing of the fields and the expectation of beginning a new season with fresh vegetations. It may be called the New Year festival. The main objective of this festival is to celebrate and worship Wangwan, the Spirit of blessing. From the first day, people invite Wangwan, giving thanks and invoking his blessings upon the crops for the whole year through their singing, dancing, feasting and other rituals. Then, on the last day, they bid farewell to Wangwan till the next year when they meet again.[66]

c) Harvest Dance

In Naga cultural tradition, harvest dance is performed during the festivals that fall just before the beginning of harvest and after the harvest is over. They celebrate the festivals and dances with great jubilation and enthusiasm. During the festivals and dances, they ask for God's protection for the harvest and also thank him for granting plentiful harvest for the members of the whole community.

d) Coronation of Konyak 'Angh' Dance

The coronation dance of Konyak Nagas is performed during the celebration of two festivals of coronation, namely, 1) the Village 'Noktoh 'Ahng' festival, and 2) the Range 'Pongwan 'Ahng' festival. Chungwang is the Chief Ahng.[67] These festivals are celebrated for two days, for the Selection and Coronation of the 'Ahng.' The Feast of merit celebration also takes place along with these two celebrations. During the celebration of these festivals, all the community members and other villagers are invited and welcomed. Together, they enjoy a grand community feast,

64 B. B. Ghosh, *Nagaland District Gazetteers: Mokokchung District* (Kohima: Government of Nagaland, 1979), p. 80.

65 Interview with Y. Leiphoa Konyak, Dimapur, on May 19th 2006.

66 Konyak Cultural Troupe, Mon, 'Aoling Dance,' in Department of Art & Culture, ed. *Echoes of Nagaland: Hornbill Festival*, 2005 (Kohima: Department of Art & Culture, 2005), p. 17.

67 "The Konyak is culturally rich, philosophically deep and artistic. Konyak have the set of intelligence and philosophy that keep their identity and social harmony. Thus, politically, the Konyak is known for its monarchical system called Ahng-Wanglam. The Monarchical head is called Ahng who rules in a hereditary system, although a nominal headship system is also found in some part of Konyak land." Ibid., p. 17.

singing, dancing and merry making.[68] In addition, both men and women dance together to mark the occasion.

ii. War Dance

War dance is one of the most striking and prominent dances among the Nagas. There are some war dances in which both men and women dance together and there are certain other dances only for men. In all these war dances, men fully arrayed in their war-dress enter with great enthusiasm to play their several parts. They exhaust themselves by perpendicular jumps and side leaps, through which they exhibit considerable agility. On the whole, it can be observed that their gesture, their countenance, and their voices are exceedingly wild, and well adapted to their various situations.[69] During the fore-parents time, these dances were used for self-glorification and for denouncing others. Today, these dances are performed not for bringing the past memories of such raids and enmity, but mainly for the purpose of the community participation, for learning from one another and to preserve their rich culture. There are different types of war dances; however, what they all have in common is that they portray the bravery and skills of the warrior, signifying their might and great achievements.

a) Youth Warrior Dance

It is also a seasonal dance, which exhibits their rich traditional attires. The dance is displayed by both men and women, forming two lines facing each other and moving backward and forward. This dance does not have the accompaniment of a song. However, the drum gives the rhythm and the tempo to the dance movement.

b) Shield Dance

This dance is always performed by men folk with shields. War songs are sung along with the dance, depicting their victorious performances and achievements. In addition, the dance displays the bravery and war skills of the warriors.

c) Spear Dance

Spear dance is a solo dance. The dancer holds the spear horizontally at both its ends. Then, he displays a high jump over it and does it without a break as much as possible. He repeats the same according to the tune and rhythm of a drum. Throughout the dance, the warrior tries to show that he is now brave and strong enough to face his enemy.

---

68 Interview with Y. Leiphoa Konyak, Dimapur, on May 19th 2006.

69 W. Robinson, op. cit., p. 395.

d) Cock Fight Dance

This dance is performed by two warriors. The dance goes along with the beating and with the rhythm of a drum. In such a dance, men with splendid physique and rippling muscles holding spears and javelins with shields, act out the story of a battle – the advance, the retreat, the wielding of weapons and the defence accompanied by terrific howls and war whoops or cries.[70]

iii. Peace-Making Dance

This dance is performed during the time of making reconciliation with other rival villages or people. The participants come in full traditional dresses and perform dances appropriate to the theme. Treaties are made within their own tribe or with other neighbouring tribes, usually in the month of January. This kind of treaty is celebrated with a great feast, and both the parties agree not to fight and never to hunt for the heads of each other. during such a celebration, both the parties come together and dance with songs related to the treaty in a peaceful manner.[71] During the celebration, people sing appropriate songs, dance together and enjoy the feast. On the closing day, the host family and village send the other villagers with portions of meat, pig's or cow's legs and those of Mithun (Bison).

iv. Feast of Merit Dance

This dance is performed during the festival of the Mithun sacrifice in front of or inside the house of a rich man who sacrificed the Mithun and offered the feast to all the community members. It is an occasion for merriment for the members of the community. Among the Ao Nagas, the dance is performed inside the house of the giver of the feast. It consists of a circle of men and women standing alternately with linked arms chanting and moving round slowly in time to the singing.[72] According to M. Busham, among the Khiamniungan Naga tribe, such feasts of merit dance and songs are performed in a rich man's house on the occasion of his offering a feast to all the villagers. During the feast, all the community members are invited to sing and dance. Roof and ceiling are removed from the house. People sit over there to watch the singing and dancing. This celebration continues for three days.[73] Through their dance, the Chang Nagas communicate saying that, even the stone and the wood dies and fade away, but the work they have done stays alive and will live forever. This dance is mainly performed for a wealthy

---

70 Alongla P. Aier, ed., *From Darkness To Light* (Kohima: Nagaland Baptist Church Council, 1997), p. 11.

71 Interview with Among Chang, Assistant Director, Art & Culture, Government of Nagaland, Kohima, on 8 May 2006.

72 J. P. Mills, *The Ao Nagas* (Bombay: Oxford University Press, 1973), p. 158. Also See, G. K. Ghosh, op. cit., p. 49.

73 Interview with M. Busham, Pastor, Khiamniungan Baptist Church, Dimapur on 5th May 2006.

person.[74] The songs and dances are dedicated not only in honour of the donor, but also to promote mutual sharing and participation among the people for their communitarian life.

v. Mimetic Dance

This dance is performed in high spirits and in moments of joy. It is done with imitations or mimics of the moments and characters of animals, birds and even humans. Regarding this, Robinson has commented that all the Naga dances are imitations of some actions; and though the music by which they are regulated is extremely simple and tiresome to the ear being dull and monotonous, some of their dances appear wonderfully expressive and animated.[75] The dance is performed along with an appropriate song or a rhythm of music. This dance is not only the imitation of the characters of animals, but it also communicates moral lessons and messages to all humankind. The following are some of the examples of this dance.

a) Fish Dance

It is an Ao traditional dance imitated or learned from the movement of the fish in the river. This dance is performed imitating the fish swimming in a big river. This dance is displayed under the conditions of good weather during Moatsü festival. In this connection, J. P. Mills says that, 'In this the dancers move in columns of four formation in quick time to the tapping of the drum, the column wheeling about in all directions, like a fish swimming.'[76] The dancers wear three hornbill feathers on their head. A shawl is fastened around their waists to which each one holds. The dance is characterized by making a long line in a queue formation and their moving together from one end of the village to the other.[77] The meaning of the dance conveys that human beings should also learn to live in unity and cooperation with one another in the same way as fish move in harmony with one another.

---

74 Interview with Among Chang, Assistant Director, Art & Culture, Government of Nagaland, Kohima, on 8 May 2006.

75 Robinson, op. cit., p. 395.

76 J. P. Mills, op. cit., p. 159.

77 "There is an Ao Naga folk tale that narrates the origin of the fish dance. It says that there was a man by the named "Mürüng" who is said to have first seen the fish dancing in a river. He was a "Tzüinketer" (the one who by his supernatural power can hear and see the sound and movement of fish in the water). One day he saw a big contingent of fish in Dheko River in the Ao area. These fish were coming from the adjoining sea to a place called "Ngapui" in the same river where both the big and small fish can be accommodated and they could live together. It says that these fish came singing and dancing. The small fish asked the big fish, "When are we going to reach Nagpui?" (Isa kuyim tongrula?). Then, the big fish replied, "Till you reach Nagpui, move on and on" (Ngapui madongdangbo senjen senang)." Interview with Sademmeren, Ungma village, on April 27th 2006.

b) Hornbill Dance

Hornbill is a symbol of bravery, valour and beauty. The bird is regarded as the king of the birds. The hornbill is a nomadic bird which is always on the move from place to place, looking for food and shelter. This dance imitates the movement of the bird as it moves from one branch to another on the top of the trees, for its survival.[78] In this dance, both men and women can dance together with emphasis on the different rhythms and body movements. The dance symbolizes and conveys the message of peace and unity among people in the society.

c) Butterfly Dance

This dance is inspired by the beautiful movements and actions of butterflies as they fly around flowers tasting its sweetness and beauty. The dance is popular among the Sangtam Nagas. It is being performed by the women folk with the accompaniment of songs and musical instruments.[79] The dance communicates and symbolizes the spreading of peace and joy to all humankind.

d) Snake Dance

In this dance, the dancers imitate the smooth, and gliding movements of the snake. The dance is accompanied by the rhythm of drum beats and songs. The dance depicts the snake as a harmless one when not harmed by us. Thus, it removes our fear of it and encourages to be kind to it.[80] The dance precisely communicates the message of acceptance and understanding of others and maintaining harmony among people and other life forms in the community.

e) Chicken Dance

It is a dance of the Chakhesang Nagas to amuse the people and collect eatables for their feast at night. Young people perform this dance after their day's work in the field. The dance is being harmonized and performed along with the song as follows.

> "We chicken know not when we'll die.
> The people will come and catch us at night for their feast.
> We wake them up in the morning,

---

78 Kosasanger Cultural Club, 'Tenem Jilu (Hornbill Dance),' in Department of Art & Culture, ed. Cultural Panaroma: Hornbill Festival 2004 (Kohima: Department of Art & Culture, 2004), p. 1. Also See, Interview with Sademmeren, Ungma village, on 27th 2006.

79 Kosasanger Cultural Club, 'Shinu Tsungsang (Butterfly Dance),' in Department of Art & Culture, ed. Cultural Panaroma: Hornbill Festival 2004 (Kohima: Department of Art & Culture, 2004), p. 1. Also See, Interview with Shirongmong Anar, Asstt. Engineer, on 6th May 2006.

80 Kosasanger Cultural Club, 'Per Tsungsang (Snake Dance),' in Department of Art & Culture, ed. Cultural Panaroma: Hornbill Festival 2004 (Kohima: Department of Art & Culture, 2004), p. 1.

but instead they kill us for their purpose.
Because we are only their domestic fowls."[81]

vi. Marriage Dance

The celebration of marriage ceremony of a young couple often provides people in the community opportunities for dancing and singing together. Interesting courtship and marriage dances are found among the Nagas. Now-a-days, marriage dance is in seldom use in the society because of the present changes that have taken place in the cultural, religious and social life of the people. In the marriage dance, both men and women dance together, although, on other occasions, they dance separately. In this connection, Kamlong pointed out that among the Phom Nagas, when a girl is married to a boy of another village, the men folk of the same village will welcome the bride with suitable songs and dances.[82] In fact, they dance to the accompaniment of musical instruments, especially, to the rhythmic beating of traditional drums. Their relentless movements of dances demonstrate their remarkable strength and vigor that gives them complete satisfaction in terms of exhibiting their skills of dance and befitting themselves to the occasion.

vii. Labour Dance

The Nagas have many labour dances, which are connected with their agricultural work, community labour and domestic labour. Most of the dances are accompanied by songs and chanting by the dancers themselves. Originally, Nagas were hard working people and they loved and enjoyed their work. There are a number of folk songs and music associated with different kinds of work, which they sing while being engaged at tasks.[83] This labour dance belongs to the Chakhesang Naga tribe, which was also performed by both men and women while singing a song. This Khuho dance is an enactment of ploughing the terrace field. The song of the dance goes like this:

"God gives strength to work and get food.
There is no rich place without doing any work,
Therefore, we want to live there.
There is no harvest place without sowing any seed,
Therefore, we want to live there.
Food cannot come to our mouth by itself.
Otherwise we want to take rest all the time.
Anywhere sincere people can get food.
So let us be sincere in our life."[84]

---

81 Interview with Veswuzao Phesao, Cultural Officer, NEIZCC, Dimapur, on 5th May 2006.

82 Interview with S. Kamlong Phom, Dimapur, on 20th May 2006.

83 Temjen Jamir, op. cit., p. 18.

84 Interview with Veswuzao Phesao, Cultural Officer, NEIZCC, Dimapur, 5th May 2006.

Labour dance is always a source of inspiration and motivation for the people, which strengthens them to work hard with a spirit of unity both for the welfare of the individuals and that of the community. Labour dance also provides people with a time of sharing and enjoyment with their friends in the work places.

viii. Community Hall Dedication Dance

During the dedication of Morung or community hall, both men and women dance together with songs to the rhythm of music. The celebration of such dedication and dance will be followed by feasting. It is also a dance for the dedication of dormitory for young men. Among the Khiamniungan Nagas, the construction of the house is permitted to only one clan. Thus, when one clan is constructing the house, the girls from another clan come and dance with the men folk. After a day of celebration, roof is fixed and the house is completed.[85] This dance conveys the message of cohesiveness and unity of the community for the purpose of mutual learning and development.

ix. Log Drum Dedication Dance

The process of making the log drum is almost the same among the Aos and other Naga tribes as well. On the appointed day, the log drum is pulled to the village with great feasting and prayer. During the process of pulling, everyone including women participate in singing and dancing. The male members do the main pulling. After reaching the village, there is much celebration followed by feasting, dancing and merry making.[86] According to Busham, among the Khiamniungan Nagas, after dragging the log drum to the village, during the ceremony, the men take part in singing and dancing. There are four leaders or owners of the log drum. They dance and worship for the arrival of good offsprings, good harvest, victorious head-hunting and other blessings for the owners and all the community members in the village.[87] According to Among Chang, the forefathers of Chang Nagas danced during the dedication of log drum. They praised and worshipped the drum, saying, "You have the best quality of head and toes; we vow to keep you in the most beautiful place and regard you as our god and we will worship you from time to time." During the dedication of the log drum, they dance with great enthusiasm and strength.[88] The process of pulling and dedication of log drum was a community event. The community dances and songs have provided an ecumenical space for all the community members for participation and sharing with one another.

---

85 Interview with Busham, Pastor, Khiamniungan Baptist Church Dimapur, 5th May 2006.

86 N. Talitemjen Jamir, op. cit., pp. 117-119.

87 Interview with Busham.

88 Interview with Among Chang, Assist Director, Art & Culture, Government of Nagaland, Kohima, 8th May 2006.

x. Tug of War Dance

This dance is performed by two groups of men and women, which is accompanied by a song. This dance also invokes God's blessings for the whole community. In this connection, Sademmeren says that during the dance, if the rope is broken off, it indicates a bad omen by which a certain misfortune might come to the village. The dance is concluded with some songs of joy. During this dance, men hold at the bigger-sized part of the rope and the ladies hold the smaller-sized part of the rope. The dance and song start with big shouts. This dance is accompanied by a song and it goes like this:

> Oh, Arü atsüteptini,
> Oh, ni yongpang arü atsüteptini,
> Oh, jenjang meshishili,
> Ni yongyongpang atsüteptini.[89]

During the dance, women pull away first, then, men will pull back; finally, the women pull. The dance wines up with big shouts of joy. Some men folk holding at the end part of the rope with the ladies signify that in the family man is the head and leader. The dance signifies that both men and women should work together harmoniously in the chores of the family at home as well as in the socio-political life.

xi. Group Dance

This dance is performed without any pause and continues as a series of dances one after the other. The rhythm and movements of the dance are led by the tapping of the drum and music. Group dance is often performed by both men and women together. According to Hekhevi Achumi, there are group dances among the Sumi Nagas being performed by the women folk. For example, Hunti Dance is performed by the women folk, which is more or less a competitive dance displayed by the dancers themselves; Buxa Dance is another group dance of Sumi Nagas, which is also being performed by the women folk of the same community.[90] Thus, it may promote the values of equality, sharing and justice among the people in the community.

xii. Mourning Dance

Dancing at the death of a person is common among several tribes of India. Such a mourning dance can also be found among some of the Naga tribes. The dance is accompanied by the rhythm of chanting and music.[91] The objective of performing such a dance is not only that of honouring of the departed, but also expressing and showing solidarity to the bereaved family as community members.

89 Interview with Sademmeren, Ungma village, on April 27th 2006.

90 Interview with Hekhevi Achumi, Notune bosti, Dimapur, on 4th May 2006.

91 Interview with Mhonrao Kikon Lotha, (Dobashi) at Wokha on 3rd May 2006.

At present, though the dance is not often in use as such, it has its own importance in the community.

The above discussion on the different types of the Naga folk dances indicates that the celebration of Naga folk dances may provide space for communication outside the church in which people can interact, participate and enjoy fellowship with one another. Further, it promotes unity and cooperation among the people in the society. Through these brilliant festivities and dances, they can reaffirm their communitarian values and identity.

4.3. Theoretical Understanding of Naga Folk Dance

Folk dance and music are effective means of communication in Naga culture, which enlivens their social life. The celebration of cultural festivals and folk dances keep them active with fresh strength and vigour. All the different types of the Naga folk dances have in common in providing entertainment and merry making to all the community members. In this connection, Naga folk dances need not only be seen as an optional entertainment but also understood as a vehicle in bringing people together on a common platform, promoting towards participation and relationship among people in the community. In addition, Naga folk dances are associated with the social, economic, political and religious life of the people in the community. Through this medium of dance performances, they communicate their inner feelings of joy, sadness and wishes to one to one another in the society.[92] Such a celebration brings the hearts of the people closer with one another and helps them to focus on the common interests promoting towards unity, harmony, sharing, participation and well being of the whole community. In this connection, since the Naga folk dance is a community dance, it strengthens and revitalizes their communitarian identity and relationship with one another.[93] for this reason and others, irrespective of their social status, background, and religious affiliation, they come together on a common platform to celebrate their cultural festivals and folk dances.

People come together as community members showing their solidarity to one another during the celebration of the cultural festival and dances. At this point, community consciousness becomes a focal point for the tribal people in the North East India in general and in Nagaland in particular. It becomes a space for the people to come together that goes beyond their denominational, linguistic and social barriers. It creates an ecumenical common sphere for the members of the community for mutual participation, interaction and sharing with one another. In this connection, such a sphere of tribal cultural dance can go beyond the traditional model of unity and dialogue within the Church to widen it to the realm of ecumenical activities related to development, freedom, peace, justice

92 Interview with Talinucha, Deputy Director, North East India Zonal Cultural Council, Dimapur, Nagaland on 5th May 2006.

93 Interview with Lanunungsang in Mokokchung on 12th May 2006.

and human dignity in the society. As mentioned earlier, the church has failed to provide an ecumenical space for the Christians of different denominations due to denominationalism, cultural, doctrinal, and linguistic barriers, to come together for mutual participation and sharing with one another. This can also be considered as failure in maintaining relationship and unity with one another in accordance to the scripture because unity is God's will for all Christians. At this juncture, the church can go beyond her exclusive denominational barriers and boundaries to bring all people together by recognizing and availing the cultural space or common ecumenical sphere. Further, the theoretical understanding of Naga folk dance will be enlightened and discussed in the following sections.

4.3.1. Anthropological Understanding of Naga Folk Dance

The anthropological understanding of Naga folk dance can be useful in recognizing human behaviour and social values in the light of studying and understanding different types of folk dances and dance movements in contexts. Anthropology is the study of language and culture in the human phenomenon where religion is part of that culture. The study of dance and human movement has become an increasingly prominent field in anthropological analyses of expressive culture. In this connection, Royce states that most of the anthropological study of dance focuses upon the form of dance and could be said to take a symbolic, structural, or semiotic approach.[94] It focuses on the form and function of dances and dancing, exploring them as systems of meaning through their structures and semantics.[95] In fact, the study of dance is intersubjective, contextual, and interrelated to human experience and behaviour. It goes beyond the conventional boundaries of dance concepts such as the 'dance,' 'dancer,' 'dancing,' or dances, and focuses on the study on a dialectical space of performative movement which is able to infuse the space with socio-religious and socio-political meaning.[96] It shows that the productive nature of human movement is an anthropological sphere in which the medium of dance and its associated characters can be viewed as a particularly important sphere of social interaction.

Cultural forms that are generated from the creative use of human bodies in time and space are regarded as dance in the anthropological literature. In this connection, Levinson and Melvin state that the aim of anthropological works on human movement is not simply to understand dance in its cultural context, but to understand society through analyzing the movement system.[97] It is important

94 Anya Peterson Royce, op. cit., p. 31.

95 Rosita Henry, Finoa Magowan & David Murray, "Introduction – Anthropology of Dance." in Australian Journal of Anthropology, December 2000, p. 1.

96 Ibid., p.1. Also see www.furl.net.com.

97 David Levinson and Ember Melvin, *Encyclopedia of Cultural Anthropology*, Vol. I. (New York: Henry Holt and Company, 1996), p. 312.

to find out the significance and usefulness of human movement, action and interaction, which are associated with religious and secular rituals, ceremonies, entertainment, sign languages, sports, and games. These structured movement systems are the systems of knowledge that are socially and culturally constructed by a group of people and primarily preserved in memory. They may be visual manifestations of social relation and may assist in understanding cultural values.[98] Such anthropological study of human movement helps to understand and explains what the movement dimensions of various activities are communicating and to whom. It also helps to understand the Naga folk dances in their context, in relation to various activities and behaviour in the society in terms of how they provide a common ecumenical sphere to people for social interaction and participation with one another reaffirming their communitarian values and identity.

4.3.2. Naga Folk Dance as Community Dance

Tribal dance in NEI in general, and Nagaland in particular, is a community dance that promotes communitarian values and its life style among the people in the society. For the Nagas, dance performance is always a community event that serves always to the interests of the community. In this connection, Hokishe Sema states that Nagas usually dance in groups, and sometimes the whole village joins in during their festivals, which is a healthy and harmless recreation.[99] In fact, folk dance is never restricted to the number of members but provides the space where everyone is respected and included. Talinucha says that the Naga folk dance is basically a community dance, which is mainly for the members of the community for their mutual participation and growth.[100] In this connection, the interests of the community are always given first preference in which each and every individual person is treated equally and recognized with importance. Thanzauva states that in the tribal society, each individual person is not isolated from the community, but the identity of the individual is attached to the community.[101] For this reason, during the celebration of the Naga festivals and folk dances, each and every individual person comes to a common platform as a community member to affirm ones' communitarian identity. Everyone belongs to the community which itself is the source of his or her main security. Each community member can seek the help of his or her community members in times of difficulties and need. In addition, many a time, his or her decisions are greatly influenced by the community in which he or she lives. Thus, the presence of each

98 Ibid., p. 309.

99 Hokishe Sema, *Emergence of Nagaland: Socio-Economic and Political Transformation and the Future*, (New Delhi: Vikas Publishing House Pvt Ltd., 1968), p. 58.

100 Interview with Talinucha, Deputy Director, North East India Zonal Cultural Council, Dimapur, Nagaland on 5th May 2006.

101 K. Thanzauva, *Theology of Community: Tribal Theology in the Making*, (Aizawl: Mizo Theological Conference, 1997), pp. 107-110.

and every individual person in the community is respected and taken care of. In addition, the individual freedom is always respected as part of the community life. In this regard, it is well to note what Sema says, that there is a large measure of individual freedom which makes one feel delighted in the welfare of his village.[102]

In the past, the individual tendency or the idea of individualism was never felt or entertained in the Naga community. In addition, they lived together and shared with one another as members of the community within the format of their common culture. However, today, due to the rapid expansion of modernization in each and every area of life, the idea of individualism has been creeping into the Naga society and confronting the very nature of the community life. In this connection, Alemchiba points out that as a result of westernization that came along with Christianity to Nagaland, there is always an alarming tendency to abolish abruptly the traditional culture and substitute individualism for the strong community feeling which had enabled the tribes to survive for so long.[103] In such a context, it is observed that the Naga folk dance may be used as a medium of communication for reviving and redeeming their communitarian values and preserving it with the people in the society. In this connection, it has the capacity to bring people together on a common sphere and could establish contact and relationship with one another. Furthermore, the folk dance of the Nagas has both the vertical dimension of worship and the horizontal dimension of community life and activities that serve its core principle and function in the community.

4.3.3. Vertical and Horizontal Dimensions of Naga Folk Dance

Dancing was an important feature of every community event in the life of the people in primordial times. They indulged themselves in dance accompanied by every joy of life and it served as a means of usefulness and as prayer. It is commonly agreed among the scholars in the field of anthropology that dance was sacred (religious connection) in its origin. In this connection, it is well to quote Iyer and Ratnam who say that dance was sacred in its origin, and there was a consensus of opinion that every other subsequent form of dance was ultimately derived from their original form.[104] It shows that the primordial people believed that their dances were taught by their gods in whom they relied upon for their sustenance and survival of life. In this connection, there is a Sumi Naga historical mythology about the origin of dance. According to the folklore, a Sumi girl was lost from her parents. After nine years, she came back home from among the heavenly angels. She asked her father to offer a feast to all the people inviting

102 Hokishe Sema, op. cit., p. 49.

103 M. Alemchiba Ao, 'Problems of Re-adjustment to a New Situation: With Reference to the Naga Tribes,' in K. Suresh Singh, ed., Tribal Situation in India, Vol 13. (Simla: Indian Institute of Advance Study, 1972), p. 479.

104 L. A. Krishna Iyer and L. K. Bala Ratnam, *Anthropology in India* (Bombay: Bharatiya Vidya Bhavan, 1961), p. 210.

from nine villages. It was not possible because he was very poor indeed. But he was given assurance that he would be provided with all the needful for the feast. Thus, her father pronounced the feast and erected a *majang* (traditional platform) of two feet high. Accordingly, he was provided with a number of wild animals such as boars, deer, etc. He was also asked to keep big baskets and they were filled with grains. Thus, provided the feast was prepared and served to all the people.

During the feast, they were asked to watch the dancing troupe of angels. Those angels were dressed in Sumi traditional attires. They taught them 36 styles of dances. In this way they taught them how to dress and dance. Finally, the dancing troupe of angels went towards North (Patkai side). It is said that from that Sumi dance began from this time.[105] This folklore indicates that the origin of the Sumi Naga dance has a divine connection and supernatural attachment. In addition, it implies that dance is associated with a community for its welfare and development. There are also similar folktales among the Nagas in relation to the origin of folk dance.

Obviously, the Naga folk dance has both the vertical and horizontal dimensions in its character and functions. The observances of Naga cultural festivals and folk dances are associated with community life and activities, agriculture, worship, rites and rituals. It shows a vertical dimension of dance in itself as it is associated with prayer and worship of God, invoking his blessings for the members of the community and offering thanksgiving prayers for his blessings. For instance, the primary purpose of the celebration of the feast of merit is to acknowledge God's blessings and to plead for further blessings on earth as well as in life after death.[106] In addition, during the spring festivals, people worship God and invoke his blessings upon the new grains in the field and protection of the new crops from all sorts of pests throughout the seasons. It is normally observed just after the completion of sowing the seeds in the new field.[107] During the festival, all the community members worship God with the performances of their cultural folk dances, invoking his favour and blessings. The community members get an opportunity to enjoy vertical communication and relationship with God. Such a vertical dimension of dance leads all the other forms of petitions and prayers for the favour of the whole community.

There is a horizontal dimension in Naga Folk dance in providing a common space for mutual participation and establishing a relationship among the people in the community. Further, it can broaden the horizon of their vision in making cooperative efforts promoting peace, unity and justice in the society. Regarding

105 Interview with Mr. Hekhevi Achumi, Public leader, Dimapur, Nagaland on 4th May 2006.

106 O. Alem Ao, *Tsungremology: Ao Naga Christian Theology* (Mokokchung: Clark Theological College, 1994), p. 53.

107 N. Talitemjen Jamir and A. Lanunungsang, *Naga Society and Culture: A Case Study of the Ao Naga Society and Culture*, (Lumami: Nagaland University, Tribal Research Centre, Department of Sociology, 2005), p. 128.

this, Gadamer says, 'The horizon is the range of vision that includes everything that can be seen from the particular vantage point. Applying this to the thinking mind, we speak of narrowness of horizon, of the possible expansion of horizon, of the opening up of a new horizon etc.'[108] In every human society, there are differences in people's socio-economic status, and they are often divided along their religious affiliation and beliefs. However, in this paradigm, the celebration of festival and folk dances can go beyond the barriers of such disparities and differences to bring the people together both the rich and the poor on a common platform for interaction, upholding their communitarian values in the society. Such a process of openness, contact and participation can establish relationship and sharing with one another.

In this regard, the horizontal dimension can be significant when a person is able to place him or her in the situation of the other. It can enable him or her to understand others and thereby, build an intimate relationship with them. It can be seen as an act of fusion of horizons in establishing a relationship between people where they fuse together to form a single horizon.[109] Consequently, a fruitful and meaningful dialogical communication which may widen the horizon can be possible between people, to work together for the welfare and betterment of the society. In this regard, Sangyusang says that during the Naga cultural festivals, all the community members come together to show their solidarity to one another and reaffirm their communitarian identity.[110] Folk dance has both vertical and horizontal dimensions towards communicative action through which an understanding and sharing of mutual interests can be made between the people in the community.

4.3.4. Naga Folk Dance as Communication

Most of the dances have communicative purpose, ranging from primitive or ethnic dance to the expression of personal emotion or physical exuberance.[111] Folk dance is one of the means of communication of the community, especially, in the tribal society that allows the people to use the art of their body movements expressing and communicating their inner feelings; the emotions of joy, excitement and sadness. Dance can take place in a concrete historical context, communicating information of various matters and ideas to the people through its forms of non verbal expressions and symbols. In this connection, Fraleigh says that dances are contextualized events; they are cultural, historical and experiential.[112]

108 Hans-Georg Gadamer, *Truth and Method* (London: Sheed & Ward, 1975). P. 269.

109 Ibid., pp. 270-273.

110 Interview with Sangyusang S. Pongener at Ungma on 14th May 2006.

111 Richard Kraus, op. cit., p. 13.

112 Sondra Horton Fraleigh, 'Family Resemblance,' in Sondra Horton Fraleigh and Penelope Hanstein, eds. *Researching Dancing: Evolving Modes of Inquiry* (Pittsburgh: University of Pittsburgh Press, 1999), p. 16.

In India, especially in the rural areas, folk forms such as drama, dance, songs, story telling and puppetry have been effectively used as a means of communicating information and messages to one another. It can create a conducive atmosphere for communication among the people in the society. In this regard, Gupta states that in India, the traditional forms of communication such as folk theatre, folk tales, folk drama, and folk dance, have been utilized by the people as a means of disseminating information for various purposes in the society.[113] Folk dance can be seen as a symbolic art form, which belongs to the members of the community and is inexpensive in character. Its simple dance movement and steps can be easily picked up by anyone without going through a skilled training, which is an effective means of communication in the society.

i. Naga Folk Dance as a Symbolic Art Form

Human beings can communicate with one another in a variety of ways: verbally, kinesthetically, artistically, and literarily. Dance in general and the folk dance in particular, is one of the symbolic art forms, which plays an important part in the society in terms of socializing and entertaining through various creative forms. According to Geertz, symbols are the vehicles of 'culture,' thus symbols should be studied and understood in terms of what they can reveal to us about culture and human behaviour.[114] It has been pointed out by many authorities that symbols and culture are interconnected in understanding and expressing community behavior. It may be pointed out that culture can be expressed meaningfully by the external symbols of music, dance, gestures, etc., that a society uses. By means of such symbolic forms, people may communicate and develop their knowledge about their worldview and attitudes toward life. Such enactment and movements of dances represent the real world of human situations, activities and needs.

Generally, in the dance, all the parts of the body are used to express or to release emotions: movements of arms and legs, hands and feet, fingers and toes, with movements of trunk, hips and heads, twitching and rippling of muscles, grimaces and protruding tongues.[115] Thereby, the movements express and communicate information, message and meaning to the people. The movements in dance may signify signs and symbols, in any combination. Essentially, dances are cultural artifacts that convey the idea that these movements belong to a specific culture or sub-culture or that a specific type of movement or dance is being activated for a particular purpose within a community.[116] In addition, it

113 V. S. Gupta, *Communication and Development: The Challenge of the Twenty-first Century* (New Delhi: Concept Publishing Company, 2000), p. 52.

114 Clifford Geertz, *The Interpretation of Cultures* (New York: Basic Books, Inc., 1973), pp. 5 & 89.

115 Alison Hingston Quiggin, "Dancing," in Chambers' Encyclopedia, New Edition, Vol. IV, Confirmation-Educational Psychology, (London: George Newnes Limited, 1959), p. 362.

116 Levinson and Melvin, op. cit., p. 310.

promotes contact and collective participation among the people, and thereby, enabling them to communicate their feelings and attitude to others.

4.3.5. Naga Folk Dances as Participatory Communication

In most of the developing countries, folk dance is recognized and considered as participatory communication as it provides people with opportunities to participate in collective manner on a common platform. In fact, participation in community initiated programmes can be seen as a human right for each individual, which needs to be encouraged for its intended result. In this connection, it is worthwhile to quote Bordenave who says that participation is the process in which a person sees himself or herself as a unique individual person and at the same time as a member of a community.[117] Unlike the classical dances, ballroom dances, Hollywood tap dance of Astaire, etc.,[118] which are characterized by the solo, duet or performing with a restricted number of members, folk dance is a community dance in character in which participation of all the members of the community is encouraged.

Folk dance can offer a participatory form of communication between the dancers and their community members. It does not reduce people into mere passive recipients of the message and information, but also encourages and facilitates them to be more active participants in the process of the community events. In this regard, participatory communication can be understood as a type of communication in which all the participants are free and have equal access to the means to express their viewpoints, feelings and experiences.[119] The celebration of folk dance as it belongs to the community as a whole provides a two-way traffic communication between people, which involves dialogue, collaboration, cooperation and group decision making. In this way, folk dance in general and the Naga folk dance in particular can promote democratic communication among the people in which the opinion and feelings of each community member is accepted and respected for the well-being and development of the whole community. In this regard, UNESCO's discourse on the ideas of access participation and self-management reaffirms the principles of democratic communication in the society.[120]

Furthermore, the widespread acceptance of Freire's notion of dialogical communication as a normative theory of participatory communication can be relevant as it insists that the subjugated peoples must be treated as full human

117 Juan Diaz Bordenave, 'Participative Communication as a Part of Building the Participative Society,' in Shirley A. White with K. Sadanandan Nair and Joseph Ascroft, eds. *Participatory Communication: Working for Change and Development* (New Delhi: Sage Publications, 1994), p. 36.

118 Alexander Bill Filson Young, op. cit., pp. 22-23.

119 Bordenave, op. cit., p. 43.

120 Ibid., p. 17.

subjects in any political process for their development and emancipation.[121] Such a dialogical communication may bring the individual to a critical reflection on his/her own living situations and can enable him or her to participate in a historical process. In Freire's conscientizing pedagogy, the receivers break out of the fetters of mental and psychological control and become more aware of their own existence.[122] In this connection we may do well to refer to Servaes who states that the right to participation and emancipation regarding social, cultural, and historical reality is a fundamental right for everyone.[123] The celebration of folk dances within the community can provide the adequate space for participation and dialogical communication in the spirit of respect and acceptance for each other. Such a process of interaction may enlighten the people about the reality of their own situations, and may encourage them to make cooperative efforts towards development, to bring about the necessary changes in the society. Ultimately it aims at promoting their common interests, solving their problems and transforming their society within the resources available to them. The fact that folk dance is participatory in character can be seen in it being a ritual dance with a cyclical performance and sacred intention during the cultural festival.

4.3.6. Ritual Dance of Communication

Ritual describes an extraordinary event involving stylized, repetitive behaviour.[124] In this connection, dance is ritualized in its repetitive enactment as cultural performance in the society. Dance can preserve and communicate people's culture, identity, and their religious beliefs and practices. Hanna points out that dance is often a set of operations in the society to ensure a certain type of communication.[125] The cultural dances that communicate and promote people's identity, their religious beliefs and practices can be validated as rituals. They are often seen as public rites of renewal and passage. For instance, Sekrenyi is one of the major festivals among the Angami Nagas. It is an annual festival of the installation of the village gate. The whole community, including the women folk can join in the stone pulling ceremony. An elderly person can perform the ritual 'terhase' pronouncing blessings and leads the pulling process. A strict compliance of the ritual is observed on the eve of the event which is held on a fair day. The gate stone is pulled and brought to the village and installed, accompanied by a

121 Jan Servaes, 'Introduction: Participatory Communication and Research in Development Settings,' in Jan Servaes, Thomas L. Jacobson and Shirley A. White, eds. Participatory Communication for Social Change (New Delhi: Sage Publications, 1996), p. 17.

122 Paulo Freire, *Pedagogy of the Oppressed.* (New York: Herder and Herder, 1971), p. 33.

123 Jan Servaes, 'Participatory Communication Research with New Social Movements: A Realistic Utopia,' in Jan Servaes, Thomas L. Jacobson and Shirley A. White, eds. Participatory Communication for Social Change (New Delhi: Sage Publications, 1996), p. 97.

124 Judith Lynne Hanna, op. cit., p. 129.

125 Ibid., p. 129.

grand feast for the whole community.[126] During this festival, other villagers are also invited to celebrate together with song and dances, which may be called inter-village celebration. During the celebration, friendship day is also organized, to strengthen their relationship with one another.[127] Among the tribals, ritual dance is a public rite and celebration of the community event that promotes and communicates their cultural values, identities and religious beliefs. It is also a community celebration with songs and dances, providing collective entertainment enabling them to share their emotions with one another. Ritual dances are usually total events that incorporate music and costumes as artifacts that cannot be divorced from the dance movement.[128]

Naga Folk dance is often connected with the worship of God as a means for appeasement, in addition to invoking his blessings on them and expressing their gratitude. Ritual dances are performed for a higher being with the hopes of success in the community endeavours of the community during harvest and war. For instance, Tsungrem-mong is the second most important festival of the Aos. It is the harvest festival observed for three days in the first week of August every year. A day of worship and sacrifice is offered to Lichaba, the creator of the earth, for good harvest. This is the last celebration of the year by the whole community including the children. They celebrate with a grand feast, songs and dancing.[129] Further, ritual war dances are performed by the people preparing to go into battle. The dances energize the actual combatants for their task ahead and rallies support from the onlookers by generating or strengthening the belief that the enemy was an evil one who needed to be defeated.[130] Further, the warrior and his family members were expected to observe *genna* in order to make the raids successful. These ritual dances are important means of communication for invoking religious favour, for strengthening cohesion among the people and for preserving their cultural identity in the society.

Furthermore, ritual dances are often passed down for generations and thus have become bearers of a people's history. They are often regarded as a means of communication in the community for preserving and transmitting the rich cultural heritage of the people. Such repetitive enactment and performances of the ritual dances are part of the process of learning for the younger generation.

---

126 Department of Art & Culture, Echoes of Nagaland: Hornbill Festival 2005 (Kohima: Department of Art & Culture, 2005), p. 8.

127 Interview with Vilalhou Angami, Art Executive, Art & Culture, Government of Nagaland, Kohima, on 10th May, 2006.

128 Fraleigh, op. cit., p. 13.

129 Jamir, N. Talitemjen, & A Lanunungsang, *Naga Society and Culture: A Case Study of the Ao Naga Society and Culture*, op. cit., p. 139. Also See, B. B. Ghosh, Nagaland District Gazetteers: Mokokchung District (Kohima: Government of Nagaland, 1979), p. 82.

130 Ian Enriques, 'The Ritual of War and Manhood,' http://www. Barbarycoast.org/ritual.html Browsed on 23-01-2008.

Cultural rituals and ceremonies extend space and time beyond the ordinary sense, being transformative on both personal and communal levels.[131] As they embody myths and cosmologies, they also interpret and integrate culture and society. In this connection, folk dance can be also considered as being a medium of social interaction as it provides space for interaction among people, promoting unity and transformation in the society.

4.3.7. Naga Folk Dance as Medium of Social Interaction

A society can be studied and understood as a system of actions, satisfying social purposes wherein social interaction can be seen as a reciprocal communication among the members of the society. Regarding this, Sutherland says that social interaction is the basic process through which human nature and social structure develop and are changed. The process can take place only when the contacts between people are social and the meanings communicated are between persons.[132] People in the community, as individuals and groups, interact with one another in attempting to solve problems and for achieving their common goals. In this regard, social interaction can be understood as a "society in action" and may be defined as the dynamic interplay of forces in which contact between persons and groups results in modification of the attitudes and the behaviour of the participants.[133]

Social interaction may take place in various socio-cultural contexts, be it at the market places, in the village home, in village meetings, in the farm fields, during the celebration of cultural festivals at community halls, or elsewhere. In such communicative situations, various forms and methods of communication, such as verbal and non-verbal forms, signs and symbols, symbolic gestures, and folk media, are used to achieve its purpose. As such, these forms of communication are essential to social interaction for communicating a message to others, and bringing change and transformation to the people in the community. Interaction is a fundamental process in any society, and the character of the society is strongly influenced by the types of interaction and contact that take place within it.[134] In this regard, folk dance can be considered as an effective medium of social interaction in the community for bringing people together on a common platform for the purpose of achieving progress and development in the society.

---

131 Ibid., p. 14.

132 R. L. Sutherland, J. L. Woodward, and M. A. Maxwell, *Introductory Sociology*, 6th edition. (Philadelphia: Lippincot, 1961), p. 100.

133 "There are four important aspects of interaction: (1) social contacts are a prerequisite to interaction; (2) communication is the medium of interaction; (3) the different ways or modes in which these forces operate are the types of interaction; and (4) social interaction always occurs within a social structure, even though that structure itself may undergo changes as a result of it." Ibid., p. 99.

134 J. B. Chitambar, *Introductory Rural Sociology: A Synopsis of Concepts and Principles* (New Delhi: Wiley Eastern Limited, 1973), p. 265.

Folk dance can be used as a means of self-expression, social interaction and entertainment in the society. Throughout the Naga history, folk dance has remained as an important component for the cultural expression of the people. Obviously, it may give an opportunity for people to get involved with others providing social entertainment and merry-making. It can also create a space for people to express and share their common goals and concerns towards community development. Sometimes it may provide an opportunity for bringing values to the community members that are not so common to each other in terms of their background, beliefs and practices. This could become a point of contact in strengthening their relationship. People's mutual contact and participation can strengthen their cooperation in working together for a common purpose, such as, construction of a village road, building a community health center, or a community hall, etc. Such a space for social interaction and communication can become ecumenically viable for promoting peace, justice, development, and unity among the people in the community.

4.4. Concluding Remarks

The Naga folk dances are the invaluable heritage of the Naga culture. It is apparent that the folk dance has an important place in the society in terms of establishing a common space for community participation and interaction with one another. This cultural space brings them into a closer contact and relationship with each other and serves the needs and aspirations of the people. It is observed that, it is a medium of communication in providing a social entertainment, and a channel for socializing with others in the community. The celebration and the movements of the various folk dances at different times and seasons can reveal the culture, behaviour and attitude of the people in the society.

It can further communicate the meanings and ideas in relation to the socio-cultural, political and religious life and activities of the people in the society. Such a space for communication can go beyond the idea of individualism and exclusive regional or denominational communication to promote an inclusive and democratic communication in which the opinion of every member in the community is respected and encouraged. It broadens the horizon of ecumenical communication in which social interaction takes place bringing about changes and transformation in the society. In addition, the anthropological study of dance and human movements has become important in which the expressive culture of a particular community is analysed. The analysis of the present chapter indicates that the celebration of the Naga folk dance can provide a common platform for contact, relationship, and participation among the people in the community. In the next chapter which is chapter five, folk dance among the Ao Nagas with special reference to Moatsu festival will be discussed. The discussion will be mainly based on the field research being conducted during the Moatsu festival in Ao Naga area, using the qualitative social anthropological method.

Chapter 5

Folk Dance for the Promotion of Ecuminical Sphere with Special Reference to Ao Naga Moatsu Festival A Social Anthropological Study

In this proceeding chapter, a social anthropological study of the folk dance among the *Ao Nagas*[1] with special reference to Moatsu festival will be taken up for discussion. The analysis of this study is based on the materials collected during the field research conducted using the qualitative methods of the participant observation and in-depth interview during the celebration of Moatsu festival in some selected Ao Naga areas in Nagaland. It examined how the celebration of cultural festivals and folk dances could bring people together as community members on an ecumenical common sphere, establishing contact, participation

1 The etymological meaning of the word *Ao* is *"going"* or *"going ones."* In this study, the word *Ao* stands for a group of people or one of the social groups in Nagaland. They are one of the tribes in Nagaland and are called the Ao Nagas. The people of Nagaland are called Nagas. Nagas belong to the Mongoloid stock settled in the region between India and Myanmar. There are many conflicting views on the origin and the meaning of the word "Naga." The term "Naga" might have originated from the Sanskrit word "*Nag*," meaning hills or mountains that ascribes the name of Nagas as those people of the hills. According to Verrier Elwin, the origin of the Naga might have come from the Sanskrit word "*Loka*" meaning people who were closely associated with the surrounding nature. In this connection, he further states that the term Naga developed later. Originally, Nagas were known by their tribe's name like Sema, Ao, and Lotha, etc., and not by the general term Naga. B.B. Kumar, "Origin of the Word *Naga*." in *Highlander*, Vol. 1/1/1973, p. 31. Thus, the term *Naga* can be understood as the hill people who are warriors. These are independent people who were never before ruled by any king or colonized but lived in freedom. A. Bendangyabang Ao, *History of Christianity in Nagaland: Social Change 1872 – 1972* (Bangalore: Shalom Ministry Publications, 2004), p. 9. In fact, they have an independent outlook and have a natural taste for colour, love of music, rhythm and dance.

and relationship among the people in the Church and society. In addition, it examined how such a space for communication in Naga folk dance, which can be recognized as a common ecumenical sphere to promote ecumenical relations between churches in Nagaland. It also analyses the attitude of Christians towards folk dance in terms of promoting positive attitude towards it in the community.

5.1. Moatsu Festival: A Social Anthropological Study

In pursuance of these goals of research as mentioned above, the social anthropological study of participant observation was conducted in Ao Naga area in three places in Mokokchung town, Ungma, and Chuchuyimlang, during the celebration of Moatsü festival from the first of May to the third, 2006.[2] These three selected places are located within the distance of twenty five kilometers in the Ao Naga area. Thus, the researcher could attend the events of the celebrations and observed the proceedings of the programmes. The researcher observed and investigated the three events in three places at different times because this particular Moatsu festival falls only once in a year during these three days.

5.1.1. Format of Data Gathering Procedure

A format of data gathering procedure was being used for the observation and verification of the events. Thus, each event was observed and recorded according to the format of the participant observation. The researcher checked how such cultural performances at Naga festival could bring people together on a common platform, enabling them to establish contact, interaction, relationship and understanding outside the church regardless of their denominational affiliation. In addition, it was studied how such a space for communication in Naga folk dance, which can be recognized as a common ecumenical sphere to promote ecumenical relations and communication between churches in Nagaland. In this connection, the behaviour, movements, participation and interaction of the Naga people were observed and studied in their real life situation during the celebration of the Moatsu festival and folk dances. Further, all the observations and the meanings of each event were entered and recorded in accordance with the theoretical framework of the study and substantial interests. In addition, photos of dance performances were taken for further surveillance, observation and comments.

2 During the post research, the researcher has been made available during the celebration of Moatsu festival in Mokokchung by participating and observing in the proceedings of the celebration. In this connection, it has noted that irrespective of gender, colour, tribal and denominational affiliation and identity, during the celebration of cultural festival, people would come together on a common platform and participated in the presentation of folk songs, dances and other cultural events. This indicates that the celebration of cultural dances and songs has a potential sphere for developing ecumenical communication encouraging contact and interaction among the people in the church and society.

5.1.2. Data-Processing and Analysis

The data and materials collected from different events of the celebration of Moatsu festival were cross-checked and corroborated with collaterals. Further, classification and cross-classifications of data, and structural diagrams and flow-charts were used that facilitated the data-analysis and interpretation. The interpretation of the data was made from the point of theoretical concept of the Naga folk dances and their performances. In addition, data-processing and analysis enabled the researcher to come up with useful hypothesis. It indicated that the performances of folk dance as the people-centered ecumenical communication act in promoting contact, sharing, relationship, participation, learning, and understanding in the community.

In addition, the method of in-depth interview was conducted in Mokokchung, Kohima, Dimapur, Ungma, Chuchuyimlang, and Changtongya town. In this connection, 23 selected people were interviewed in their own respective places (Appendix II. A). Through this method, the levels of people's understanding, their idea, and vision in the promotion of ecumenical relationships and their actions in the society and the church were investigated and studied. In this connection, structural diagrams were used that facilitated the data-analysis and its interpretation. This analysis indicates the importance of people's role and participation in the celebration of the Moatsu festival and folk dance.

5.2. Role of People in Moatsü Festival

Moatsü festival is one of the major festivals of the Ao Nagas. This festival falls in the early first week of the month of May. All the members of the entire community celebrate it after sowing the grains and seeds in the fields. Moatsü is a festival of asking God for a bountiful harvest. During the festival, all the community members, both men and women folk enjoy lots of sharing and fellowship with dances, songs and feasting with one another.[3] Celebration of folk dances is one of the important features of this festival which promotes interaction, participation, sharing, unity, and relationship among the people in the community.

In Nagaland all the celebrations of cultural festivals, folk dances and music are people-centered events. The research shows that they are important in the society because they give meaning to the lives of the people. It is a festival of dancing with music and traditional dresses. During this festival both men and women wear their best traditional dresses and enjoy the festivity with one another. For this purpose they work hard throughout the year, which strengthens their skilled labour such as weaving and handicraft.

The celebration of cultural festival is organized by the people themselves that facilitate an opportunity to all the members of the community to come

3 L. Imtisüpong Aier, *Aor Sobaliba Temzüng Ozüng, (Ao Naga Customary Law)* Second Edition (Mokokchung: Published by the Author, 1991), pp. 41-42.

together on a common ecumenical sphere to participate in the events. The events of cultural celebration were organized and initiated by the cultural groups and lay people of the same community. This shows that the celebration of festivals and folk dances is a community event that promote towards the welfare of the members of the community.[4] In addition, the community leaders and students' leaders conducted all the events of celebration. This indicates that the celebration of Moatsü festival and folk dances is people-centered that advocates the interests of the people in strengthening the whole community life. For this reason and other, people come together on a common platform to reaffirm their communitarian values and identity which can be considered as a cultural space or a common ecumenical sphere promoting towards relationship, interaction and participation with one another.

5.2.1. Folk Dance Towards Community Participation

The research indicates that Moatsu festival is characterized by people's participation including children in which dance with colourful dresses, singing, tug of war and other activities are displayed. In addition, the people with their traditional attires and ornaments go round and round in the open street, dancing and singing songs of joy and blessings. During the festival, both young boys and girls can get an opportunity to make interaction and participation with each other through various cultural activities and presentations exhibiting their best talents. In this connection, Akok who is one of the local folk dancers pointed out that the celebration of the festival and folk dance often provides an opportunity to get into interaction, sharing and participation with friends in the community.[5] Since it is a community celebration, everyone is given an ample opportunity to participate with one another, contributing his or her best to the community. In addition, during the festival, no one is allowed to remain as a mute spectator just because he or she is poor and cannot afford to participate in the celebration. In this connection, Chib points out that the community as a whole appropriately looks after such a person and provides him or her all that is required for the celebration of such festivals.[6] In fact, during the festival, everyone in the community is given attention with respect, and enjoys together the community celebration. It was observed that the representations of the people including the participants (dancers) during the festival were from the same village or community, from other

---

4 In Ungma the Moatsu festival celebration was organized by the students Union on May 1st 2006 at 10 AM. While in Chuchuyimlang, the Moatsu festival was organized by the village community on May 2nd 2006 at 11.00 AM. In Mokokchung town, the festival celebration was being organized by the Mokokchung Town Art and Culture Council on May 2nd 2006 at 3.00 PM.

5 Interview with Akok, a local folk dancer, at Ungma village, on 30th April 2006.

6 Sukhdev Singh Chib, *This Beautiful India Nagaland* (New Delhi: Light and Life Publishers, 1980), p. 94.

villages, and also from the other tribes of Nagas. In addition, children, youths, adults and elders make up the representation of the people who come to the celebration mostly on voluntary basis.

5.2.2 Inter-village and Inter-tribal Representations

The representation of people indicates that the celebration of Moatsu festival itself is inclusive, democratic and ecumenical in character, inviting community members and others to participate and share with one another. In addition, the representation and participation of both men and women during the festival is significant and usually given importance in the society. However, in all the three events, it was noticed that the representation of men outnumbered the women and children. This shows a sign of men's domination in leadership and participation in the community.

During the celebration of cultural festivals, all the community members are invited and welcomed. The participation of all the members of the community including children is the unique feature of this festival. During this season, they enjoy dancing and singing in colorful dresses and ormanents. For this reason, Moatsu festival is the most common and popular among the Ao Nagas. It does not only bring people to a common platform for interaction and sharing but also indicates that all the community members are equally important as active participants by being part of the celebration and making significant contributions in relation to moral, ethical and social values to the community.

It has been observed that the people's participation during the celebration of Moatsü festival and folk dances takes place not only within the intra-village sphere but within the inter-village and inter-tribal relationships as well.[7] The representations of the people including the participants (dancers) during the festival are from the same village or community and also from other villages such as Unger, Longmisa, Sungratsu, and the tribes of Nagas such as the Phom tribe, the Lotha tribe, the sumi tribe, the Chang tribe, the Angami tribe, the Chakhesang tribe and Nepali community. In addition, children, youths, adults and elders make up the representation of the people who come to the celebration mostly on voluntary basis. This shows that people come together with community consciousness irrespective of their geographical, cultural and linguistic differences, to reaffirm their communitarian identity. Further, it may promote social interaction, participation and mutual understanding with one another. At this point, one can see an ecumenical overtone in all these cultural

---

7 In Ungma, during the celebration, out of the total number of participants about 980 from Ungma, Mokokchung and Kohima, about 600 were men, while 380 were women; in Chuchuyimlang, the the total number of participants were about 2270 representing Ao, Phom, Chang, and Angami, Chakhesang tribes, out of which 1100 were men and 970 were women; while in Mokokchung town, the total number of representations were about 4900 from Ao, Nepali, Lotha, Chang, and Sumi tribes, out of which 3700 were men and 2900 were women.

performances and participation. It indicates the feeling of unity among the people which may promote and strengthen their relationship and identity.

5.3. Ao Naga Folk Dance as the People-Centered Communication for the Promotion of Ecumenical Relationship

Folk dance is people's dance, which is originated from the hearts of the people in the socio-cultural and religious contexts. It belongs to the community which can be used by the people themselves at any given opportunity as a medium of communication for the welfare and development of the members of the community. It expresses their inner feelings and emotions in communicating their way of life.

Folk dance can be seen as a mirror of the whole community life through which their community activities and aspirations can be reflected and communicated to others. In this connection, Pooranam states that the alternative media such as drama, dance, music, and puppetry are the people-centered media, which have people as their focus.[8] Folk dance can play an important role in bringing people together not only for the purpose of entertainment and fun but also for communicating and promoting ecumenical relationship, communitarian values of fellowship, sharing, and unity among the members of the community. The analysis of this study shows that the celebration of Naga Folk dances can provide the space for communication and relationship for the following in the community.

5.3.1. Naga Folk Dance Towards a Common Ecumenical Sphere

Traditionally, the Arijumen[9] decides the date, usually the first week of May every year. The celebration of Moatsü festival among the Ao Nagas goes on for six days beginning from the first day of May. It is also called *teroknu mong*, which means a six-day festival. The first three days act as the preparatory period with strict *anempong* which means *genna* from sex, travel, guest and hard work during which all the necessary arrangements are made for the celebration. The next three days are the real festival which is marked by feasting, dancing and singing in sharing the joy, happiness and blessings of Moatsu with one another.[10] However, at present,

---

8 Pooranam M. X. "People's Media: An Alternative in Information Bulletin." (3/1993), Catholic Media Council, Aachen, p. 2.

9 "The *Ariju*, popularly known as 'dormitory' or 'bachelors' house' (morung in Assamese) is one of the most significant social institutions found among the tribal societies of the world in different forms. This institution is the fundamental basis of the Naga cultural heritage...... The membership of Ariju is extended to all the male members irrespective of their status since they are entitled into its system at the age of 12 to 13 years. The oldest *zunga* (age group) retires every three year at about 25 years. Therefore, the tenure of *Ariju* for a person is about ten to fifteen years after which he would automatically become a village councilor in the village administration, *Putu Menden*." See, N. Talitemjen Jamir and A. Lanunungsang, op. cit., pp. 75, 83.

10 *Ibid*., pp. 128-129.

the festival is being celebrated only for three days: from 1st to 3rd May, throughout the Ao area, during which people organize various special cultural programmes to mark the occasion.[11] The village elders or the community leaders can decide a particular date for the whole community celebration and participation. In this connection, all the twenty three interviewees agreed that the celebration of folk dance as non-material culture could provide a common platform or an ecumenical sphere for people toward achieving contact and relationship with one another in the community. It indicates that culture can act as a powerful force in bringing the members of the community together to a common ecumenical sphere irrespective of their denominational affiliation, age, gender, and social status, to enjoy a closer interaction, participation and fellowship with one another.

5.3.2. Initiating Contact and Sharing among the People

Celebration of festivals and folk dances is a community based activity in a more organized way. Naga folk dance is basically a community dance, which includes all the community members irrespective of their social status, background, religious affiliation, tribe, and gender. The researcher observed that the people come to the common platform as community members, to celebrate the cultural festival and folk dances together with one another. Since it is a community event, it does not only strengthen the social life of the people but also enables them to reaffirm their communitarian values and identity. It gives the people ample opportunities to come together to share in table-fellowship or for sharing food with one another as part of the celebration of the festival. It brings the hearts of the people closer with a meaningful interaction with one another.

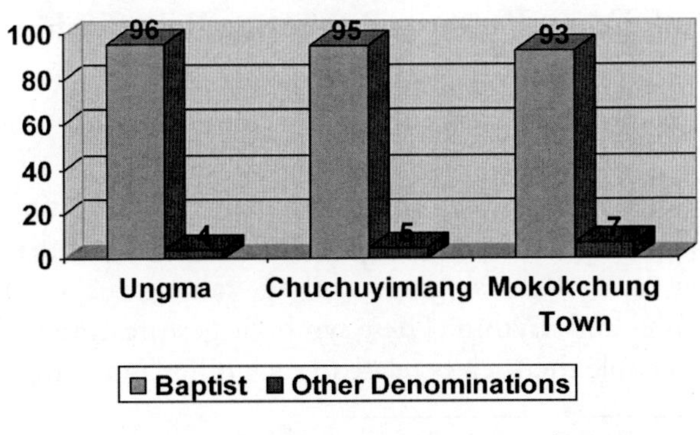

Chart 1: Denominational Representations (In percentage)

11 During this study, the researcher noticed that the celebration of Moatsü festival took place at Ungma on 1st May 2006. Further, the other two different cultural programmes of the celebration of the festival were organized and held on 2nd May 2006 in Chuchuyimlang and in Mokokchung Town respectively on the same day. Such a choice of particular date and time for the occasion enables people to invite one another and celebrate together. In this connection, all the three events of Moatsü celebration took place at the public ground where most of the community activities and functions are organized and held.

The representation and participation of other Christian denominations[12] are noticed including Nagaland Christian Revival Church, Pentecostal Church, Catholic Church, about 4 percent in Ungma, about 5 percent in Chuchuyimlang and about 7 percent in Mokokchung Town respectively (Chart 1). It indicates that though the percentage of their representation is low, still their active participation during the festival is continued as part of the community life. One reason for their low percentage of representation could be due to there being less number of members in the community. For this reason and other, they are not able to come forward with confidence to participate. In this connection, it is also worth noting that, all the twenty three interviewees agreed that the celebration of folk dance could provide a common ecumenical sphere for people toward establishing contact, communication and sharing with one another in the community.

Such a common platform may be seen as a common ecumenical sphere where people can interact and relate to each other. In addition, it further facilitates and promotes better relationship, sharing and interaction within the members of the community. The kind of contact and sharing being established may encourage a wider participation and cooperation among the people.

Further, apart from the dance performances and other cultural activities, in all the three events of Moatsü festival celebration, the Pastors and church leaders were given the opportunity to participate.[13] It shows that the participation during the cultural programmes were not limited only to the lay people but included the Church leaders as well. Obviously, such a mutual participation of the church leaders and the people on the same platform can be a significant feature of ecumenical communication.

5.3.3. Naga Folk Dance Towards Promoting Relationship

Celebration of cultural festival and folk dances can be a time of revitalizing friendship and relationship within the community and with other communities as well. The researcher's observation in all the three events of Moatsü festival celebrations, brings to light that the participants tried relating to each other, maintaining interpersonal relationship with one another through symbolic actions, such as holding each other, singing, smiling, talking, using and maintaining appropriate gestures and rhythm. These symbolic gestures and bodily movements can exhibit how people themselves relate to each other and maintain a close social

---

12 The tentative percentage regarding the representation of other Christian denominations during the celebration of Moatsu festival in three selected places were established through researcher's personal observation and interaction with the people.

13 In Ungma, Mr. Noklen, Pastor, Ungma Baptist Church, offered the opening prayer and the Associate Pastor (Women) offered the closing prayer. In Chuchuyimlang, Rev. Lanu, Pastor of the Chuchuyimlang Baptist Church pronounced the opening prayer, and the Pastor of the Alempang Baptist Church, Mokokchung, offered the closing prayer. In Mokokchung Town, one of the Associate Pastors of the Mokokchung Town Baptist Church offered the opening prayer.

relationship with others. In this connection, all the interviewees opined that the celebration of cultural festivals and folk dances could strengthen relationships among people in the community at the family, inter-village and inter-tribal levels. It shows that during the celebration of the festival, people do not emphasize their differences but on the common interests, aspirations, values and identity that bind them together as a people of a particular community.

Moreover, this event gives people a common space where people can come together face-to-face and share their experiences in terms of upholding their communitarian values and practices, such as contact, relationship, sharing, unity, and caring. Such an act of interaction, retrospection and introspection at interpersonal level can be seen as a dialogical communication which is characterized by acceptance and respect of another person. It may become a point of establishing mutual understanding and relationship with one another. At this point, it can be a means of education especially for the younger generation to learn about their cultural traditions and practices in the society.

Communication through symbolic objects: The researcher observed and examined the symbolic objects, for instance, the cultural dresses and ornaments, the people displayed during the celebration of the cultural dances as follows: hornbill feathers, mekala, earrings, necklaces, bangles, bracelets, shawls, ivory, sash, spear, dao, headgear, etc. These clourful traditional dresses and ornaments are tools in studying and understanding the rich culture of the Nagas and indicate their social relationship, behaviour, cultural identity, tradition and way of life in the community. Further, it shows that they come together and dance because of their community consciousness and attachment and thereby, allows people to participate and reaffirm their communitarian identity.

5.3.4. Naga Folk Dance Promoting Towards Education and Learning

Performance of dance and celebration of the festival can be a learning experience for the participants and spectators by enjoying the presentations with positive approval. In this connection, it is worthwhile to quote Sebastian Periannan who says that the celebration of the alternative media of communication, such as folk songs, folk dance, dramas, folktales, and puppetry, can become effective means of learning and education in the society, especially among the younger generation.[14] In fact, this can be a means of inculcating the importance of cultural values and practices in the minds of the people in the society.

Post-Dance Behaviour: It was observed that all the dance performances in all the three events were melodious and harmonious with appropriate gestures and body movements. Their performances were accepted with joy and appreciated by spectators, which strengthened their communitarian values and identity. The festival is a great opportunity to bond with fellow dancers and meet

14 Sebastian Periannan, "Modern Methods of Communication for an Effective Education," in *Journal of Dharma* (Religion and Education) April-June 2006, Vol. 31, No. 2. pp. 219-236.

other dancers from the neighbouring villages and tribes in terms of sharing and learning new dances from one another. In fact, one can say that such a celebration of cultural festivals and folk dances can provide the space for communication wherein the areas that are partly known and unknown to each other are perceived and understood. The data analysis of the in-depth interview shows that the folk dance could facilitate a learning experience among the people in the community in terms of expressing mutual appreciation displaying their cultural heritages, which strengthen their culture in general and their tribal communitarian values such as peace, unity, fellowship and particularly friendship with one another. The participation of people, especially the young people, in the cultural festival and folk dances can enliven their culture that may be passed on from one generation to the other. Such a learning experience and interaction among the people can establish a mutual understanding with one another in the society.

5.3.5. Naga Folk Dance Towards Communal Harmony

It has been observed that the cultural festivals and folk dances have a positive strength to support and encourage appreciative and perceptive attitude towards each other in the community. In this connection, the researcher found out that the participation of the people from different sections of the society including people from different Christian denominations can promote acceptance, respect and better understanding among the people in the community.

Most of the Naga folk dances go along with folk songs accompanied by traditional instruments. The participants played some traditional instruments such as the drum, the horn, the flute, the log drum, and stringed instruments, along with their dance performances. In this connection, the data analysis of the in-depth interview indicates that the different colourful traditional dresses and ornaments they wore during the festival portray their communitarian values and cultural heritages. It depicts that the Nagas have a lot of things in common in terms of their cultural values and practices, which gives them the opportunity to explore and understand one another and affirm their identity. Furthermore, it encourages people to maintain and uphold the values of acceptance, unity and participation in the midst of diversity and differences in the society. It is such a mutual understanding that motivates people to move towards decision-making and action in the society.

5.3.6. Naga Folk Dance Towards Community Development

The researcher observed that the celebration of cultural festivals and folk dances not only establish contact, sharing and understanding but they also facilitate each and every community member in reaffirming their commitment towards achieving welfare, development and unity in the community. It provides them with a common platform to come together to discuss their needs and enables them to come to a consensus decision based on their common interests for the betterment of the society. In this connection, decision-making is praxis-oriented in nature that allows people to come out from the ghettoes of their own world to communicate and promote the values of human dignity, justice, integrity and the quality of life among the people in the society.

Naga festivals and folk dances are closely associated with agriculture, the rites and ceremonies of purification, display of heroism, depiction of work places, and their way of life. It has always contributed towards community welfare and its interests. Celebration of folk dance does not only serve the purpose of entertainment and merry-making but it also gives an opportunity and space to discuss and talk about people's common concerns and needs in relation to their community development and progress. In this connection, it is worthwhile to remember Lanunungsang who says that the celebration of cultural festival has always had a vision for the promotion of peace, justice, unity and development in the society. We need to encourage inter-cultural participation towards social harmony, global peace and justice.[15] One can say that the Naga dance takes place throughout the year, nurturing and promoting common interests of development, peace, justice and unity in the society. Thus, it must be stated that dancing for ecumenism is a life-long task for every community member achieving towards harmony, peace and holistic development in the church and society.

5.4. Folk Dance for the Promotion of Ecumenism

The analysis of this study indicates that the Naga folk dance is a viable medium of ecumenical communication in terms of advocating and communicating the common interests and goals in the church and society. The celebration of Moatsu festival and folk dance can establish a common ecumenical sphere for community participation and interaction in promoting ecumenical values of contact, sharing, relationship, understanding, learning, and decision-making among the people. In addition, the study reveals that folk dance has a capacity to promote ecumenical relationships and participations both outside and inside the church.

5.4.1. Folk Dance Towards Ecumenism Outside the Church

Irrespective of their different tribal identities, religious and denominational affiliations, and different social status, people still come together outside the Church during the festival on a common ecumenical sphere for communication and participation. It shows that people want to maintain social relationship and association with one another through their involvement in the celebration of cultural festivals and folk dances. It may enable them to reaffirm their communitarian values and identity in the society. Consequently, it can keep their community life vigorous and vibrant one. Such an ecumenical presence and values in dance performances in the community may also promote the participation of

---

15 Interview with Lanunungsang in Mokokchung on 12th May 2006.

the Christians of different denominations in the church through similar dance performances and presentations.

5.4.2. Folk Dance Towards Ecumenism in the Church

Folk dance can be seen as a medium of ecumenical communication in the church and society in expressing their aspirations, needs and inner feelings to one another.

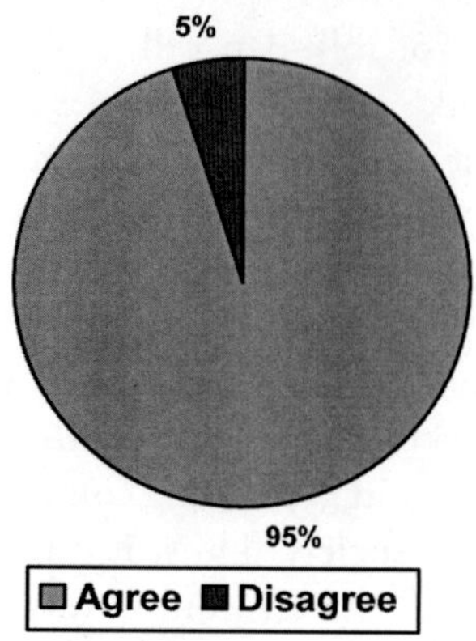

Chart 2: Folk Dance towards Ecumenism in the Church

In this connection, about 95 percent of the interviewees agreed that folk dance could be used not only outside the Church but also in the Church for the purpose of promoting ecumenical fellowship, relationship and participation among the Christians of different denominations. While 5% opined that unless the members of the church are well informed and educated, it may take time to achieve. In addition, it was pointed out that the use of folk dance in the church can be modified with gospel meanings, so that the communication of the Christian message can be meaningful and relevant in people's context. There are some folk dances and songs being performed during the Moatsu festival which had incorporated gospel meanings. It shows that while preserving their cultural folk dance in the society, the people themselves are also interested in the use of folk dance to symbolize and communicate Christian message to others. Such a folk dance that conveys the Christian message or gospel message can be called as Christian folk dance.[16] It may preserve not only their communitarian identity but also maintain their Naga Christian identity in which their faith and the gospel can be relevantly expressed and demonstrated.

16 Most of the Naga folk dances that are performed and enjoyed by the people during the celebration of Moatsu festival are being associated with the traditions, beliefs and practices of our fore-parents in the past. These folk dances can be revitalised and popularised in the church by incorporating and adopting the gospel meaning to the rhythm of dance movements and music, which may be known as Christian folk dance.

The mutual celebration of folk dance in the church can be organized and conducted as special programmes such as, youth cultural and talent presentations and Naga dance festivals. It may not only promote participation and interaction among the people but also motivate the churches to incorporate their own in worship. In fact, folk dance is a community dance and community medium as well through which people could meaningfully express and share their emotions, feelings and their way of life to others.

It is a general understanding that the folk dance can be a means of communication in bringing people together on a common platform for promoting and sharing peace and relationships among people in the church and society. In this connection, it is worth quoting Joseph Edakkudan who says that in order to create more ecumenical character in the church and society, we need to encourage inter-tribal and inter-denominational performance of dance, not on the basis of competition but on the basis of humility and acceptance of others.[17] Dance performance needs to be encouraged in the church for mutual growth of Christian faith among the people and for the promotion of ecumenical values such as, peace, unity, justice, freedom and human dignity among the people in the society.

5.5. Findings and Discussion

As mentioned earlier in the theoretical framework of the study, the research was being guided by theology, namely the theology of ecumenism, and theology of Communication. It was also being guided by the theoretical frameworks of dance as a medium of communication, in general and the Naga folk dance in particular. In addition, the research was carried out using a social anthropological approach and used two qualitative methods of participant observation and in-depth interview which are approved by the school of scientific social research. The researcher observed and checked the performances of the Naga folk dances in the field work as independent variables and collected the data in the data gathering format. The following are the findings emerging from the field work and analysis of the data.

a) **Ecumenical Relationship:** The celebration of the Naga cultural dances has a capacity to promote contact, sharing and relationship with one another in the community. In the context of the existing problem of non-ecumenical spirit and denominationalism among the people in the church, such a space for communication in Naga folk dance can promote sharing, building relationships and participation with one another can be a positive sign of ecumenical progress among the people in the church and society.

17 Interview with Joseph Edakkudan, Society of Don Bosco (SDB) at Kohima on 10th May 2006.

b) **Community Participation:** The gamut of Community participation in the celebration of cultural dances can include the way they organize the programme, taking leadership roles, active participation as members of the community, the representations of people both men and women, including the inter-village and inter-tribal representations. The celebration of the Naga cultural dance has a potential to provide people with a wide range of opportunities to participate reaffirming their communitarian identity and values.

c) **Ecumenical Communication:** Folk dance can bring people to an interpersonal level for developing interaction with one another. The elements of interpersonal relationship and inter-personal communication are essential in the study of dance in developing a dialogical and free flow of communication between people in the church and society. Since dance performance is a group activity and community event, it can enhance group interaction and participation among the people irrespective of gender, tribe, and denominational affiliation, which can be seen as an ecumenical communication.

d) **Community Development:** The research analysis of the data indicates that ecumenical unity and relationship goes beyond the church to include wider ecumenism in promoting towards common interests of community development leading to social development such as, human dignity, quality of life, freedom, unity, peace and justice.

e) **Promoting Tribal Soil and Culture as Ecumenical Resources:** The people, land culture and their spirituality can be considered as gifts from God, thereby, they can remain as resources to promote ecumenical relationships and participations in the society.

f) **Communal Harmony:** The celebration of cultural dances is a process and means of education and learning in the society. It may provide a space to work towards mutual understanding, communal harmony and unity among the people in the society. Further, it may provide new opportunities for co-operation with the people of other faiths on issues such as that of communication, communal harmony, peace and justice.

5.6. Concluding Remarks

Folk dance can be considered as a community-centered communication in promoting ecumenical relationships with one another in the church and society. In this connection, the chapter dealt with the following, such as, meeting people, initiating contact and relationship, participation, sharing, learning, understanding and decision-making. The celebration of Naga cultural festivals and folk dance could also bring people together on a common ecumenical sphere in establishing interaction, relationship and participation among the people in the community. Further, it may strengthen their communitarian identity. At this point, one can say that it is the celebration of cultural festivals and folk dance that connects people with one another irrespective of their social status, background and religious status, while it is the church that people are divided on a denominational line.

The study shows that the celebration of folk dance can provide a cultural space outside the church promoting ecumenical relationships and participation among the people in the church and society. In this connection, such a space can be used in the church for the same purpose in which Christians of different denominations may need to promote a positive attitude towards its use in the church. In addition, there is a tendency of domination and control of folk dance by the rich and elite in the society for the purpose of promoting their own political power and commercial intention. This can be checked and safeguarded by the community members emphasizing on their common interests and goals, and also by not giving in to their offers and demands.

Chapter 6

Folk Dance as Ecumenical Communication in the Church and Society

The analysis of the materials in this study shows that folk dance is a people-centered communication in the community in which the participation of the people is of utmost importance. It also revealed that the celebration of the cultural festivals and folk dance can establish a common ecumenical sphere in which all the members of the community irrespective of their status, background, religious and denominational affiliation, can come together and participate in promoting relationship, unity, peace and justice in church and society.

The folk dance is being considered as a common ecumenical sphere: a theological vision and mission. In this connection, it deals with the theological understanding of folk dance as the common ecumenical sphere in terms of communicating the Christian faith and also promoting people's participation, unity, and sharing in church and society across borders. Such an act of communication and expression can be seen as an ecumenical communication. In addition, the chapter will take up for discussion the findings, implications of the study and the recommendations, for various future course of action towards promoting the celebration of folk dance for ecumenical relationship and participation among the people in the church.

6.1. Theological Understanding of Folk Dance as Ecumenical Communication

Dance has a prominent place in Christian Scriptures. From the Biblical and theological perspectives, dance can be seen as connected to God's creation. One can say that the cosmic dance is an ever-expanding dance of the planets and the stars. The whole creation, including humanity has emerged out of the divine dance. Creation exists because God continues to act and play. In this connection, Amaladoss states that the creation of the cosmos is the expression and manifestation of God's gift of love in which God shares his life and joy with the humans and the universe.[1] In this regard, God provides a space to all humankind and the whole universe inviting them to dance along with him in which he sustains and supports them. It can be considered as the dance of God that provides and promotes justice, peace, unity, life and joy to all his creation. The dance of God starts with creation which is free, gratuitous and self-giving, actions revealing his love and grace to all.[2] God reveals himself in dances composed of creative movements and actions. Human beings can also understand and know him intimately through dance in worship.

God who became human in Jesus Christ invites all human beings to dance in the celebration of the gift of life and the joy of his salvation. In this connection, Jesus' incarnation, ministry, death and resurrection can be seen as the dance of God in Jesus Christ in bringing the eternal hope and salvation to all humankind. One can say that the dance of the risen Christ brings the whole creation together in accordance with his eternal purpose. In this regard, it is worthwhile to remember Sara Grant who says that 'the Word who became flesh and dwelt among us, who underwent death and is alive unto endless ages, can surely be called Lord of the Dance, who makes visible for us the hidden rhythms of the Creator Spirit at work within us and in our confused and torn-apart world to bring all things to their mysterious consummation.'[3] The dance of Jesus itself is the creative and redemptive act of God that brings healing, relationship and liberation to all creation. In this connection, Sydney Carter visualizes the birth, life, ministry, suffering, death and resurrection of Jesus Christ in his famous hymn entitled 'Jesus-Lord of the Dance,'[4] (see the hymn in Appendix III). This hymn has been widely used, especially in the United Kingdom and the United States

---

1 Michael Amaladoss, *The Asian Jesus* (New Delhi: IDCR & ISPCK, 2005), pp. 182-185.

2 "If we are imaginative enough we may see the loving and creative interaction between the three persons of the Trinity as a never ending dance. But with regard to us the dance of God starts with creation." *Ibid.*, p. 185.

3 The term 'Lord of the Dance', was previously used by the author referring to *Nataraja* – the dancing Shiva, however, she reinterprets it as a name for Jesus, the Word incarnate'. Sara Grant, *The Lord of the Dance* (Bangalore: Asian Trading Corporation, 1987), p. 195. "For those who are not familiar with Indian tradition it is good to note that the dancing Shiva is not a human manifestation or *avatar* of Shiva, as Rama and Krishna are *avatars* of Vishnu, but a symbolic image that expresses and manifests God's significance for us and for the cosmos." Michael Amaladoss, *The Asian Jesus*, op. cit., p. 184.

4 Sydney Carter, 'Hymn-Lord of the Dance', in *The New English Hymnal,* Part IV General Hymns, no. 375, (Norwich: The English Hymnal Company Ltd., 1986), pp.806-807. Also see, http://www. stainer.co.uk, 1963 Stainer & Bell Ltd. London. Browsed on 27-04-2006. "Lord of the Dance is a hymn with words written by Sydney Carter in 1963. He adapted the tune from the famous American shaker dance song "Simple gifts." The hymn is widely performed in the United Kingdom and the United States, and is often mistakenly thought

which portrays Jesus as the Lord of the dance. The hymn is sung in churches, and in another way in a folk club. It can be sung as a carol - a dancing kind of song, the life of which is in the dance as much as in the verbal statement.[5] In fact, this song has been popularly used in churches in promoting the dance of Jesus' sacrificial and redemptive act for all humankind in which he personally involved. It can continue to promote relationship, unity, and mutual participation among people in the church and society.

In this connection, it is worthwhile referring to Francis Peter Barboza who says that Jesus is truly the Lord of the Dance, the dancing prophet who danced through and communicated his message in and through his body.[6] The whole redemptive work of God in Jesus Christ can be seen as the dance of Jesus Who restores the broken relationship with God and with one another through his personal involvement and participation in the human history. At this point, one can say that Jesus, who is the Lord of the dance, provides a common sphere for dancing, promoting and communicating his message of love, freedom, peace, unity, justice, integrity and development among all the people in the society.

In this connection, dance in general and the folk dance in particular can be understood as God's gift and the medium of communication for all humankind in expressing their emotions, feelings and joy. During Jesus' ministry, he recognized dancing as a normal means of communication and expressing joy, when he relates the story of the prodigal son that there was dancing and rejoicing over his return (Luke 15:25). This shows that dance can be used as a means of ecumenical communication for the promotion of friendship, relationship, unity and participation among the people in the church and society.

As mentioned earlier, the Naga Folk dance can also be recognized as God's gift to people which can play an important function in the religious and social life of the people. It may be used for people's participation, sharing, learning and building relationship with one another in the community. In this regard, the common ecumenical sphere that takes place outside the church in providing participation and interaction among the people during the celebration of Naga cultural festivals and folk dances can be identified as the expression of God's gift of dance in the society. In addition, such an expression and celebration of Naga folk dance can be recognized in the church in continuing God's creative work in the world and expressing their Christian faith in terms of promoting unity,

---

to be a much older traditional hymn." en.wikipedia.org/wiki/Lord of the Dance. Browsed on 22-03-2008.

5 "I Danced in the Morning," in Hymn: Claves Regni-St. Peter's Church, Nottingham, England on-line Magazinethe On-line Magazine, http://www.stpeternottingham.org/hymns/dance.htm 01-07-2007. Browsed on 28-03-2008. There are some Christians who expressed their view that the third stanza suggests rather an anti-Semitic notion or message that the Jews were being the Jesus killers.

6 Francis Peter Barboza, *Christianity in Indian Dance Form*, op. cit., p. 11.

mutual relationship, sharing and participation among Christians of different denominations.

6.1.1. Folk Dance as the Expression of Christian Faith

God himself makes known to human beings not only through his creative, redemptive and liberative acts, but also through the movements and expressions of human presence. Dance can translate faith into art in those spaces where our words cannot reach, but where the human spirit moves forward and where Christ himself ventured ahead of us.[7] In this connection, James B. Nelson points out that 'the body can be word itself... the Word made flesh...Christian faith is an incarnational faith, a faith in the repeatable and continuing incarnation of God. God is uniquely known to us through human presence, and human presence is always embodied presence.'[8] In fact, an understanding of God and incarnation can be reflected in the articulateness of physical dimension and the expressiveness of folk dance as well. In this regard, Susan Bauer states that "when God is perceived as a creative source of being who acts in and expresses intentions through human bodily form, arms reach out to and/ or touch others, costuming facilitates bodily expression, and use of energy is also strong and quick."[9] Human movements and expressions of folk dance can be the effective means of communication in knowing and experiencing God, and also for conveying the personal experience of God and his message to others.

Folk dance itself is a symbolic[10] means of communication for conveying one's personal experience of God through body movements and actions. Such a symbolic way of communication does not only lead the spirit but also moves the heart and the body. In this regard, it is worthwhile to remember Pierre Babin when he says that the symbolic way of communication is a language full of resonance and rhythms, dance, music, stories and images, through which the Christian

7 "Look at this: Christianity is a religion of the body- the body of Christ incarnate, the body of the Word crucified, the body of the Son lifted up, the Eucharist body. The Church is Christ body. This shows what Christ achieved when he gave birth in himself to a transfigured humanity...Dance is art because it is work, change, a reaching out toward an other. With its work, it joins itself to the movement of faith." Albert Rout, *Liturgy and the Arts*, (Collegeville: The Liturgical Press Book, 1997), pp. 148-149.

8 James B. Nelson, *Embodiment: An Approach to Sexuality and Christian Theology* (Minneapolis: Augsburg Publishing House, 1978), pp. 35-36.

9 Susan Bauer, "Dance as Performance Fine Art in Liturgy," in Doug Adams and Diane Apostolos-Cappadona, eds. *Dance As Religious Studies* (New York: The Crossroad Publishing Company, 1990), p. 180.

10 "The term "Symbol" means basically to bring together. The function of a symbol is to bring together various relationships into a simple whole, to make something more meaningful through this relationship and to gather significance for members of a group so that they understand what the symbol represents." Marilyn Daniels, *The Dance in Christianity: A History of Religious Dance Through the Ages* (New York: Paulist Press, 1981), p. 12.

faith and message can be communicated in bringing freedom, healing, unity and spiritual fulfillment to the lives of the people in the church.[11] The performance of the Folk dance in worship can be also seen as a symbolic way of communication which may enable the congregation not only to express and affirm their faith, but also can enable them to fully celebrate and affirm the physical body as God's instrument. In this regard, dance in worship or liturgy can provide a visible and moving affirmation of a congregation's faith in the incarnation, the Word made flesh through Jesus Christ and the ongoing incarnation takes place in the lives of the people through their participation.[12] The movement of the body in dance performance can demonstrate the Word, the truth of words and communicate the message meaningfully. It may bring healing, promoting unity, and freedom in the lives of the community and church as well.

6.1.2. Folk Dance Towards Christian Participation

From the beginning of human history, dance was used as part of religious worship,[13] and community participation. Dance was used for the purpose of basic human need to communicate through bodily gestures and movements with other humankind and with the gods. In Christianity, God can be seen as the active moving God, who dances and participates along with the people in their struggle for achieving freedom, unity, peace and justice. One can say that it is not only humans who dance, God is also a dancer and he is immanent, dancing along with humans and experiencing their joy, feeling their pain when it occurs. In this connection, Barboza points out that conceptualizing God as the supreme dancer is quite familiar to the Indian mind, whereas it is apparently not normal to the Christian concept of God. However, if one gives careful thought to the Old Testament, New Testament and to the Christian tradition, this idea does not appear foreign to Christianity.[14] In the following Old Testament passages such as Psalm Ps. 30:11, 149:3; and Ps. 150:4 [15] in which religious dancing is recorded there is no hint of disapproval. It is therefore, evident that it must have been looked upon as a usual and integral part of worship.[16] In addition, it indicates that such religious dancing was participatory in nature and was explicitly connected

11 Pierre Babin & Mercedes Iannone, *The New Era in Religious Communication*, Translated by David Smith (Minneapolis: Fortress Press, 1991), pp. 149-154.

12 Susan Bauer, op. cit., p. 181.

13 Diane Apostolos-Cappadona, "Scriptural Women Who Danced." in Doug Adams and Diane Apostolos-Cappadona, eds. *Dance As Religious Studies* (New York: The Crossroad Publishing Company, 1990), p. 96.

14 Francis Peter Barboza, op. cit., p. 9.

15 "You have turned my mourning into dancing; you have taken off my sackcloth and clothed me with joy." (Ps. 30: 11); "Let them praise his name with dancing, making melody to him with tambourine and lyre." (Ps. 149: 3); "Praise him with tambourine and dance; praise him with strings and pipe!" (Ps. 150: 4).

16 Marilyn Daniels, op. cit., pp. 10-11.

with rejoicing[17] and the participation of each and every member was respected and encouraged.

As mentioned earlier, traditionally, most of the performances of the Naga folk dance are associated with religious worship and the participation of the whole community during the celebration. It is God the creator and sustainer who dances for the welfare of the whole community. During the celebration of the cultural festivals and folk dances, the community members express their thanksgiving to God and invoke his blessings and favour for the whole year. During the festivals, the Nagas irrespective of social status, religious and denominational affiliation, can come together and participate in the celebration of the folk dances. At this point, one can say that the supreme God who can dance with the humans and experience their emotions and feelings, can also dance alongside the Nagas in the celebration of their folk dances. In this connection, the Naga folk dance which establishes a common ecumenical sphere for people's participation and interaction outside the church can also be extended as a common platform in the church for promoting sharing, unity, contact, and relationship among the Christians of different denominations. In addition, it may enable the Christians to dance and work towards a wider ecumenism in promoting peace, harmony, human dignity and justice among the people in the society.

6.2. Ecumenical Communication as Christian Imperative

Ecumenical relations, unity and participation are not an option but imperative for every Christian because it comes from the heart of the Triune God as revealed by Jesus. Communion and unity are given in Christ Jesus because he is the source of the unity. He prayed for the unity of his disciples - as he is one with the Father.[18] The underlying principle of unity promotes relationship, sharing, equality, justice and human dignity for all people. In this connection, it is worthwhile to quote Traber when he says that, "Cultivating an ecumenical spirit should be the life-long-task of all Christians and all churches. In the deepest theological sense,

17 In both the Old Testament and the New Testament, there are sufficient examples of explicit connection with dancing and rejoicing. When the Israelites were delivered from Egypt, Miriam, the Prophetess, led the women folk out with Timbrels, dancing and rejoicing in the victory (Exodus 15:20ff.); young girls danced and rejoiced at the feast of the Lord (Judges 21: 19-21); and there was rejoicing at the feast of the harvest (Exodus 23:16). During the time of Jesus, dancing was understood by a Jew as being the means to rejoice. Dance, for a Jew meant that he was happy and joyful, and so expressed it, so it was a means for rejoicing and leaping for joy (Luke 6:23 and Mathew 5:12). Barboza, op. cit., pp. 8-9. In Aramaic which Jesus spoke, the word for 'rejoicing' is the word for 'dance'. Mathew Black, *The Aramiac Approach to the Gospel and Acts* (London: 1967), p. 158.

18 The Canberra Assembly of the WCC had described thus, "The Holy Spirit as promoter of *koinonia* (11 Cor. 13:13) gives to those who are still divided, the thirst and hunger for full communion. We remain restless until we grow together according to the wish and prayer of Christ that whoever believes in him may be one." WCC, "The Unity of the Church as *Koinonia*: Gift and Calling," in *Ecumenical Trends*, Vol. 20, no. 3, 1991, p. 42.

churches and Christians have no option but to be genuinely ecumenical."[19] At this point, one can say that to live an authentic Christian life is to live in better ecumenical relations and interactions with all men and women as God's children, which is an indispensable task for all Christians. In this regard, K. J. Thomas says that "Commitment to ecumenism and active participation in this movement is a duty of every Christian."[20] It affirms the biblical principle of one body, one Spirit, one Hope, one Lord, one Faith, one Baptism, one God, and Father of all, who is above all and through all in all. (Eph.4: 4-6). At this juncture, the churches in the North East India in general and in Nagaland in particular, need to take a new thought to go beyond the idea of non-communication and denominationalism to promote inclusive and ecumenical community within the church by identifying the cultural space in their tribal dances. Christian communication opposes any form of non-communication that divides people destroying relationship. In this connection, the Naga folk dance that can bring the people together on a common platform for participation and interaction can be considered as an ecumenical communication. Such a dance performance itself is communal in character as it is usually performed in group which can be known as community dance or communal dance.

6.2.1. Folk Dance in Christian Worship

Dance in general and the folk dance in particular, had been given an important place in worship throughout the history of the Jewish and the Christian worship. It plays as a means of communication in providing a common space for mutual participation and expression of faith in worship. Dance, in various forms, continued to be a part of the believers' expression of faith. There was the development of dance forms around the eucharist, baptism, ordination of priests, processional for entering and leaving the sanctuary, and holiday dances. Dancing has been used in Christian worship to reveal God and those close to God as active, as well as to help people identify themselves with this active moving God through their own movement.[21] Dance can not only allow the people to express their faith in Jesus but also enables them to understand and express their vertical and horizontal relationship with God and the members of the community. Without dance and other corporate expressions in worship, one could see the relationship with God as opposed to the demands of the community, and therefore withdraw from the community.[22] Folk dances in many developing countries have been rediscovering its rightful place in the church and its importance in Christian worship. In this

---

19 Michael Traber. "Ecumenical Relations in Communication." *Media Development*, 27/1,1980, p. 1.

20 K. J. Thomas, *Ecumenism A Call to Unity*, St. Peter's Guide Book Series No. 10. (Bangalore: St. Peter's Pontifical Institute Publications, 2007), p. 18.

21 Doug Adams, *Congregational Dancing in Christian Worship*, op. cit., p. 119.

22 Doug Adams, "Communal Dance Forms and Consequences Biblical Worship," op. cit., p. 39.

connection, Barboza points out that the origin, aim, goal and purpose of dance is for communication to God and humankind in history. In this connection, one does not find a great deal of dance in practice among the Indian Christians, but a closer, critical and historical survey reveals that dance has been part and parcel of the religious and social life of various groups of Christians in different regions of India.[23] In fact, dance can play a significant role in the socio-religious life of the people in fulfilling their various needs in the church and society.

Naga folk dance which is regarded as a community dance with ecumenical characteristics can be used in worship as well as for ecumenical worship. During our fore-parents' time, folk dance had an important place in worship. It played a vital role in their community worship especially during the celebration of festivals at different seasons and occasions. They used it for the sacred purpose for the praise and worship of God and also for the welfare of the people in the community. However, as mentioned earlier, after the advent of Christianity in Nagaland, the use of Naga folk dance was discouraged in the society as the early missionaries might have thought that it was associated with evil practices, such as, drinking and worship of evil spirits. Consequently, a negative attitude has been created in the minds of the people considering that the Naga folk dance is unworthy for Christian worship and ecumenical worship as well. The immaterial culture, such as folk music, folk dance, and folk theater, is regarded as God's blessings for the members of the community which can be used for religious, social, economic and political purpose. It is a medium of communication in the society which may be used for good or bad intentions in the society. It depends upon how people use it for a particular purpose in a specific context or situation. Thus, it may not be right to judge and call the Naga folk dance as devilish or unworthy to be used in Christian worship simply because it was used in secular contexts in the past.

At this point, it must be stated that since the Naga folk dance is considered as a gift from God and the heritage of the people, such misconception about their culture and folk dance can be corrected by giving proper education and awareness to the people. In addition, it can be used in the church as a means of communication for fellowship, interaction, and participation by discarding the elements that are being contrary to Christian faith and practices. In this connection, when the Psalmist says in Psalm 149: 3, "Let them praise His name with dancing," it can be understood that the Nagas can also dance as a community in group to the Lord in praise of His name through their own cultural dance as being gifted by God. In fact, the Nagas can meaningfully use it in the church by expressing their faith in Jesus and also for enriching one another through their participation.

23 Francis Barboza, "Dictionary of Indian Christian Theology: Dance," in www.drbarboza.com/dictionary.htm Browsed on 26-11-2007.

i. The Celebration of Folk Dance as Ecumenical Worship

The celebration of folk dance in Christian worship needs to be understood in inclusive terms in bringing together all the Christians of different denominations for mutual participation in common ecumenical worship which may bring their hearts closer and strengthen their relationship, interaction and promote a sense of unity and love among the people. In this connection, Iringting points out that the Naga folk dance can be used as an ecumenical communication towards establishing contact, unity and relationship among the Christians of different denominations not only outside the church but also in the church promoting cooperation and participation with one another.[24] Such a mutual participation and interaction through the celebration of the folk dance can demonstrate the unity of the body of Christ in which each and every Christian is a member which can be seen as an ecumenical worship. It may create an atmosphere of mutual understanding, respect and acceptance among the people which may break through various barriers that hinder them from coming together. In fact, God works through all customs and ethnic cultures, but also transcends all cultures which can be reflected in the use of the folk dance in worship.[25] The Naga folk dance can display the love of God incarnate in creation when it is performed in a context of genuine humility, openness, respect and Christian unity. In addition, it may strengthen the vision and mission of the Christian community to work towards a wider ecumenism in promoting the kingdom values in all realms of life in the society.

ii. Community Dance as Ecumenical Communication

Community dance bears an ecumenical character that promotes and encourages community participation and interaction with one another. It always aims at promoting the communitarian interests and values, such as, relationship, unity, peace and justice in the religious and social life of the people in the church and society. In this regard, community dance can be seen as an ecumenical communication. According to the Old Testament, communal dancing or group dancing has been more in practice than the individual dances. Throughout the history of the Jews, the shape of dances has been conditioned by the desire to have all caught up in the community.[26] It shows that the performances of the Jewish folk dances could be seen as communal dance which intended towards the worship of the living God and for the welfare of the whole community. Community dance is often inclusive in character in terms of recognizing and accepting the movement and participation of each and every member in the group or community.

---

24 Interview with Iringting Zeliangrong. Youth Secretary, NBCC, Kohima on May 9th 2006.

25 Kelly Johnson-Hill, "Dance and Worship in the Pacific Islands: A Comparative Study with Implications for an Emerging Ecumenical Consciousness," *Asia Journal of Theology*, Volume 18 Number 2 (October 2004), p. 371.

26 Francis Peter Barbosa, op. cit., p. 8.

The communal nature of dance in worship as a community has a scriptural basis, for instance, Psalm 149: 3, says, "Let them praise his name with dancing." In addition, God's heavenly restoration of Zion is a form of Community dance,[27] "And go forth in the dance of the merrymakers," and "Then shall the young women rejoice in the dance, and the young men and the old shall be merry."[28] These underlined scripture passages portray not only the importance of the community dance in the praise and worship of God but also indicate that the community participation in dance affirming their faith, communion, dignity, and solidarity is indispensable.

In the New Testament, the Christian church is built upon the deepest understanding of the Jewish tradition of worship by supporting communal or choral dancing, while suppressing individual dancing. In this connection, it is worthwhile to quote Doug Adams when he says that, the two scriptural references to individual dancing, *orchoumenos* depict decidedly non-worshipful scenes. First is the dance of Salome before Herod, Mathew (14:6 & Mark 6:22). The second instance requires careful attention as the passage has often been misread as Jesus' call for individual dance (Luke 7:31-34 & Mathew 11:16-19). Christ is not calling for the people to individual dances. Rather, "this generation" acted like the children in the marketplace expecting such a performance. This passage focuses on the false expectations and the resulting errors in judging others. From the concluding verse it is obvious that as John the Baptist does not fulfill the dancing expectation, Jesus does not fulfill the weeping one.[29]

In fact, community dance is preferable to individual dance so that one comes to look upon the constraints of living in community as a part of the response to God. In this connection, the communal or group dance accompanies the return of the prodigal son to his father[30] which may be seen as pragmatic for Christian worship. It underlines the importance of corporate expressions of community faith in worship. In this regard, it must be stated that our human relationship with God in Christ Jesus is personal and not to be considered only in terms of community life. Thus, personal worship and expression of faith in Jesus Christ need to be encouraged and realized. In addition, each and every individual person is important in the body of Christ and need to grow together in the community of corporate expression and affirmation of faith in Jesus Christ.

---

27 "Often based on circling and leaping forms found in earlier Jewish dance, twentieth-century folk dances regularize the movements and produce more uniform results than one would find in earlier periods." Doug Adams, "Communal Dance Forms and Consequences Biblical Worship," in Doug Adams and Diane Apostolos-Cappadona, eds. *Dance As Religious Studies* (New York: The Crossroad Publishing Company, 1990), p. 36.

28 Jeremiah 31:4 & 13.

29 D. Adams, "Communal Dance Forms and Consequences in Biblical Worship," op. cit., p. 3 7.

30 Luke 15:25.

Furthermore, in this paradigm, basing on the biblical directives, community dance can be considered as an ecumenical communication in which the participation of all the members of the community is respected and recognized. In this connection, Doug Adams states that "Our coming together to God includes a coming together with people in community."[31] Adams stresses the fact that the community dance can be a means of ecumenical communication in fostering mutual understanding, relationship and interaction between the worshippers of all ages and all denominational and ethnic backgrounds. In this regard, the Naga folk dance which is often performed in group may be called as community dance. It may be an effective means of ecumenical communication in bringing the people together on a common platform irrespective of their cultural differences, social status and religious and denominational affiliation, promoting unity, relationship, sharing, interaction and participation among the people in the church and society. In addition, it can support and communicate the message of freedom, love, peace, justice, human dignity and development among the people in the society.

The Hebrew Scriptures and subsequent Jewish traditions show that the dance celebrations mark the end of slavery in the past and the beginning of a new freedom to act in the world and to create a new community.[32] At the Exodus, Miriam, the prophetess, sister of Aaron, led the women folk in dance to celebrate the overthrow of the Egyptians and the end of the Israelites' slavery. It is found in the biblical account of the community dance,[33] which is an appropriate watershed between slavery and freedom, the past and the future. In fact, the Naga folk dance can create an ecumenical community in fostering freedom from all forms of divisions, discriminations, oppressions, exploitations and injustice. Further, the Naga folk dance may be used as an ecumenical communication in promoting unity, cooperation, participation, change and transformation in the church and society.

iii. Promoting Communitarian Identity and Values among the People

In the present multi-religious and diverse cultural contexts, folk dance in general and the Naga folk dance in particular, can play a significant role in bringing the members of the community on a common platform during the celebration of cultural festivals. The Naga folk dance is basically a community dance which can provide an opportunity for each and every individual to come to a common platform as a community member to affirm his or her communitarian identity. In addition, since the celebration of the Naga folk dance is inclusive in character, it provides space for inter-village and inter-tribal participation and interaction that enhances and expresses their common tribal identity.

---

31 Doug Adams, *Congregational Dancing in Christian Worship*, op. cit., p. 317.

32 Doug Adams, "Communal Dance forms and Consequences in Biblical Worship." op. cit., p. 39.

33 Exodus 15:20.

Further, it may not only allow people to establish contact, relationship, interaction and participation with one another but also can enable them to reaffirm their communitarian identity and values, such as, love, sharing, caring, helping one another, peace, and justice. It shows that such an act of affirming the values of the community can strengthen their social lives in terms of supporting and promoting their common interests for the welfare and development of the society. Consequently, it may help to preserve and promote the Naga folk dance, the cultural heritage of the people, in the church and society for communicating various information, ideas and messages including gospel message to the people. In this regard, the Christian worship may become culturally and theologically relevant and meaningful to the members of the community by incorporating certain indigenous elements into the order of worship, such as folk dance and folk music.

iv. Folk Dance as Promoting People's Spirituality

Most dances are not only about the body movements and expressions, but also about being in relation to God and with other dancers and music. The participants and spectators can understand dance as a spiritual experience through their body movements and other physical activities in a religious milieu. In ancient India, fine arts, the art of dance, painting and sculpture were developed and inspired by religion. All arts like all stages of life are embodied in religion. Indian art is life suffixed by religion and philosophy. Art was dedicated to producing objects of worship in a life ordered by faith. Indian art of all periods had been close to life both divine and traditional.[34] In fact, dance has been used over the ages as an expression of the deepest aspects of life, of the dancer's relationship with the Earth, the animal and vegetable kingdoms, and, perhaps most importantly, the connection with the Divine. In this connection, Margaret H'Doubler states that 'art cannot be divorced from life – it is life's essence and emotional value not fact. The art which expresses emotional values is dance that needs to be explored and studied.[35] In tribal societies, folk dance is a natural means of communication which expresses joy, sadness, and love. It also pleads with the God to provide food, rain, sun, and celebrates all the meaningful stages of life - birth, puberty, initiation, marriage, death. In this connection, one can see the spiritual dimension of dance in terms of communicating and relating themselves with God and others. In addition, the folk dance can remain as a means of communication in expressing their physical, spiritual and psychological needs. It may portray people's spirituality and promote interaction, unity, participation and relationship with one another.

---

34 Leela Ganapathy, "Spiritual Dance: Dance in Spiritual Indian Art," in Spiritual Dance in Indian *Art,* www.experiencefestival.com/a//Spiritual_Dance/id/4158. Browsed on 19-11-2007.

35 Margaret H' Doubler, *Dance: A Creative Art Experience* (London: The University of Wisconsin Press, 1940), p. xxi.

v. Folk Dance as Promoting Ethical Values in Society

The spiritual dimension of dance relates to the ethical dimension of dance in expressing and promoting the truth in the interest of the people and to protect human rights and dignity for all. In this connection, it is worthwhile to quote Sebastian Periannan when he says that 'Ethical dimension includes the prophetic function of communication which binds every human being by doing ones duty, witnessing to the truth and human dignity through conviviality.'[36] In fact, genuine communication presupposes respect for human dignity, equality, freedom and justice for all human beings. In this regard, the celebration of folk dance can be a means of ecumenical communication in promoting and protecting human rights, peace, justice, freedom, quality of life and human dignity among the people in the society. In this connection, Traber states that communication has to provide human rights for all without which there can be no integrity of life, no life in fullness, no community, no worship, and no human dignity.[37] In this connection, the celebration of folk dance can provide a common space for promoting and supporting the ethical values and human rights in the lives of the people in the church and society.

6.3. Implications of the Study

The above discussion has indicated the outcome of the research in relation to the presence of a common ecumenical sphere in the celebration of Naga folk dance. In this connection, research indicates its importance in facilitating and encouraging Christians to identify such an ecumenical sphere in the folk dance promoting ecumenical relations and action in the church and society.

6.3.1. Facilitating the Church's Recognition of Ecumenical Sphere in the Folk Dance

The study of this research shows that the presence of a common ecumenical sphere in the celebration of the Naga folk dance can be a dynamic force not only in the society but also in the church for promoting unity, ecumenical relationship and participation with one another. In this regard, this research may facilitate the churches to recognize their own culture as important in understanding the gospel meaningfully in their own context and also to encourage using their cultural dance in the church. As mentioned earlier, initially, the mutual celebration of folk dance in the church can be organized and conducted as a special programme such as, youth cultural and talent presentation, and Naga dance festival. It may not only promote participation and interaction among the people but also motivate the churches to incorporate their own in worship. Further, such a space for

36 Sebastian Periannan, "Eucharist in a New Media Age," presented in the Conference on "Eucharist as Communication." FABC Office of Social Communication, Bangkok, 2007. p. 9.

37 Michael Traber, "Communication for Peace and Justice," in John Bluck, ed. *Beyond Technology: Contexts for Christian Communication* (Geneva: WCC Publications, 1984), p. 61.

communication can also improve the networking and public relations between the churches. It may enable them to transcend all the barriers and establish a mutual understanding and acceptance of one another which may promote not only a sense of unity and participation among them but also towards achieving common interests and aspirations in the society.

6.3.2. Encouraging a Wider Ecumenical Awareness on Common Interests

The sphere of ecumenical presence need not be limited to the church and for the purpose of unity alone. In this connection, the celebration of folk dance has a wider ecumenical vision for the purpose of supporting and advocating peace, justice and the integrity of creation. Further, it is basically a community dance and is characterized by active participation of the people, stressing on transformation and liberation, narrative format, dramatic structure, didactic focus, and cultural appropriateness. Such cultural expressions and dance performances may become participatory, dialogical, meaningful, transformative and liberative, and geared to God's mission in the world. The celebration of Naga folk dance can be a means of ecumenical communication in allowing the Christians to work and dance together on behalf of the women, poor, needy, marginalized, downtrodden, etc. for their emancipation and restoration of human dignity in the society.

In the socio-cultural and political context of North East India in general and in Nagaland in particular, peace, justice, human dignity and development are crucial for their survival and maintaining their identity. In this situation, such an ecumenical endeavour may bring about transformation, changes in the lives of the people and also can promote growth in all the realms of God's creation. As such, Christian participation and involvement for the common interests and aspirations through the celebration of cultural dance can be considered as the ecumenical development in the society.

Christian and ecumenical communication strongly advocates social justice and peace in the context of oppressions, discriminations and exploitations against women, poor people and poor nations in many forms in the world. In this context, the church needs to get involved and work together with an ecumenical vision and mission in achieving transformation and change in the society. In this connection, this research may create a wider ecumenical awareness among the people for working together on common interests of development, freedom, unity, peace and justice. Thus, it encourages every individual to contribute to or restore the community life among the people in a wider ecumenical perspective in the context of tribalism, casteism, denominationalism, religious pluralism, mass media and globalization.

6.3.3. Enhancing the Role of the People in the Ecumenical Movement

The celebration of the Naga cultural festivals and folk dance is people-centered communication in the society. The celebration of these events are adequately focused and organized by the people themselves, for the welfare of the members of the community. In this connection, one can see the vital role of the people in the celebration of cultural festivals and folk dance in the community which can strengthen and promote relationship, unity, participation, communitarian values and identity in the church and society. In this paradigm, the presence of common ecumenical sphere in the folk dance which brings people together for interaction, fellowship and participation with one another can be seen as ecumenical movement. In this regard, the celebration of folk dance in the church can overcome and ward off prejudices and fears from the minds of the Christians of different denominations resulting in showing openness towards one another with a spirit of cooperation and unity. Such a positive attitude and an atmosphere of openness and sharing as being equal partners in the celebration of folk dance can provide a space for dialogical communication among the Christians which can strengthen mutual understanding and relationship with one another. In this regard, it may further enhance the importance of the role of the people which includes the folk dancers, dance leaders, public leaders and religious leaders in ecumenical movement in the region. Further, it can sharpen their parts in relation to planning, coordination, cooperation, and participation, in the celebration of cultural festivals and folk dances for the purpose of promoting ecumenical relationship, sharing, unity, interaction, participation, peace and justice in the church and society. Further, it may also reaffirm their communitarian identity and values in the church and society. In this connection, the gospel can be meaningfully communicated to the people through the expressions and movements of their cultural dance in the context of worship. Perhaps, it may help the churches to move towards an ecumenical fellowship, sharing, and learning its true sense.

6.3.4. Promoting Folk Dance in the New Media Age

The human community in general and the Nagas in particular, are living in the new media age which is characterized by accessing to the cyberspace. It happens in the domains of digital communication and information that includes 'the Internet, email, chat rooms, MUDs, (Multi User domains) digital imaging systems, virtual reality, new biomedical technologies, artificial life and interactive entertainment systems.[38] New Media has become a significant element in everyday life. It allows people to communicate, bank, shop and entertain. New media rely on digital technologies, allowing for previously separate media to converge.[39] In addition, it is also related to information communication technology (ICT) which can bring together different types of analogical communication media and forms

38 Andrew Dewdney and Peter Ride, *The New Media Handbook* (London: Routledge, 2006), p. 74.

39 "New Media." en.wikipedia.org/wiki/New_media. Browsed on 21-02-2008.

into a single digital system which may be called convergence.[40] This technological advancement has enabled people to communicate and interact meaningfully with one another in the society. In Nagaland, especially, in the towns and cities, where the computer, Internet, social, and telecommunications, facilities are available, people can use them for recording, sharing, and preserving their cultural heritage such as, folklore, folk songs, folk dance, dramas, and folktales. In addition, people from the rural areas can also enjoy having access to these facilities through proper coordination among the people. This can be done not only for the purpose of getting information and entertainment but also for the promotion of ecumenical relationship, unity, peace, justice, participation, development and human dignity among the people in the church and society. In this connection, copyright of each and every programme may be maintained so that their rich cultural heritage may be protected and preserved from commercialization and exploitation from within and outside.

6.4. Recommendations Towards Ecumenical Communication

The present research has found the presence of ecumenical common sphere in the Naga folk dance which can be extended to the churches for establishing ecumenical relationship, sharing, interaction and participation between Christians of different denominations. It shows that Christians of different denominations are realizing its importance in worship for mutual participation in the church. However, Christians are not familiar with the use of folk dance in the church as they have neglected it for many years. In addition, they need to use it for the purpose of enjoying fellowship and sharing with one another and also for expressing and communicating the gospel message relevantly and meaningfully in the church and society. The following recommendations can be considered and moved with a view to popularize the celebration of the Naga folk dance in the church and society. In addition, it may promote not only ecumenical relationship and participation among Christians of different denominations, but also may support towards a wider ecumenism in all the realms of God's creation in the society.

6.4.1. To Promote People-Based Indigenous Communications Towards Ecumenical Relations

A society or a community can harmoniously and meaningfully exist through various means of communication available therein. In Naga society, the people-based indigenous communications such as, folk music, folk dances, and folklore, are powerful media of communication both in the religious and social life of the people. In this connection, during our fore-parent's time, folk dance and music

40 "Convergence is a technological phenomenon through which telephone, radio, television, VCR's Cameras, and so on, are becoming an integral function of the multimedia personal computers." John Joshva Raja and Samson Prabhakar, eds., op. cit., p. 367.

had an important place in community worship and celebration. The Naga folk dance is the medium of communication and interaction in the society which can strengthen their social relationship and also can promote their communitarian values. Since it belongs to the community, and is participatory in nature, it serves as the people-centered communication in catering to the needs of the people by providing as a means of entertainment and enjoyment to people in the community. In addition, it can be used by the members of the community for the welfare and development of the society.

As mentioned earlier, the present theoretical concept and models of ecumenism were practically unsuccessful, especially in North East India, mainly because these models were of the top-down kind and centered within the sphere of the church under the high-level church leadership, comprising official representatives where the lay people were sidelined. In this context, research shows that the celebration of Naga folk dance can serve as the people-centered communication in the church at a micro-level in terms of bringing together Christians on a common platform for participation and interaction, hence promoting unity, relationship and cooperation with one another.

In fact, today, this indigenous media can play an important role in the church and society in bringing the whole community together on a common platform for promoting interaction, sharing, relationship, unity and participation among the people. Hence, the people-based indigenous communications can be popularized among the people in the church so that their faith and the gospel message can be meaningfully communicated. In this connection, the experts of folklore in the community, folk dance teachers, folk dancers, youth leaders and church leaders who have a lot of experiences, knowledge and understanding about the importance of people-based indigenous communications can take the initiatives in organizing and inviting people to participate in the celebration of folk dance in the church. In addition, as mentioned earlier, such Christian folk dance can be encouraged and promoted in the church which may convey the gospel message through the dance movements and music as well. It may create a space for communication among the people for wider mutual participation, interaction, sharing, understanding, and learning with one another in the church.

6.4.2. To Promote Dialogical Communication between Christians of Different Denominations

The celebration of folk dance can promote dialogical communication between Christians of different denominations. Dialogical communication has a capacity to create a healthy atmosphere of learning experience with one another with a spirit of respect and appreciation. Such an attitude of interaction and communication among the people can help them to sort out and overcome such misconception of ideas, prejudices, fears and doubts. Consequently, it can provide a better understanding and participation among Christians in the church. In addition, it also may establish a mutual relationship and interaction with one another which may allow them to grow together as a community. As mentioned earlier, the celebration of folk dance that promotes dialogical communication among the people can be a means of developing an ecumenical relation between churches. Thus, such a dialogical communication can be promoted and encouraged in the church for the enrichment and growth of the people in faith and unity.

6.4.3. To Communicate Social Justice and bring about Communitarian Communication

Folk dance can be a means of ecumenical communication in promoting peace, unity, justice, development and human dignity in society. In this connection, the Christian denominations can be encouraged and motivated to come together on a common platform and work for promotion of common interests of the people in the society in relation to the development and emancipation of the poor, women, and the neglected sections of people from all forms of oppression, suppression, discriminations and exploitations in the society. It may be seen as an ecumenical development among the people through their mutual participation and cooperation.

a) Communicating Justice towards Women

Furthermore, it encourages and promotes the role and status of women in the Church and society in the context where women are denied the exercise of their rights and privileges, as they experience discrimination and unequal treatment compared to their male partners. It is therefore, aimed to give voice to the women so that they may be able to articulate their own inner feelings, experiences and pains, and also thereby give meaningful contribution and service to the Church and society.

b) Communicating the Principles of Community Development and Justice

In the context of economic liberalization and globalization which widens the haves and have-nots, ecumenism challenges the Church to make a meaningful partnership with God and in communion with the poor, women and the victims of globalization, to intervene and alter equations, relationships and structures which degrade people.[41] In such a context, the Church and all the Christian communicators need to side with the poor for their liberation and development.

c) Communicating Socio-political Peace

The relentless wars and tensions between nations, ethnic conflicts, terrorism, communal conflicts, and ecological destruction, are the realities that always

41 R. Devadoss, "Ecumenism: A Framework for Praxis," in Vinod Victor, Leslie Nathaniel & P. Surya Prakash, eds., *Ecumenism: Prospects and Challenges.* (New Delhi: ISPCK, 2001), p. 246.

promote fear and uncertainty in the lives of the people. It demands socio-political peace and justice among the global community. In the context of Northeast India, peace, justice and development are crucial not only for their survival but also for maintaining peace, justice, identity and human dignity. It is in this context that the mutual participations and cooperation of Christians will be significant to achieve the needs and aspirations of the people in the region.

6.4.4. To Establish an Institute for the Study and Promotion of Folk Dance

The Nagas are rich in folk dances which are communal in character. There are different types of folk dances available in the community that is associated with various contexts and situations in the society. These folk dances need to be collected, studied and promoted by means of teaching and training the younger generations. In order to put this into action, an institute or an academy for the study and promotion of the Naga folk dance need to be set up. In fact, this will facilitate and promote their cultural heritage, such as, folk dance, and folk music among the people in the church and society. It can help them to get familiar with their cultural heritage and practices. In addition, such an institute can remain resourceful in making their dance meaningful and relevant in accordance with the context and needs of the people in the community. It also may play a vital role in imparting education and updated knowledge on folk dance and music to the people, especially the younger generation.

6.4.5. Conduct a Workshop and Education Seminar

The present research shows that the people are slowly realizing the need and importance of using folk dance in the church and society for the purpose of promoting interaction, participation and relationship with one another. However, there are many people who have the narrow understanding about their culture by projecting their own dance as unfit to be used in the church. In addition, people do not have a proper understanding and knowledge about the importance of ecumenism in the church and society. In this connection, workshops and education seminars should be organized and conducted in the church, colleges and schools, in order to inculcate proper education and understanding about Naga culture, and create awareness about the importance of celebrating folk dance in the church. It may encourage ecumenical endeavours and values among the people in promoting contact, interaction, relationship, sharing, justice, peace, and development, in the church and also in all the realms of God's creation.

6.4.6. Scope for Future Research

The presence of ecumenical common sphere in the folk dance and its application in the church for the purpose of promoting ecumenical relations can be further strengthened and its intentions by understanding its relationship with the liturgical and cultural factors in worship such as, the indigenization of worship, liturgical dance in Christian worship and ecumenical worship. In this connection, a deeper and a wider cultural, liturgical and theological research can be done in order to reconceptualise the issues mentioned above.

6.5. Concluding Remarks

The above discussion has dealt with the theological vision and mission in relation to the presence of the ecumenical relationship in the Naga folk dance. In this connection, basic principle of the church is to establish an ecumenical community within the church. It shows that the church has failed the ecumenical connection in creating an ecumenical space within the church, enabling people to come together irrespective of culture, language, denomination, and social status, promoting towards interaction, sharing, relationship, participation, peace, justice, unity and development in the church and society. However, there is a lack of ecumenical spirit within the church in endeavouring toward sharing, relationship, participation and unity among the people in the church, because of denominationalism, and power struggles within the church. In such a context, one can find an ecumenical space in the celebration of Naga tribal dances, in terms of bringing people together as community members on a common platform. This shows that the concept of community for the tribal people begins to exist outside the church. Here, such community consciousness is crucial for the tribal people as it becomes a cultural space for them to come together during the cultural celebration. Such a space goes beyond their cultural, linguistic and denominational barriers to include others in establishing contact, relationship, participation and unity in the society. At this juncture, the church needs to go beyond her exclusive and comfort zones to recognize such a cultural space outside the church, to bring all people together from within and outside the churches, creating an ecumenical community.

At this point, it must be stated that if the celebration of Naga cultural festivals and folk dance provides a cultural-ecumenical space outside the church where God works with the people allowing them to practice and realize ecumenism through their interaction and participation with one another, then, it is theologically relevant for the church to recognize and enhance the process within the church or use such available cultural space for ecumenical understanding, relationship and participation among the members of the church and society. In this connection, the recommendations of the research can be taken with commitment and dedication by all the Nagas, so that they may experience change and transformation in relation to ecumenical progress and endeavours in the church and society.

Appendix I

A. Data Gathering Procedure for Participant Observation

1. Demographic Data

1. Who organizes the programme?
2. Date of Dance Performance
4. At what time the programme starts and how long it lasts?
5. Who leads the programme?
6. Who are the people coming to the dance programme?
7. What are the representations of people according to age wise?
8. What is the total representation of men and women?
9. What is the denominational representation?
10. How many villages have participated?
11. How many tribes have participated?
12. How is the seating arrangement?
13. Do they sit together or separately?
14. How do they perform and use gestures such as feet, body movements, facial expressions, etc.
15. What kind of tribal attires and ornaments do they wear?
16. What kinds of traditional instruments do they play?

2. Dance Performance

1. Who dances with whom?
2. What are the types of dances they perform?
3. How do men and women relate with each other and maintain interpersonal relationship in the group?
4. What kind of group do they form?
5. What is the content of the dances?

3. Post Dance Behaviour

1. How do they go home?
2. How do people appreciate them?
3. How do they appreciate each other?
4. Whether other personalities like Pastor, other tribal leaders are given opportunity and participate in the event actively?

Appendix II

A. Names of the Interviewees taken for the In-depth Interview

1. Mr. Sademmeren Lkr
2. Mr. Mhonrao Kikon
3. M. Busham Pastor
4. Mr. Hekhevi Achum.
5. Mr. Veswüzao Phesao NEIZCC
6. Mr. Talinucha NEIZCC
7. Mr. L. K. Among Pastor
8. Mr. Shirongmong
9. Mr. Among Chang
10. Rev. Keviyiekieliu Pastor
11. Rev. Iringting Zeliangrong
12. Mr. Alemchiba.
13. Fr. Joseph Edakkudan
14. Mr. Vilalhou Angami
15. Mr. Neivilieo Zuyie. Youth Secretary, ABCC
16. Prof. Dr. Lanunungsang
17. Mr. Bendangangshi
18. Mr. Sangyusang S. Pongener
19. Mr. Y. Leiphoa Konyak
20. Mr. S. Kamlong Phom
21. Rev. P. Solomon Pastor (Pentecostal church)
22. Mr. Heirang Lungalang. Zeliang
23. Mr. Daniel Associate Pastor (NCRC)

B. The types of questions asked during the In-depth Interview

1. During the festivals, whether all the members of the community are invited and welcomed?
2. Can a folk dance provide a common platform for people towards achieving contact and relationship among the people?
3. During the festivals, whether both men and women dance together or separately?
4. Can a folk dance promote peace, unity and justice in the church and society?
5. Can we use folk dance in the church?

Appendix III

Hymn-Lord of the Dance by Sydney Carter

1. I danced in the morning when the world was begun,
   And I danced in the moon and the stars and the sun,
   I came down from heaven and I danced on the earth;
   At Bethlehem I had my birth.
   Refrain:
   Dance, then, wherever you may be;
   I am the Lord of the Dance, said he,
   And I'll lead you all, wherever you may be,
   And I'll lead you all in the dance, said he.

2. I danced for the scribe and the Pharisee.
   But, they would not dance and they would not follow me
   I danced for the fishermen, for James and John.
   They came with me and they went on.
   Refrain:

3. I danced on the Sabbath and I cured the lame;
   The holy people said it was a shame.
   They whipped and they stripped and they hung me on high;
   They left me there on a cross to die.
   Refrain:

4. I danced on a Friday when the sky turned black
   It's hard to dance with the devil on your back.
   They buried my body and they thought I'd gone;
   But, I'm the dance and I still go on.

Appendix IV

Photos of Naga Folk Dancing Troupes During the Moatsu Festival

Photo 1: Moatsu Festival dance

Photo 2: Children Dance

Photo 3: War Dance

Photo. 4: Festival Dance in Progress

Photo 5: Group Dance

Photo 6: Hornbill Dance

Photo 7: Seasonal dance

References

Abraham, K. C. ed. *Christian Witness in Society*. Bangalore: BTESSC, 1998.

Adams, Doug. *Congregational Dancing in Christian Worship*. Texas: The Sharing Company, 1980.

Adams, Doug and Diane Apostolos-Cappadona, eds. *Dance as Religious Studies*. New York: The Crossroad Publishing Company, 1990.

Aier, Alongla P. ed. *NBCC: From Darkness To Light*. Kohima: Nagaland Baptist Church Council, 1997.

Aier, L. Imtisüpong. *Aor Sobaliba Temzüng Ozüng (Ao Naga Customary Law)*. Mokokchung: Author, 1991.

Aier, Toshi. "A Study of the Ecumenical Movement in North East India," *M.Th. Thesis,* (2000).

Alemchiba, M. *The Art and Crafts of Nagaland*. Kohima: Naga Institute of Culture, 1968.

_______. *A Brief Historical Account of Nagaland*. Kohima: Naga Institute of Culture, 1971.

Ao, A. Bendangyabang. *History of Christianity in Nagaland: A Source Material*. Mokokchung: Shalom Ministry, 1998.

_______. *History of Christianity in Nagaland: Social Change 1872 – 1972* Bangalore: Shalom Ministry Publications, 2004.

Ao, L. Kijung. *Nokinketer Mongchen: Nagaland nung Arogo Tetenzük Otsü,* (The Genesis of the Ao Naga Church History). Guwahati: Ao Baptist Arogo Mungdang (ABAM), 1972.

Ao, O. Alem. *Tsüngremology: Ao Naga Christian Theology*. Mokokchung: Clark Theological College, 1994.

Ao, Tajen. *Christianity Versus Ao Nagas*. Mokokchung: Author, 1984.

Ahuja, Ram. *Research Methods*. Jaipur: Rawat Publications, 2001.

Amaladoss, Michael. *The Dancing Cosmos: A Way to Harmony*. Anand: Gujarat Sahitya Prakash, 2003.

________. *The Asian Jesus*. New Delhi: IDCR/ISPCK, 2005.

_______. *Beyond Inculturation: Can the Many be One?* New Delhi: ISPCK, 2005.

Amirtham, Samuel & Cyris H. S. Moon, eds. *The Teaching of Ecumenics*. Geneva: WCC Publications, 1987.

Appavoo, James Theophilus. *Folklore for Change*. Madurai: TTS Publications, 1986.

Arens, Edmund. *Christopraxis: A Theology of Action,* Translated by John F. Hoffmeyer. Minneapolis: Augsburg Fortress Press, 1995.

Ariarajah, S. W. *Gospel and Culture: An Ongoing Discussion within the Ecumenical Movement*. Geneva, WCC Publications, 1994.

Arthur, Chris, ed. *Religion and The Media: An Introductory Reader*. Cardiff: WACC & University of Wales Press, 1993.

Atsongchanger, Mar. *The Historical Memoranda of the Nagas and their Neighbours*. Mokokchung: Tribal Communication & Research Centre, 1995.

Babin, Pierre and Iannone, Mercedes. *New Era in Religious Communication*. Philadelphia: Fortress Press, 1991.

Balling, Jakob. *The Story of Christianity: From Birth to Global Presence*. Grand Rapids: William B. Eerdmans Publishing Company, 2003.

Bangkok Assembly 1973: Minutes and Report of the Assembly of the Commission on World Mission and Evangelism of the World Council of Churches, December 31, 1972 and January 9-12, 1973, WCC, 1973.

Barboza, Francis Peter. *Christianity in Indian Dance Forms*. Delhi: Sri Satguru Publications, 1990.

Bareh, H. M. ed., *Encyclopedia of Northeast India-6: Nagaland*. New Delhi: Mittal Publications, 2001.

Barnard and Jonathan Spencer eds. *Encyclopedia of Social and Cultural Anthropology.* London and New York: Routledge, 1996.

Barpujari, H. K. *The American Missionaries and North- East India (1836-1900)*. Guwahati: Spectrum Publications, 1986.

Bauerochse, Lothar. *Learning To Live Together*. Geneva: WCC Publications, 1996.

Bea, Augustine Cardinal. *Unity in Freedom: Reflection on the Human Family*. New York: Harper & Row, Publishers, 1964.

Beattie, John. *Other Cultures: Aims, Methods and Achievements in Social Anthropology.* London: Routledge, 1999.

Bell, G. K. A., ed. *Documents On Christian Unity*, 1948-57. Fourth Series. London: Oxford Press, 1958.

Bell, Judith. *Doing Your Research Project: A Guide for first-time Researchers in Education and Social Science*. Third Edition. New Delhi: Viva Books Private Limited, 1999.

Bent, Ans J. Van der. *Vital Ecumenical Concerns: Sixteen Documentary Surveys.* Geneva: WCC Publications, 1986.

Berger, Arthur Asa. *Media and Communication Research Method.* Thousand Oaks: Sage Publications, 2000.

Best, Thomas F & Dagmar Heller. eds. *Worship Today: Understanding, Practice, Ecumenical Implications.* Faith & Order Paper no. 194. Geneva: WCC, 2004.

Bhavnani, Enakshi. *The Dance in India: The Origin and History, Foundations, the Arts and Science of the Dance in India - Folk and Tribal.* Bombay: Taraporevala's Treasure House Books, 1970.

Black, Mathew. *The Aramiac Approach to the Gospel and Acts*. London: 1967.

Bluck, John. *Beyond Technology: Contexts for Christian Communication*. Geneva: WCC Publications, 1984.

Blumer, Herbert. *Symbolic Interactionism: Perspective and Method.* Englewood Cliffs, NJ: Prentice-Hall, 1969.

Bogdan, Robert. *Participant Observation in Organisational Settings.* Syracuse, NY: Syracuse University Press, 1972.

Bridston, Keith R. & Wagoner, Watter D. *Unity in Mid-Career: An Ecumenical Critique*. New York: Macmillan Company, 1963.

Briggs, John, Mercy Amba Oduyoye and George Tsetsis, eds. *A History of the Ecumenical Movement. Volume 3, 1968-2000*. Geneva: WCC Publications, 2004.

Bruyn, Severyn. *The Human Perspective in Sociology: The Methodology of Participant Observation.* Englewood Cliffs, NJ: Prentice-Hall, 1966.

Caplan, Lionel. *Religion and Power: Essays on the Christian Community in Madras.* Madras: CLS, 1989.

Cardijn, Joseph. *Laymen into Action.* London: Geoffrey Chapman, 1964.

Carey, James W. *Communication as Culture: Essay on Media and Society.* New York: Routledge, 1989.

Castro, Emilio. *A Passion for Unity: Essay on Ecumenical Hopes and Challenges.* Geneva: WCC Publications, 1992.

Chatterji, Saral K. ed. *Society and Culture in North-east India: A Christian Perspective.* New Delhi: ISPCK, 1996.

Chethimattam, John B. *Towards a Theology of Intercommunion.* Bangalore: Dharmaram Publications, 2001.

Chib, Sukhdev Singh. *This Beautiful India Nagaland.* New Delhi: Light and Life Publishers, 1980.

Chitambar, J. B. *Introductory Rural Sociology: A Synopsis of Concepts and Principles.* New Delhi: Wiley Eastern Limited, 1973.

Christians, Clifford G. & Michael Traber, eds. *Communication Ethics and Universal Values.* Thousand Oaks: Sage Publications, 1997.

Christian Conference of Asia, *The Communication Revolution and NWICO: The Challenge to the Churches.* Tao Payoh: CCA, 1985.

Clark, M. M. *A Corner in India.* Guwahati: Christian Literature Centre, 1978.

Congar, Yves M. J. *Lay People in the Church: A Study for a Theology of Laity.* London: Geoffery Chapman, 1985.

Collingwood, R. H. *The Principles of Art.* London: Oxford University Press, 1974.

Collins, Richard, ed. *Media, Culture and Society: A Critical Reader.* Edited by Curran, James. Newbury Park: Sage Publications, 1986

Copland, Roger and Marshall Cohen, eds., *What is Dance?: Readings in Theory and Criticism.* Oxford: Oxford University Press, 1983.

Cross, F. L. & Livingstone, E. A. *The Oxford Dictionary of the Christian Church.* Oxford: Oxford University Press, 1997.

Dance: The Study of Dance and the Place of Dance in Society. Proceedings of the VIII Commonwealth and International Conference on Sport, Physical Education, Dance, Recreation and Health, Conference '86 Glasgow, 18- 23 July. London: E. & F. N. Spon Ltd., 1986.

Daniels, Marilyn. *The Dance in Christianity: A History of Religious Dance Through the Ages.* New York: Paulist Press, 1981.

David Levinson and Melvin Ember eds. *Encyclopedia of Cultural Anthropology.* New York: Henry Holt, 1996.

Davies, J. G. *Liturgical Dance: An Historical, Theological and Practical Handbook.* London: SCM Press LTD, 1984.

Deitering, Carolyn. *The Liturgy as Dance and Liturgical Dancer.* New York: The Crossroad Publishing Company, 1984.

Denzin, Norman K. and Yvonna S. Lincoln, eds. *Handbook of Qualitative Research.* Thousand Oaks: Sage Publications, 1994.

Department of Art & Culture, ed. *Cultural Panaroma: Hornbill Festival 2004.* Kohima: Department of Art & Culture, 2004.

Department of Art & Culture, ed. *Echoes of Nagaland: Hornbill Festival, 2005* Kohima: Department of Art & Culture, 2005.

Deshmukh, Sandeep. *Group Communication: Theory and Methods.* New Delhi: ANE Books India, 2008.

Dewdney, Andrew and Ride, Peter. *The New Media Handbook* London: Routledge, 2006.

Dissanayake, Wimal, ed., *Communication Theory: The Asian Perspective.* Singapore: Asia Mass Communication Research and Information Centre, 1988.

Doohan, Leonard. *The Lay-Centered Church: Theological and Spirituality.* Minneapolis: Winston Press, 1984.

Dorson, R. M. *American Folklore.* Chicago: The University of Chicago, 1954.

Doshi, S. L. & Jain, P. C. *Social Anthropology.* Jaipur: Rawat Publications, 2002.

Douglas, J. D. ed., *The New International Dictionary of the Christian Church* Grand Rapids: Zondervan Corporation, 1978.

Downs, Frederick S. "Church Union in the North East India" (1965).

______. "Church Union: News and Views" 1965.

______. "Church Union: Theological and Non-Theological Factors" (1965).

______. "A Reply to 'A Picture of an Organic Church Union,'" Guwahati: Published by the Author, 1970, pp. 1-16.

______. *The Mighty Works of God.* Guwahati: CLC, 1971.

______. *Christianity in North East India: Historical Perspectives.* Delhi: ISPCK, 1983.

______. "Ecumenical Developments" in *Christianity in North East India: Historical Perspective.* Guwahati: ISPCK, 1983, pp. 155-171.

______. "Tribal Ecumenism in North East India: The Christian Role in Solidarity Movement," in Renthy Keitzar, Ed., *A Trainer of Leaders: Essays in Honour of Jonathan H. Thumra,* Special issue of ETC Journal, Vol. 2, No. 2, 1989.

______. "Import Substitution: Reflections of Indigenization of Ecclesiastical Conflict in North East India," in *Indian Missiological Review* (Special Issue on the Centenary of the Church of North East India, 1890-1990), Vol. 12, No. 3 & 4, 1990. pp. 71 – 80.

______ . *History of Christianity in India: North East India in the Nineteenth and Twentieth Centuries.* Vol. V, Part 5, Bangalore: CHAI, 1992.

Dozo, Phuveyi. *The Growth of the Baptist Church in Chakesang Naga Tribe.* Kohima: Chakesang Baptist Church, 1978.

D'Souza, Henry, ed. *A Communicating Church In India.* New Delhi: CBCI Media Centre, 2002.

Duchrow, Ulrich. *Conflict over the Ecumenical Movement: Confessing Christ Today in the Universal Church.* Translated by David Lewis. Geneva: WCC Publications, 1981.

Eilers, Franz-Josef. *Church and Social Communication: Basic Documents.* Indore: Satprakashan Sanchar Kendra, 1996.

Eilers, Franz-Josef. *Communicating between Cultures: An Introduction to Intercultural Communication.* Indore: Satprakashan Sanchar Kendra, 1993.

Eilers, Franz-Josef. *Communicating in Ministry and Mission: An Introduction to Pastoral and Evangelizing Communication.* Indian edition. Manila: Logos (Divine Word) Publications, Inc., 2004.

Ellfeldt, Lois. *Dance From Magic to Art.* Dubuque: Wm. C. Brown Company Publishers, 1976.

Elwin, Verrier. *Nagaland.* Shillong: P. Dutta, Research Dept. Advisor's Secretariat, 1961.

______. *The Nagas in the Nineteenth Century.* Bombay: Oxford University Press, 1969.

Ember, Carol R. and Melvin Ember, *Cultural Anthropology*, 7th Edition, Englewood Cliffs, N. J.: Prentice Hall, 1993.

Emmanuel, Dominic. *Challenges of Christian Communication and Broadcasting: Monologue or Dialogue?* Hampshire & London: Macmillan Press Ltd, 1999.

Evans, G. R. *Method in Ecumenical Theology: The Lessons So Far.* Cambridge: Cambridge University Press, 1996.

Ferraro, Gary. *Cultural Anthropology: An Applied Perspective*. St. Paul: West Publishing Company, 1992.

Firth, Cyril Bruce. *An Introduction to Indian Church History*. Revised Edition. Madras: CLS, 1976.

Fore, William F. *Television and Religion: The Shaping of Faith, Values and Culture*. New Haven: SBS Press, 1987.

Fraleigh, Sondra Horton & Hanstein, Penelope, eds. *Researching Dance: Evolving Modes of Inquiry*. Pittsburgh: The University of Pittsburgh Press, 1999.

Freire, Paulo. *Pedagogy of the Oppressed*. New York: Herder and Herder, 1971.

Gadamer, Hans-Georg. *Truth and Method*. London: Sheed & Ward, 1975.

Gagne, Ronald, Thomas Kane and Robert VerEecke, *Introducing Dance in Christian Worship*. Washington: The Pastoral Press Washington, D.C., 1984.

Gandhi, P. Jegadish, & George Cheriyan, eds. *Ecumenical Perspectives in Asia Beyond 2000: Towards Demarginalisation*. Chennai: Association of Christian Institutes for Social Concern in Asia (ACISCA), 2000.

Gandhi, P. Jegadish & K. C. John, eds. *Upon the Wings of Wider Ecumenism: Essays and Tributes in Honour of Rev. Dr. M.J. Joseph ECC*. New Delhi: ISPCK/ECC, 2006.

Ganguli, Milada. *A Pilgrimage to the Nagas*. New Delhi: Oxford & IBH Publishing Co., 1984.

Geertz, Clifford. *The Interpretation of Cultures*. New York: Basic Books, *Inc.*, 1973.

George Newnes Limited. *Chambers's Encyclopedia: Confirmation – Educational Psychology*, New edition, Vol. IV. London: George Newnes Limited, 1959.

Ghosh, B. B. *Nagaland District Gazetteers: Mokokchung District*. Kohima: Government of Nagaland, 1979.

Ghosh, G. K. *Tribals and Their Culture in Manipur and Nagaland, Vol. III*. New Delhi: Ashish Publishing House, 1995.

Granfield, Patrick, ed. *The Church and Communication: Communication, Culture and Theology*. Kansas City: Sheed & Ward, 1994.

Grant, Sara. *The Lord of the Dance*. Bangalore: Asian Trading Corporation, 1987.

Goodal, F. N. Norman. *The Ecumenical Movement: What it is and what it does*. 2nd ed. London: Oxford University Press, 1964.

_______ . *Ecumenical Progress: A Decade of Change in the Ecumenical Movement*, 1961-71. London: Oxford University Press, 1972.

Goose, Gideon. *Bringing Churches Together: A Popular Introduction to Ecumenism*, Revised and Enlarged Edition. Geneva: WCC Publications, 1993.

Gunter, Barrie. *Media Research Methods*. London: Sage Publications, 2000.

Gupta, V. S. *Communication and Development: The Challenge of the Twenty-first Century*. New Delhi: Concept Publishing Company, 2000.

Habermas, Jurgen. *The Theory of Communicative Action, Volume 2, Lifeworld and System: the Critique of Functionalist Reason*. Translated by Thomas McCarthy. Cambridge: Polity Press, 1987.

________ . *Structural Transformation of the Public Space*. Cambridge, Mass: MIT Press, 1989

Haimendorf-Fürer, Christoph Von. *Return to the Naked Nagas: An Anthropologist's View of Nagaland 1936-1970*. New Delhi: Vikas Publishing House, 1976.

Hamelink, Cees J. *The Politics of World Communication: A Human Right Perspective* London: Sage Publications, 1994.

Hanna, Judith Lynne. *To Dance is Human: A Theory of Nonverbal Communication*. Austin: University of Texas Press, 1979.

H'Doubler, Margaret. *Dance: A Creative Art Experience.* London: The University of Wisconsin Press, 1972.

Hillerbrand, Hans J. ed. *The Encyclopedia of Protestantism,* Vol. 2, D-K, (New York: Routledge, 2004.

Hoover, Stewart M. and Knut Lunby, ed. *Rethinking Media, Religion and Culture.* New Delhi: Sage Publications, India Pvt. Ltd., 1997.

Herskovits, Melville F. *Cultural Anthropology.* Culcutta: Oxford and IBH Publishing Co.1955.

Horam, M. *Naga Polity.* New Delhi: B. R. Publishing Corporation, 1975.

_______. *Nagas Old Ways and New Trends.* New Delhi: Cosmos Publications, 1988.

_______. *North East India.* New Delhi: Cosmos Publications, 1990.

Horsfield, Peter G. *Religious Television: The American Experience. Communication and Human Values.* London: Longmans, 1984.

Horton, Walter Marshall. *Christian Theology: An Ecumenical Approach.* New York: Harper and Brothers Publishers, 1955.

Hooft, W. A. Visser't, ed. *The New Delhi Report: The Third Assembly of the World Council of Churches 1961.* London: WCC Publications, 1962.

Hooft, W. A. Visser't. *No Other Name: The Choice between Syncretism and Christian Universalism.* London: SCM, 1963.

Hrangkhuma, F. ed. *Christianity in India: Search for Liberation and Identity.* New Delhi: CMS/ISPCK, 1998.

Hutton, J. H. *The Sema Nagas.* Bombay: Oxford University Press, 1968.

_______. *The Angami Nagas.* London: Oxford University Press, 1969.

Iyer, L. A. Krishna and L. K. Bala Ratnam, *Anthropology in India.* Bombay: Bharatiya Vidya Bhavan, 1961.

Jamir, A. Temjen. *Popularisation of Folk Music in Christian Worship.* Mokokchung: Published by the Author, 2001.

Jamir, N. Talitemjen. *Asen Sobalibaren (Our Cultural Heritage).* Mokokchung: Author, 1993.

Jamir, N. Talitemjen & Lanunungsang A. *Naga Society And Culture: A Case Study of the Ao Naga Society and Culture.* Lumami: Nagaland University, Tribal Research Center, Dept. of Sociology, 2005.

Jamir, Nungshitula. *Naga Images of Human Being: A Source for Theological Anthropology.* Jorhat: Tribal Study Centre, 2001.

Jayaweera, Neville. "The WACC and the NWICO," *Document.* London: WACC, 1982.

Jensen, Klaus Bruhn and Nicholas W. Jankowski, eds. *A Handbook of Qualitative Methodologies for Mass Communication Research.* London & New York: Routledge, 1991.

Jorgensen, Danny L. *Participant Observation: A Methodology for Human studies* (Applied Social research Methods, vol. 15). Thousand Oaks: Sage Publications, 1993.

Joseph, Sarah. *Interrogating Culture: Critical Perspectives on Contemporary Social Theory.* New Delhi: Sage Publications, 1998.

Joshi, P. C. *Culture, Communication and Social Change.* New Delhi: Vikas Publishing House, 1989.

Jurji, Edward J., ed. *The Ecumenical Era in Church and Society.* New York: Macmillan Company, 1959.

Karotemprel, Sebastian, ed. *The Tribes of Northeast India.* Shillong: Centre for Indigenous Cultures, 1998.

Kealiinohomoku, Joann Marie Wheeler. *Theory and Methods for an Anthropological Study of Dance.* Ann Arbor: University Microfilms International, 1981.

Keitzar, Renthy, ed. *Triumph of Faith in Nagaland.* Kohima: NBCC, 1987.

Kennedy, Douglas. *England's Dances.* London: G. Bell & Sons, Ltd., 1950.

Kessler, Diane, ed., *Together On the Way.* Geneva: WCC Publications, 1999.

Kinnamon, Michael. *Truth and Community: Diversity and Its Limits In The Ecumenical Movement.* Geneva: WCC Publications, 1988.

Kinnamon, Michael and Cope, Brian E., (eds). *The Ecumenical Movement: An Anthology of Key Texts and Voices.* Geneva: WCC Publications, 1997.

Kraus, Richard. *History of the Dance: In Art and Education.* Englewood Cliffs: Prentice-Hall, Inc., 1969.

Kumar, B. B. *An Introduction to Naga Tribes.* Meerut: K. K. Mittal, 1997.

Kumar, Keval J. *Mass Communication in India,* Revised Edition. Bombay: Jaico Publishing House, 1989.

Kothari, C. R. *Research Methodology: Methods and Techniques.* Second Edition. New Delhi: Wiley Eastern Limited, 1990.

Leeming, Bernard. *The Vatican Council and Christian Unity: A Commentary on The Decree on Ecumenism of the Second Vatican Council, Together with a Translation of the Text.* London: Darton, Longman & Todd Ltd., 1966.

Leibrecht, Walter. *Religion and Culture: Essays in Honour of Paul Tillich.* New York: Harper & Brothers Publishers, 1959.

Likok, T. *A Picture of an Organic Church Union.* Impur: Author, 1970.

Livinson, David and Ember, Melvin eds. *Encyclopedia of Cultural Anthropology.* Vol. 1. New York: Henry Holt, 1996.

Longchar, A. Wati. *The Traditional Tribal Worldview and Modernity: Focus On North East India.* Jorhat: N. Limala Lkr, 1995.

Longchar, A. Wati and Davis, Larry E., eds. *Doing Theology with Tribal Resources: Context and Perspective.* Jorhat: Tribal Study Centre, ETC, 1999.

Longchar, A. Wati. *An Emerging Asian Theology: Tribal Theology.* Jorhat: Tribal Study Centre, ETC, 2000.

Longchar, A. Wati, ed. *In Search of Identity and Tribal Theology: A Tribute to Dr. Renthy Keitzar.* Jorhat: Tribal Study Centre ETC, 2001.

Longkumer, Nüklu. *The Growth of Baptist Churches among the Aos of Nagaland.* Changtongya: Changtongya Baptist Church, 1988.

Lossky, Nicholas, Jose Migruez Bonino, John Pobee, Tom Stransky, Geoffrey Wainwright, and Pauline Webb, eds., *Dictionary of the Ecumenical Movement.* Geneva: WCC Publications, 1991.

Lotha, John. "The Church Union Movement in North East India with Special reference to the Response of the Kyong (Lotha) Baptist Churches from 1963 to 1988." *M.Th Thesis,* 1989.

Lotha, Yanbemo. *Making a Theology of Naga Community.* Dimapur: Abeni Lotha, 2005.

Lotsüro, Angeline. *The Nagas: A Missionary Challenge.* Shillong: Vendrame Institute Publications, 2000.

Mackay, John A. *Ecumenics: The Science of the Church Universal.* Englewood Cliffs, N. J., Prentice-Hall, Inc., 1964.

Mackenzie, Kenneth, ed. *Union of Christendom.* London: Macmillan Company, 1938.

Macquarrie, John. *Christian Unity and Christian Diversity.* London: SCM Press LTD, 975.

Majumdar, D. N. and Madan, T. N. *An Introduction to Social Anthropology.* Bombay: Asia Publishing House, 1963.

Manuel, A. D. *Communication and the Church*. New Delhi, ISPCK, 1994.

Martini, Carlo Maria. *Communicating Christ to the World.* Kansas City: Sheed & Ward, 1994.

Mattam, Joseph & Sebastian Kim, eds., *Mission Trends Today: Historical and Theological Perspectives.* Bangalore: St. Pauls, 1997.

Massey, James, ed. *Communication and Community and Prophecy.* New Delhi: Asian Region-WACC-ISPCK, 1989.

McKenzie, John L. *Dictionary of the Bible.* New York: Geoffery Chapman, 1975.

McLuhan, Marshall and Powers, Bruce R. *Global Village: Transformations in World Life and Media in the 21st Century.* New York: Oxford University Press, 1992.

McQuail, Denis. *McQuail's Mass Communication Theory*, 4th Edition. London: Sage, 2000.

Melkote, Srinivas R. and Sandhya Rao, eds. *In Critical Issues In Communication Looking Inward For Answer: Essays in Honor of K. E. Eapen.* New Delhi: Sage Publication, 2001.

Menamparampil, Archbishop Thomas. *The Challenge of Cultures: Cross-cultural Relationships, Conflicts, Inculturation.* Bombay: St. Pauls Publications, 1996.

Meshack, Samuel W. and Eberhard von de Heyde, eds., *Communication of the Gospel: In the Context of Globalisation, Religious Pluralism and Nationalism.* Chennai: Gurukul Publications, 2002.

Miller, Gerald R., ed., *Explorations in Interpersonal Communication: Sage Annual Reviews of Communication Research Vo. V.* Beverly Hills: Sage Publications, 1976.

Mills, J. P. *The Ao Nagas.* Bombay: Oxford University Press, 1973.

________. *The Lotha Nagas.* Kohima: Directorate of Art and Culture, Government of Nagaland, 1980.

________. *The Rengma Nagas.* Guwahati: Spectrum Publications, 1980.

Mohanraj, R., ed. *Communicating for an Alternate Humanity.* Chennai: The Department of Communication of the Churches of South India, 2003.

Monteiro, Evelyn. *Church and Culture: Communion in Pluralism.* New Delhi: ISPCK, 2004.

Murphy, Sally. "Why Dance? A Functional Perspective," in *Dance: The Study of Dance and the Place of Dance in Society,* Proceedings of the VIII Commonwealth and International Conference on Sport, Physical Education, Dance, Recreation and Health, Conference '86 Glasgow, 18-23 July. London: E. & F. N. Spon Ltd., 1986.

Naga Institute of Culture. *A Brief Historical Account Of Nagaland.* Kohima: NIC, 1970.

Nelson, James B. *Embodiment: An Approach to Sexuality and Christian Theology* Minneapolis: Augsburg Publishing House, 1978.

Niebuhr, H. Richard *Christ and Culture.* London: Faber and Faber Limited, 1956.

Noverre, Jean-Georges. *Letters on Dancing and Ballets,* translated by Cyril W. Beaumont. London: C. W. Beaumont, 1951.

Nuh, V. K. *A Thelogical Reflection on Naga Society.* Kohima: Research Wing, Council of the Baptist Churches, 1993.

________. *Struggle for Identity in North-east India: A Theological Response.* New Delhi: Spectrum Publications, 2001.

Nuovo, Victor, ed., *Visionary Science.* Detroit: Wayne State University Press, 1987.

Oberdorfer, Donald N. *Electronic Christianity: Myth or Ministry.* Tylors Falls: John L. Brekke and Sons, 1982.

Oxley, Simon. *Creative Ecumenical Education.* Geneva: WCC Publications, 1988.

Pachuau, Lalsangkima, ed. *Ecumenical Missiology: Contemporary Trends, Issues and Theme.* Bangalore: UTC, 2002.

Palakeel, Joseph. *Towards a Communication Theology.* Bangalore: Asian Trading Corporation, 2003.

Pasayat, Chitrasen. *Tribe, Caste and Folk Culture.* Jaipur: Rawat Publications, 1998.

Prasad, Kiran, ed. *Political Communication: The Indian Experience, Vol. I The Domain, Political Process and News Presentation.* Delhi: B. R. Publishing Corporation, 2003.

Pearsall, Judy, ed. *The Concise Oxford Dictionary.* Tenth Edition. Oxford: Oxford University Press, 1999.

Philip, Puthuvail Thomas. *The Growth of the Baptist Churches in Nagaland. Guwahati:* CLC, 1976.

Philip, T.V. *Edinburgh To Salvador: Twentieth Century Ecumenical Missiology.* Delhi: CSS & ISPCK, 1999.

Pothirajulu, Doraisamy. *Laity Formation: An Educational Model.* Madras: CLS, 1993.

Potter, Philip. *Life in all its Fullness.* Geneva: WCC Publications, 1981.

Presler, Henry H. *Primitive Religions in India: A Textbook on the Primitive Religious Type among India's Tribals.* Bangalore: Christian Literature Society, 1971.

Priest, Susanna Hornig. *Doing Media Research: An Introduction.* Thousand Oaks: Sage Publications, 1996.

Pritchard, Evans. *Social Anthropology.* London: Cohen & West Ltd., 1962.

Puthenpurakal, Joseph. *Baptist Missions in Nagaland: A Study in Historical and Ecumenical Perspective.* Shillong: Vendrame Missiological Institute Publications, 1984.

Quiggin, Alison Hingston. "Dancing," in *Chambers' Encyclopedia,* New Edition, Vol. IV, Confirmation-Educational Psychology. London: George Newnes Limited, 1959.

Rahner, Karl and Herbert Vorgrimler, eds. *Theological Dictionary.* New York, Herder and Herder, 1965.

Ramunny, Murkot. *The World Of Nagas.* New Delhi: Northern Book Centre, 1988.

Raiser, Konrad. *Ecumenism in Transition: A Paradigm Shift in the Ecumenical Movement.* Geneva: WCC, 1991.

________. *To be the Church: Challenges and Hope for a New Millennium.* Geneva: WCC Publications, 1997.

Raja, John Joshva. *Facing the Reality of Communication: Culture, Church and Communication.* New Delhi: ISPCK, 2001.

Raj, Ebe Sunder, Jeyakumar, and Varghese, eds. *Management of Christian Services in India,* Vol. I. (Chennai: Christian Institute of Management, 2004.

Raja, John Joshva & Samson Prabhakar, eds. *Introduction to Communication and Media Studies.* Bangalore: BTESSC/ SATHRI, 2006.

Rao, O. M. *Focus on North East Indian Christianity.* Delhi: ISPCK, 1994.

Ritter, Richard H. *The Arts of the Church.* Boston: The Pilgrim Press, 1947.

Robinson, Gnana. *Communicating the Gospel Today.* Madurai: T. T. S., 1986.

Roberge, Gaston. *The Faithful Witness: On Christian Communication.* Anand: Gujarat Shaitya Prakash, 1999.

Rouet, Albert. *Liturgy and the Arts.* Collegeville: The Liturgical Press, 1997.

Royce, Anya Peterson. *The Anthropology of Dance.* Bloomington: Indiana University Press, 1977.

Saberwal, Satish, ed. *Towards a Cultural Policy.* Delhi: Vikas Publishing House, 1975.

Samartha, S. J. *Courage for Dialogue: Ecumenical Issues in Inter-religious Relationship.* Geneva: WCC Publications, 1981.

Samartha, S. J. *One Christ – Many Religions: Toward a Revised Christology.* Second Indian Edition. Bangalore: SATHRI & Wordmakers, 1994.

Samorar, A. Larry, & Porter, Richard E., *Intercultural Communication: A Reader.* Seventh Editions. Belmont: Wadsworth Publishing Company, 1994.

Sangma, Milton S. *History of American Baptist Mission in North East India 1836-1950,* Volume I, Delhi: Mittal Publications, 1987.

______. *History of American Baptist Mission in North East India,* Volume II, Delhi: Mittal Publications, 1992.

Sema, Hokishe. *Emergence of Nagaland: Socio-Economic and Political Transformation and the Future.* New Delhi: Vikas Publishing House Pvt Ltd., 1986.

Sema, Piketo. *British Policy and Administration in Nagaland 1881-1947.* New Delhi: Scholars Publishing House, 1972.

Servaes, Jan, Thomas L. Jacobson and Shirley A. White, eds. *Participatory Communication for Social Change.* New Delhi: Sage Publications, 1996.

Sharma, R. N. *Social and Cultural Anthropology*. Delhi: Surjeet Publications, 2005.

Shimray, R. R. *Origin and Culture of Nagas*. Delhi: Published by Mrs. P. Shimray, 1985.

Shimray, Shimreingam, ed. *Tribal Theology: A Reader*. Jorhat: Tribal Study Centre, ETC, 2003.

Singh, Prakash. *Nagaland*. New Delhi: National Book Trust, 1972.

Singh, K. Suresh, ed., *Tribal Situation in India* Vol. 13. Simla: Indian Institute of Advance Study, 1972.

Singson, D. "The Baptist Involvement in the Church Union Movement in India." *M.Th. Thesis*, 1975.

Snaitang, O. L., ed. *Churches of Indigenous Origins in Northeast India*. Delhi: ISPCK, 2000.

__________. *A History of Ecumenical Movement: An Introduction*. Bangalore: BTESSC/SATHRI, 2004.

Sogaard, Viggo. *Media in Church and Mission: Communicating the Gospel*. Bangalore: Theological Book Trust, 1998.

Soukup, Paul A. *Communication and Theology: Introduction and Review of the Literature*. London: WACC, 1983.

Spencer, Paul, ed., *Society and the Dance: The Social Anthropology of Process and Performance*. Cambridge: Cambridge University Press, 1985.

Srinivas, M. N. *Village, Caste, Gender and Method: Essays in Indian Social Anthropology*. New Delhi: Oxford University Press, 2001.

Stanislaus, L. ed. *Education as Mission*. New Delhi: ISPCK, 2004.

Stauffer, S. Anita. *Worship and Culture in Dialogue*. Geneva: Lutheran World Federation, 1994.

Stout, A. Daniel and Judith M. Buddenbaum. *Religion and Mass Media, Audiences and Adaptation*. New Delhi: Sage Publications, 1996.

Sumi, Akheto, ed. *Perspectives: Current Issues in Theological Thinking*. Mokokchung: Jongshinokdang Trust Clark Theological College, 2002.

Sutherland, R. L., Woodward, J. L., and Maxwell, M. A. *Introductory Sociology*, 6th Edition. Philadelphia: Lippincot, 1961.

Syiemlieh, David. *A Brief History of the Catholic Church in Nagaland*. Shillong: Vendrame Institute Publications, 1990.

Takatemjen. *Studies on Theology and Naga Culture*. Mokokchung: Author, 1997.

Thangasamy, D. *A. Towards Involvement: The Theory and Practice of Laity Education*. Madras: CLS, ISPCK & LPH, 1972.

The Report of the International Conversations between the Anglican Communion and the Baptist World Alliance. *Conversations around the World 2000-2005*. London: The Anglican Communion Office, 2005.

Thanzauva, K. *Theology of Community: Tribal Theology in Making.* Aizwal: Mizo Theological conference, 1984.

Thomas, Helen. *Dance, Modernity and Culture: Explorations in the Sociology of Dance.* London: Routledge, 1995.

Thomas, K. J. *Ecumenism A Call to Unity,* St. Peter's Guide Book Series No. 10. Bangalore: St. Peter's Pontifical Institute Publications, 2007.

Thomas, J. Heywood. *Paul Tillich: Makers of Contemporary Theology.* Atlanta: John Knox Press, 1965.

Thomas, J. Heywood. *Tillich: Outstanding Christian Thinker.* London: Continuum, 2000.

Thomas, M. A. *Towards Wider Ecumenism.* Bangalore: ATC, 1993.

Thomas, M. M. *The Nagas Towards A.D. 2000.* Madras: Centre for Research on New International Economic Order, 1992.

Thomas, Pradip, ed. *An Ecumenical Wordsmith: The Writings of T. K. Thomas.* Tiruvalla: Christava Sahitya Samithya, 2002.

Thomas, T. K., ed. *Ecumenical Communication in Asia.* Singapore: Christian Conference in Asia, 1981.

Thompson, Betty. *A Chance To Change: Women and Men in the Church.* Geneva: WCC Publications, 1982.

Tillich, Paul. *Systematic Theology,* Volume III. Chicago: The University of Chicago Press, 1963.

Tylor, Edward B. *Primitive Culture: Researches into the Development of Mythology, Philosophy, Religion, Art, and Custom.* London: John Murray. 1871.

Traber, Michael, ed. *Communication in Theological Education: New Directions.* Delhi: ISPCK, 2005.

Turner, Victor W. *The Forest of Symbols: Aspects of Ndembu Rituals.* Ithaca and London: Cornell University Press, 1967.

Tüngoe, Merithung. *Administrators Missionaries and a World Turned Upside Down.* New Delhi: ISPCK & ETC, 2000.

Unterkoefler, Ernest L. and Andrew Harsanyi, *The Unity We Seek: A Statement by the Roman Catholic/ Presbyterian-Reformed Consultation.* New York: Paulist Press, 1977.

VanElderen, Marlin. *Finding A Voice: Communicating The Ecumenical Movement.* Geneva: WCC Publications, 2000.

VanElderen, Marlin & Martin Conway, eds. *Introducing the World Council of Churches.* Revised and enlarged edition. Geneva: WCC Publications, 2001.

Victor, Vinod, Leslie Natheniel & P. Surya Prakesh, eds. *Ecumenism: Prospects and Challenges.* New Delhi: ISPCK, 2001.

Vilanilam, J. V. *Religious Communication in India.* Vol. 1. Trivandrum: Kairali Books International, 1987.

WACC. *Statements on Communication.* London: WACC, 1997.

Walling, C. Walu, Comp. *All is Light! All is Light!: Sources Materials on History of Christianity.* Impur: ABAM, 2001.

Wardin, Albert W. *Baptists in Oregon.* Portland: Judson Baptist College, 1969.

WCC. *Joint Working Group between the Roman Catholic Church and the World Council of Churches: Seventh Report.* Geneva: WCC Publications, 1998.

WCC. *Laity Formation.* (Proceedings of the Ecumenical Consultation, Gazzada, 1965). Rome: Department of Laity, WCC & the Permanent Committee for International Congresses of the Lay Apostolate (Rome), 1966.

WCC. *Laos: The Whole People of God.* Plenary, WCC Central Committee Meeting in Johannesburg, South Africa, 1994.

WCC. *The New Delhi Report: The Third Assembly of the World Council of Churches 1961*. London: WCC, 1962.

WCC. *Sharing In One Hope: Reports and Documents from the Meeting of Faith and Order Commission, Bangalore, 1978*. Faith and order Paper No. 92. Geneva: WCC Publications, 1978.

WCC. *What Kind of Unity?* Faith and Order Paper No. 69. Geneva: WCC Publications, 1974.

Weber, Hans-Ruedi. *Living in the Image of Christ: The Laity in Ministry*. Geneva: WCC Publications, 1986.

Webb, Pauline, ed. *Faith and Faithfulness: Essays on Contemporary Ecumenical Themes*. Geneva: WCC Publications, 1984.

Wesley, Arun Kumar. *Millennium Miscellany: Essays on Current Theological Issues*. Bangalore, Asian Trading Corporation, 2003.

________. *Liturgy As Worship: Towards a Form of worship in Song, Word and Drama*. Bangalore: Asian Trading Corporation, 2002.

White, Shirley A. with K. Sadanandan Nair and Joseph Ascroft, eds. *Participatory Communication: Working for Change and Development*. New Delhi: Sage Publications, 1994.

Wilcox, David P. & Kelly, W. A., eds. *Laity Education and the Theological Colleges*. (The Report of a Consultation on the Role of Theological Colleges in Lay Training, held at UTC). Bangalore: Department of Lay Training, UTC, 1968.

Williams, Raymond. *Keywords: A Vocabulary of Culture and Society*. New York: Oxford University Press, 1983.

Wintle, Brian, James, Emmanuel, Jeyaraj, Jesudason B., Raj, Paul Mohan and Wintle, Richard S., eds. *Work Worship Witness: Essays Dedicated to a Vision and a Visionary*. Bangalore: Theological Book Trust, 2003.

Yonuo, Asoso. *The Rising Nagas: A Historical and Political Study*. Delhi: Vikas Publishing House, 1974.

Young, Alexander Bell Filson. "Dance," in *The Encyclopedia Britannica*, Fourth Edition, Volume 7, Damascus to Education. (London: The Encyclopedia Britannica Company, Ltd., 1929

Zachariah, Mathai. *Ecumenism in India: Essays in Honour of the Rev. M. A. Thomas*. New Delhi: ISPCK, 1980.

______. Beyond *Ecumenism: A Journey Into Light*. Tiruvalla: Christava Sahitya Samithy, 2002.

Articles from Periodicals and Journals

Adler, Richard. "Ecumenical Co-operation in Papua New Geuinea." *Media Development* 27/1, 1980.

Ambroise, Raymond. "Ecumenical Collaboration an Indian Point of view." *Media Development* 27/1, 1980, pp. 28-30.

Arokasamy, F. "Classical Indian Dance: Understanding its Significance for our Liturgy and Catechetic." *Word and Worship* Vol. 38, No. 4, (July – August 2005), pp. 243- 260.

Bahadur, Shamsher S. "Communicative Theology in Faith and Practice" (an article), p. 20.

Bluck, John. "Ecumenical Debate on Communication: A New Beginning." *Media Development*. 31/1, 1984.

Broz, Ludek. "Theological Foundation of Christian Communication." *WACC Journal* 26:4, 1979.

Collet, Giancarlo. "Communication and Freedom: Reflection on the Task of the Church." *Media Development* Vol. 28, No. 4, 1981, pp. 17-23.

Coventry, John. "Ecumenical Communication." *The Way*. 12:2, 1972.

"Growing Together." The Baptist News Volume 50, Nos. 1 & 2, Jan – Apr. 2000, pp. 1-2.

Henry, Rosita, Magowan, Finoa & Murray, David. "Introduction – Anthropology of Dance," in *Australian Journal of Anthropology*, December 2000, pp. 1-4.

Hooft, W. A. Visser 't. "The Calling of the World Council of Churches." Report of the General Secretary to the Third Assembly of the WCC at New Delhi, in *Ecumenical Review* Vol. 14. No. 2, 1962, p. 224.

John Paul II, Homily in the Basilica of St. Paul, Rome, on January 25th, 1993, in *OR*, no. 4, January 27, 1993, p. 1.

Johnson-Hill, Kelly. "Dance and Worship in the Pacific Islands: A Comparative Study with Implications for an Emerging Ecumenical Consciousness." *Asian Journal of Theology* Volume 18 Number 2 (October 2004), pp. 362- 373.

Joseph, M. P. "Search for a Liberating Culture." *Asian Journal of Theology* Volume 11 Number 1 (April 1997), pp. 117-127.

Jyrwa, J. Fortis. "Church Union Movement in North East India," p. 71.

Kung, Lap-yan. "Globalization and Ecumenism: A Search for Human Solidarity, with Reference to Pentecostalism/Charismatism in Hong Kong." *Asian Journal of Theology* Volume 17 Number 2 (October 2003), pp. 378-402.

Lee, Philip. 'Communicating is Peace: WACC's Mission Today.' *Media Development.* Vol. LIV 1/2007, pp. 49-52.

Longchar, A. Wati. "Tribal Theology in Changing Context," Paper presentation in CISRS Golden Jubilee Convention, 12-14 February 2007, at Indian Social Institute, Bangalore. p. 7.

Manning, Frank E. "Victor Turner: An Appreciation." *The Association for the Anthropological Study of Play Newsletter* 10 (4), 1984, pp. 20-22.

Morgenstern, Julian. "The Etymological History of the Three Hebrew Synonyms for 'To Dance,' "in *American Oriental Society Journal*, 36, 1916, pp. 321- 332.

Murphy-O'Connor, Cormac. "Unity on a Knife edge." *The Tablet*, 20/11, 2004. p.14.

Periannan, Sebastian. "Modern Methods of Communication for an Effective Education," in *Journal of Dharma* (Religion and Education) April- June 2006, Vol. 31, No. 2. pp. 219-236.

Periannan, Sebastian. "Eucharist in a New Media Age," presented in the Conference on "Eucharist as Communication." FABC Office of Social Communication, Bangkok, 2007.

Pooranam, M. X. "People's Media: An Alternative in Information Bulletin." (3/1993), Catholic Media Council, Aachen, p. 2.

Raja, John Joshva. "Communication for Alternative Human Technological Perspective." *Bangalore Theological Forum* UTC. Vol. XXXV, No.1, 6/2003, p. 109.

_________. "The Internet in the Ecumenical and Mission Work of Churches in India" presented at Consultation Meeting on "The Internet in Mission and Ecumenism – Mission and Ecumenism in the Internet." at Stuttgart, 11th – 12th November 2003.

_________. "Dramatizing and Dancing for Building Authentic Christian Communities in India." in *Saplings 2005-2006*, UTC, pp. 73-77.

Snaitang, O. L. "Ecumenical and Hill People's Culture in Northeast India." *Journal of Tribal Studies* (Jan – June 1998).

_________. "Development of the Ecumenical Movement in Northeast India." *Indian Church History Review* Vol. XXXVII Number 1, June 2003, pp. 41-52.

Scott, Stephanie S. "The Language of Liturgical Dance in African-American Christian Worship," in *Journal of the Interdenominational Theological Center*, Volume XXVII, Numbers 1 and 2, Fall 1999 / Spring 2000, pp. 245-263.

Traber, Michael. "Ecumenical Relations in Communication." *Media Development* 27/1, 1980, pp. 1-2.

Traber, Michael. "Group Communication in Different Cultures." *Media Development* Vol. XXVII, 2/1981, p. 3.

Wanless, David. "Wasted Opportunities in Ecumenical Communication." *Media Development* 27/1, 1980.

WCC, "The Unity of the Church as *Koinonia*: Gift and Calling," in *Ecumenical Trends*, Vol. 20, No. 3, 1991, p. 42.

Wellman, B. "The Community Question: The Intimate Networks of East Yonkers." *American Journal of Sociology*, 84, 1979, 1201-1231.

Wesley, Arun Kumar. "Dancing in the Aisle: Towards a Form of Worship in Drama," in *Masihi Sevak*, Volume XXV No. 2, July 2000, pp. 65-92.

Willem, Visser't Hooft. "The Basics: Its History and Significance," in *Ecumenical Review*, Vol. 37, No. 2, 1985, p. 173.

Zelditch, Morris. "Some Methodological Problems of field Studies." *American Journal of Sociology* Vol. 67, No. 5, 1962, pp. 566-576.

Online Articles and Website

Barboza, Francis. "Dictionary of Indian Christian Theology: Dance," in www.drbarboza.com/dictionary.htm Browsed on 26-11-2007.

"Diocese of Kohima," http://www.dioceseofkohima.org Browsed on 10-09-2006.

Dumitrana, Magdalena. "In Quest of Lost Ecumenism. http://www.org/book/serieso4/IVA-24/chapter-xi.htm pp. 9-10 & 22. (03/13/2006).

Carter, Sydney. 'Hymn-Lord of the Dance', http:// www. stainer.co.uk, 1963 Stainer & Bell Ltd. London. Browsed on 27-04-2006.

"Christianity_Ecumenism,"http://www.britannica.com/eb/article-67623/Christianity Browsed on 14-12-2007.

"Culture," http://en.wikipedia.org/wiki/Culture Browsed on 10-02-2008. en.wikipedia.org/wiki/Lord of the Dance. Browsed on 22-03-2008.

Enriques, Ian. 'The Ritual of War and Manhood,' http://www.Barbarycoast.org/ritual.html. Browsed on 23-01-2008.

Ganapathy, Leela. "Spiritual Dance: Dance in Spiritual Indian Art," in *Spiritual Dance in Indian Art*, www.experiencefestival.com/a//Spiritual_Dance/id/4158. Browsed on 19-11-2007.

http://anthro.palomar.edu/culture/culture. htm. Browsed on 03-02-2006.

http://www.tourismnagaland.com/Festivals.html, 2007 Nagaland Tourism. Browsed on 19-01-2008.

"I Danced in the Morning," in Hymn: Claves Regni-St. Peter's Church, Nottingham, England on-line Magazine the On-line Magazine, http://www.stpeternottingham.org/hymns/dance.htm, 01-07-2007. Browsed on 28-03-2008.

"Minute of Concern about "Lord of the Dance," Approved by the New England Yearly Meeting Committee on Prejudice and Poverty on sixth month, fifth day 1999, *A periodic newsletter* from the Committee on Prejudice & Poverty of New England Yearly Meeting of Friends; Issue #3: Summer, 1999, in http:// www.neym.org/PrejudiceAndProverty/Issue3.summer99.pdf. Browsed on 25-02-2008.

"Nagaland," www.http://en.wikipedia.org/wiki/nagaland, Browsed on 28-03-2020.

"New Media," en.wikipedia.org/wiki/New_media Browsed on 21-02-2008.

Ondrusova, Vlasta. 'Utilization and Safeguarding of Folk Handicraft as Intellectual Property sui generic,' Geneva, in www.unctad.org/trade-env/docs/czech.pdf.

"Participant Observation," en.wikipedia.org/wiki/participant_observation. Browsed on 16-07-2005.

"Sociology: Material and Non-material Culture," cliffsnotes.com/WileyCDA/CliffsReviewTopic. Browsed on 07-02-2008.

Tinder, D. G. "Denominationalism," http://mb-soft.com/believe/text/denomina/htm 01/01/2007. Browsed on 15-12-2007.

Universiteit Twente, the Netherlands, "Symbolic Interaction," http://www.tcw.utwente.nl/theorieenoverzicht/Theory%20clusters/Inte 09/09/2004. Browsed on 15-02-2005.